Visitor's (
CALIFO:

UNITED STATES
OF AMERICA

CALIFORNIA

The Authors
Brian Merritt is an American who has travelled widely in his native country. After 4 years 'touring' America with the Air Force, he spent 10 years marketing computer systems in Britain. In 1989 Brian formed a travel writing team with his British photographer-wife, Jackie, who recieved her first photography award aged 10. They have negotiated 50,000 miles of American Highway (including 10,000 miles in California to research this guide) in their motorhome, and have re-visited every state in the USA. Brian and Jackie are the author/photographer of *Visitor's Guide: USA* and *Visitor's Guide: Florida*, both published by MPC.

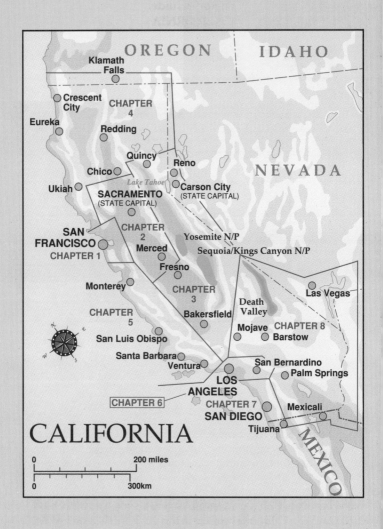

OREGON   IDAHO

Klamath
Falls

Crescent
City   CHAPTER
4
Eureka
Redding

Quincy   Reno   NEVADA

Chico
Lake Tahoe   Carson City
Ukiah   (STATE CAPITAL)
SACRAMENTO
(STATE CAPITAL)

CHAPTER
SAN   2
FRANCISCO   Yosemite N/P
CHAPTER 1   Merced   Sequoia/Kings Canyon N/P

Fresno

Monterey   CHAPTER
3   Las Vegas
Death
CHAPTER   Bakersfield   Valley
5
Mojave   CHAPTER 8
San Luis Obispo   Barstow

Santa Barbara
Ventura   San Bernardino
Palm Springs
LOS
ANGELES
CHAPTER 6   CHAPTER 7   Mexicali
SAN DIEGO
CALIFORNIA   Tijuana   MEXICO

0   200 miles

0   300km

VISITOR'S GUIDE:
CALIFORNIA

Jackie & Brian Merritt

MPC

HUNTER

Published by: Moorland Publishing Co Ltd,
Moor Farm Road West, Ashbourne, Derbyshire DE6 1HD England

ISBN 0 86190 464 8

Published in the USA by: Hunter Publishing Inc,
300 Raritan Center Parkway, CN 94, Edison, NJ 08818

British Library Cataloguing in Publication Data:
A catalogue record for this book is available from the British Libraray

Colour origination by: P & W Graphics Pty Ltd, Singapore
Printed in Hong Kong by: Wing King Tong Co Ltd

MPC Production Team: Editorial & Design, John Robey; Cartography, Alastair Morrison

Front Cover: Golden Gate Bridge, San Francisco (International Photobank);
rear cover: Death Valley (MPC Picture Collection).
Illustrations have been supplied by: Anaheim CVB page 147 (lower); Lake
Tahoe VA 14, 86 (top); MPC Picture Collection 30, 31, 35, 75, 115; Palm Springs
CVB 187; Reno CVB 86 (lower); San Diego CVB 3, 174; Sonora COC p66;
Universal Studios 150 (top); The Walt Disney Co 150 (top).
All the remaining photographs have been taken by Jackie Merritt.

Acknowledgments

The authors are deeply indebted to Fred Slater of the California Office of Tourism
and to the California Department of Parks and Recreation. Many thanks are due
to every Convention & Visitors Bureau and Chamber of Commerce, as well as the
Beverley Garland Hotel and Sportsman's Lodge who provided excellent bases
from which to explore Los Angeles. This book is especially dedicated to Fred and
Sid Merritt, whose San Jose home was a semi-permanent campsite for our motorhome, and to all our supportive relatives home and abroad.

Note on the maps
The maps drawn for each chapter, while comprehensive, are
not designed to be used as route maps, but rather to locate the
main cities, towns and places of interest.

CONTENTS

Key to Symbols Used in Text Margin and on Maps

大	Recommended walks	&	Accessible to the handicapped
❀	Garden	⊞	Building of interest
▮	Fort	⊼	Archaeological site
✳	Other place of interest	⌂	Museum/Art Gallery
➤	Birdlife	⚘	Beautiful view/Scenery, Natural Interest
⚕	Nature reserve/Animal interest	♣	Park/recreational area
☗	Church	⤜	Aquarium
↗	Beach	✈	International Airport

Key to Maps

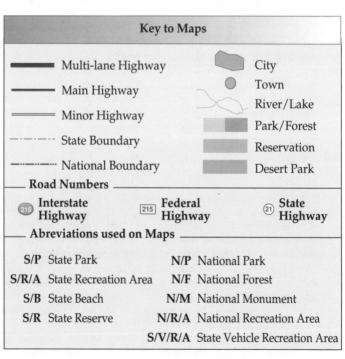

▬▬▬ Multi-lane Highway

▬▬▬ Main Highway

══════ Minor Highway

─·─·─·─ State Boundary

─··─··─·· National Boundary

City

Town

River/Lake

Park/Forest

Reservation

Desert Park

Road Numbers

(215) **Interstate Highway**   [215] **Federal Highway**   (21) **State Highway**

Abreviations used on Maps

S/P	State Park	**N/P**	National Park
S/R/A	State Recreation Area	**N/F**	National Forest
S/B	State Beach	**N/M**	National Monument
S/R	State Reserve	**N/R/A**	National Recreation Area
		S/V/R/A	State Vehicle Recreation Area

INTRODUCTION

B old and golden, California is a kaleidoscope of contrasts. To the
well known wonders — sensational San Francisco, sunny, sophisticated San Diego and the delights of Disney — add the gold-
rush ghost towns of Bodie and Calico, the incomparable Big Sur
coastline, rugged desert landscapes and lofty Lake Tahoe.

Other Californias also spring to mind: a blaze of poppies lapping
an old Spanish Mission; an alpine meadow's first fragile blossoms; a
green cathedral formed of towering redwoods. The fruited plains of
Central Valley sweep up to Mount Whitney, the highest point in the
contiguous United States, and then plummet to Death Valley, lowest
point in America. In the Sierra Nevada foothills prospective '49ers
still pan for gold, bringing home a glittering souvenir from the
Golden State.

The Land

The third largest state after Alaska and Texas, California is geographically diverse and geologically wealthy. Mount Whitney in the
Sierra Nevada is the highest point in the contiguous forty-eight
states, while just 85 miles (135km) away Death Valley is the lowest.
Variations in climate are equally immense, varying from subtropical
to subarctic. Death Valley claims the hottest temperature recorded in
the Western Hemisphere while peaks in the Sierra Nevada remain
snow-capped year-round and the annual snowfall of 20ft (6m) is the
highest in the USA. Southern Californians can ski on water and fresh
snow on the same day. The wet season is winter, when the skies
surrounding Los Angeles are much cleaner and clearer. Rainfall
varies from less than 2in in Imperial Valley to over 100in in the
northwest. Coastal temperatures are mild year round, though fogs

formed at sea drift onshore in summer. This moisture keeps the northern coast green and is essential for the mighty redwoods.

Most rivers and natural lakes are in the north of the state, with Yosemite Falls the continent's highest. With the higher population and agricultural areas most water is needed in the south. This requirement has spawned many dams and reservoirs throughout the state while runoff from the Sierra Nevada and the White Mountains is a major water source for Los Angeles.

Geologically speaking, the main fault with California must be the San Andreas which, like the state's other major physical features such as mountain ranges and valleys, runs parallel to the coast.

Flora and Fauna

Just as varied as the land and climatic zones, Californian flora boasts as many records. Near the coast are large stands of redwood trees, at over 350ft (107m) the world's tallest living things. On the western slopes of the Sierra Nevada between 4,500-8,000ft (1,300-2,500m) their cousins the giant sequoias are the largest while up in the White Mountains the gnarled Bristlecone pines are the oldest with some dating back over 4,500 years. Unfortunately over 1,000 of California's 5,000 plant species have become rare and are now monitored and protected, some having special reserves such as the Torrey pine north of San Diego and the California poppy in Antelope Valley.

Inland hills are covered with scrubby chaparral and oak while pine and juniper grow in the mountains. Desert flora, well adapted to the harsh environment, includes Joshua trees, fan palms, agave and other succulents, cacti, ocotillo, mesquite and creosote bushes. The most colourful time is spring when cacti and wildflowers bloom.

Many places along the coast are good for whale, dolphin, porpoise, seal and sea lion spotting, with Point Lobos a favourite. Most of the 2,000 delightful sea otters are found between Monterey and San Luis Obispo and may be seen floating on their backs while using stones to crack open shellfish. Tide pools offer a wide assortment of animal life but when exploring keep a watchful eye on the tide.

National Parks provide excellent opportunities for observation and photography of wildlife. However, animals such as elk, deer, bear, raccoons, coyotes, squirrels and chipmunks in the parks are really too tame. Remember these are wild animals with which contact is potentially dangerous — *all* bite or kick. Do *not* be tempted to feed them and in bear habitat heed warning signs as serious injury or even death could be the result of an encounter.

In remote areas the lucky traveller may get a glimpse of the endangered mountain lion or, high in the desert, a rare bighorn sheep. In the desert look for mammals and reptiles at dusk or early in the morning as most find burrows or cracks to hide in during the heat of the day. Animals such as rattlesnakes and scorpions do not usually pose a threat unless disturbed suddenly as they avoid contact with humans.

Birdlife in California is plentiful and varied with northern California a wintering ground for the Bald eagle. Many birdwatching opportunities exist along the coast and at the Salton Sea where birds such as the peregrine falcon and osprey may be spotted.

History

The first inhabitants of this rich land were diverse tribes of Native Americans. Language and lifestyle varied, many northern tribes being hunter-gatherers who used the prolific acorns as a staple diet, supplemented by deer and elk. The Pomo Indians from the Clear Lake area were expert basket-makers while the southern Chumash built fine canoes and ate fish and shellfish as evidenced by large mounds of shells. These peoples prospered for 10,000 years before white man intervened, bringing European diseases which few Indians had immunity to. As thousands died on early contact when brought into the mission system, accurate figures for the original population are not available but estimates put numbers anywhere from 100,000 to 300,000. Many of those remaining were displaced when the Gold Rush started and others were forcibly relocated.

In 1542 Juan Rodriguez Cabrillo (Portuguese navigator of a Spanish expedition) discovered California, named after the island inhabited by Amazons, according to an early sixteenth-century novel. Sir Francis Drake claimed *Nova Albion* (around San Francisco or possibly Santa Barbara), the first New England, in 1579, leaving a plaque behind. Sebastian Vizcaino, who named San Diego, San Clemente and Santa Catalina Island, endorsed the Spanish claim in 1602.

The progress of Russian fur traders down the Pacific coastline from Alaska prompted Spain to launch the Gaspar de Portala expedition, reaching San Diego in 1769. With Portola was Father Junípero Serra, founder of the missions, commencing with Mission San Diego and establishing San Francisco in 1776. Most Indians who survived European diseases were increasingly drawn into the Mission fold. Pueblo de Los Angeles came soon after in 1781, founded not by missionaries but Spanish families. The disastrous 1812 earthquake set back the mission effort, but by 1821, when Mexico broke away from Spain, twenty missions had been established. Mission Sonoma, founded in 1823, was the northernmost and the only Californian mission created under Mexican rule.

In 1834 the Mexican government passed the Secularization Acts in which mission property and land was given over to the people. Californian Indians were ill-equipped to be land owners. Henry Dana, author of *Two Years Before the Mast*, described the Mexican rancheros who took over the land as an idle lot given over to gambling, prostitution and cruel sports, such as bear baiting and bull fights. However Monterey, capital of Spanish and Mexican *Alta* (Upper) California, received glowing reports from Dana as the most civilized town on the Pacific Coast.

The United State's Monroe doctrine had warned Europe to keep their greedy hands off the New World, and that all land between the Atlantic and Pacific Oceans was America's 'Manifest Destiny'. President Andrew Jackson attempted to purchase California from the impoverished Mexican government for a paltry sum, then President Polk declared war on Mexico and sent in troops. US sympathizers won the Bear Flag Revolt just before Commodore John Sloat raised the Stars and Stripes in Monterey. So while the revolt did not actually give California to America, it did give California its Bear Flag.

Gold was discovered in a canyon north of Los Angeles, but the strike which captured the world's imagination was Sutter's Mill discovery in 1848. Early prospectors, which history dubbed '49ers, had the easy pickings, while San Francisco harbour bristled with masts of abandoned ships. Many nationalities rushed to make their fortunes, including a significant number of Chinese. As prospectors became more sophisticated, panning gave way to the faster sluice boxes. When river bottoms and banks were dug over, mine shafts were sunk to exploit hidden seams. Still this was not fast enough for some and the idea of directing jets of water at hillsides was invented. Hydraulic mining washed away tons of earth, flooding the Sacramento Valley with sludge, while the Comstock Lode of Virginia City, Nevada, inundated San Francisco with silver.

California finally achieved statehood in 1850. Monterey, with its Mexican sympathies, could not be allowed to govern, so the legislature met at San Jose, Vallejo, Benicia, and finally Sacramento in a series of political double-dealings dubbed 'the Capital on Wheels'.

Other wheels were also coming, replacing the short-lived Pony Express. The first overland stagecoaches reached San Diego in 1857 and the railroad arrived in 1869, oiled with the greed of Central Pacific's Big Four: Charles Crocker, Mark Hopkins, Collis Huntington and Leland Stanford. Later renamed Southern Pacific, the railroad that was to bring prosperity carried cheap Eastern goods,

California is blessed with twenty-one Spanish missions

decimating Californian industry. The hordes of immigrants brought by the railroad fuelled the growth which has made California America's most populous state.

San Francisco continued to grow, and when space became too scarce the town's grid system was extended over the irregular terrain behind. Horse drawn carriages could not manage the steep slopes, so in 1873 the cable car was born. Prosperity skyrocketed until the 1906 earthquake, when ruptured firefighting mains failed to extinguish the ensuing fire. The same year saw the founding of Beverly Hills and the first film studio, while oil had been discovered in Los Angeles back in 1891, ensuring that city's prosperity for years to come.

Between the coastal cities and the 'golden hills' lay the fertile San Joaquin and Sacramento Valleys. In the 1930s refugees arrived from the Midwest's 'Dust Bowl', a period highlighted in John Steinbeck's *The Grapes of Wrath*. This decade saw the completion of the Golden Gate Bridge in 1937, while San Francisco was the inaugural home to the United Nations in 1945. Supporters of 'The City' profess the world would be in much better straits if the UN was there still.

Modern California is living proof of Martin Luther King's proclamation that America is not so much a melting pot as a vegetable soup, with each ingredient separate yet adding to the whole. California boasts an extreme of ethnicity, a gargantuan melange of cults and cultures that are always on the boil and occasionally erupting. The cross-fertilization of peoples and ideas has put California into the forefront of technology, and the future will be anything but dull.

Economy

California produces one-tenth of America's crops by value, most being grown in the fertile Imperial Valley with a significant contribution of cotton from the San Joaquin (pronounced Hwa-keen) Valley. A wide range of fruit and vegetables is harvested, with most of the USA's dates, figs, sultanas and olives being produced here. Viticulture has thrived on Californian soil since the introduction of the first vines by Spanish missionaries, who produced sacramental, medicinal and table wines. Commercial wine production began in 1820, and having survived 13 years of Prohibition the industry currently yields some 80 per cent of the country's wine.

California benefits significantly from its size and geographic diversity, a state rich in natural resources. Apart from tourism, California possesses significant mineral wealth, massive oil reserves, and ranks high in enterprises like aircraft, electronics, lumber, shipbuilding, defense, banking, mining and construction. California's glitter-filled movie and entertainment industry attracts more visitors annually than many countries can muster.

Population

According to the 1990 Census, just under 30 million people make their home in California, with a racial mix of: White 69.0 per cent, Black 7.4 per cent, Asian & Pacific Islanders 9.6 per cent, Native Americans 0.8 per cent, others 13.2 per cent.

Food and Drink

San Francisco offers world class cuisine, having more restaurants per capita than anywhere else in America (although Southern California comes close behind). Excellent Chinese, Italian and Japanese restaurants are ubiquitous, as are Mexican and especially 'Tex-Mex' establishments. Along the coast fresh seafood and chowders are excellent, while the ever present diners, drive-ins, snack bars and restaurant chains provide good service and dependable food all day long.

British visitors should remember that tea usually comes iced unless *hot* tea is requested. Coffee cups are normally refilled continuously, whilst iced water is generally free and refreshing. Beer is served cold and is usually light, more like lager, but may be strong — drivers be warned! A number of independent micro-breweries are now produce excellent lagers, ales and bitters — explore and enjoy.

California wines have won world acclaim, the most expensive vintages being matured in oak barrels which impart a distinctive woody flavour. Inexpensive varieties tend to be labelled Chablis or Cabernet, depending upon whether they are white or red, with many of the grapes coming from the hot central valley. Wine tastings are available everywhere, but for atmosphere seek out the smaller wineries (Chambers of Commerce give wine tour maps and offer suggestions). Contrary to popular opinion, Napa Valley has numerous smaller concerns, as does neighbouring Sonoma — both excellent excursions from San Francisco. Santa Barbara and Santa Ynes are popular day trips from Greater Los Angeles, and can be combined with Danish Solvang and La Purisima Mission State Historic Park. Bus tours are excellent options, allowing those who would otherwise drive to enjoy a few glasses with lunch. Finally, do not ignore the larger wineries, many of whom provide interesting tours.

Entertainment and Leisure

California offers an incredible variety of pastimes, from marathon theme parks, world-class museums and art galleries to surfing, diving, and wilderness treks. Stay in LA or Anaheim to enjoy the bustle and excitement of theme parks — Disneyland is pure magic while Knott's Berry Farm offers monster roller coasters and a 'kiddies' village. Universal Studios recreates those special moments of cinema in a themed park incorporating original movie studios and sets. Sea World San Diego is fun and educational — the perfect double bill when combined with San Diego Zoo. The arts also have a high profile with a choice of world class art galleries and museums, music, theatre and cinema. Hands-on children's museums provide educational entertainment for youngsters and parents alike.

As California has been settled recently, much emphasis has been placed on preserving wild areas. California is a prime destination for experiencing the great outdoors, with an exceptional network of state parks, national parks, recreation areas, wilderness areas, wild-life refuges, and deserts to explore. In sunny southern California many activities revolve around the beaches. Popular pursuits include sunbathing, swimming, surfing, jogging, fishing and boating. Northern California boasts great redwood forests, rugged wilderness areas, top American ski resorts and a fantastic coastline stretching from the Big Sur to the Oregon border.

Northern California has some of America's top ski resorts

1

SAN FRANCISCO AND THE BAY AREA

Rome has its seven hills, but San Francisco boasts forty. The cable car, a San Francisco tradition since 1873, was a by-product of the city's topsy-turvy topography and land speculation during the gold rush boom. Money-hungry property developers extended the city's grid pattern over the rather irregular terrain, and when horses balked at the resulting slopes the cable car was born.

Of course the visitor need not ascend each hill, and places of most interest — Union Square, Fisherman's Wharf, and Golden Gate Park — are all on the level. However, an indisputable part of San Francisco's charm *are* those picture-postcard cameos afforded from her various vantage points.

Yet the undeniable attraction of The City is invisible, even from Coit Tower. It can only be felt. The entire city is a conspiracy, a rich and stimulating assault on the senses which, if the visitor is not careful, brings about a permanent love affair. Of course lovers embrace fine company: join the ranks of Frank Lloyd Wright, George Stirling, John Steinbeck and Rudyard Kipling. It was Kipling who declared, 'San Francisco has but one drawback — 'tis hard to leave.'

Downtown San Francisco

The **San Francisco Visitor Center** at Hallidie Plaza (Powell and Market Streets) is a good starting point for bay city sightseeing. Their *San Francisco Book* has useful maps, information, and current events — the selection of festivities highlighting the city's rich cultural diversity. Chinese New Year includes fireworks and marauding dragons, while the Hispanic both commemorate and celebrate Cinco de Mayo (literally 5th of May). Japanese festivals rejoice cherry blossoms in spring and falling leaves in autumn, and for an old-

Getting Around San Francisco

San Francisco International (SFO) Airport is 15 miles (24 km) south of Union Square in San Mateo County. Airporter Coaches link travellers with the financial district and Union Square, Good Neighbors and Super Shuttle offer a hotel to airport service.

Public transport is excellent, and a growing number of MUNI buses offer wheelchair access. The fun and functional cable cars are also operated by MUNI, with maps and a daily pass (otherwise have plenty of change) good for both buses and cable cars — get the map at the San Francisco Visitor Center at Hallidie Plaza (Powell and Market Streets). Two cable car routes lead north: the Powell-Mason service to Fisherman's Wharf and the Powell-Hyde service to Hyde Street Pier. The latter passes Lombard, the 'crookedest street', while both pass Union Square en route. California Street offers the east-west cable car service, linking the Embarcadero to Nob Hill via Chinatown.

Bay Area Rapid Transit (BART) runs underneath Market Street with stations at Powell Street and the Embarcadero, both convenient for MUNI buses and cable cars. BART runs west to Daly City and under San Francisco Bay east to Fremont, Concord and Richmond, the latter line servicing Oakland and Berkeley. Trans-Bay Terminal at Mission and First hosts Greyhound Buses and provides connections to Amtrak rail in Oakland, while CalTrain leaves south for San Jose and points between from its terminus on Townsend and Fourth.

For drivers US101 is the main north-south route, while I-80 leads east over Oakland Bay Bridge. The tourist's San Francisco is primarily the northeast corner, starting just below busy Market Street and continuing north to Fisherman's Wharf. Sightseeing tours provide useful orientation, but to truly sample San Francisco's carnival-like atmosphere go on foot. Allow *days* rather than hours, wear comfortable shoes, and use public transport to save shoe leather. Drivers may visit outlying places of interest along the acclaimed 49-Mile Scenic Drive. Remember when driving downtown that cable cars have right of way and beware of driving on the tracks in wet weather as they may cause wheel-spin or a skid. To prevent runaway vehicles all drivers must park with wheels turned in to the curb, hand-brake set and parking gear applied.

Finally, smart visitors to blustery San Francisco bring several warm and/or windproof layers, even in summer, when chilling fogs can roll in without warning.

fashioned parade arrive the Sunday nearest St Patrick's Day.

Most places of interest are north of the Hallidie Plaza Visitor Centre on Powell and Market, but first take a two block sidestep south on 5th Street. San Francisco's roots are inexorably linked to the gold rush, and during the heyday considerable amounts of the yellow metal passed through the **Old US Mint**. Now a museum of that era, several rooms house period displays while the exhibits of gold are a firm favourite.

Tracing the cable car route north of Hallidie Plaza along Powell leads to **Union Square**, always brightly dressed in the season's flowers. People-watchers find the square offers an excellent cross-section of San Francisco life, while the vicinity is Mecca to the discerning shopper. Surrounding Union Square are Saks 5th Avenue, Neiman-Marcus, Burberry's and Bally, plus a host of speciality stores including Bullock and Jones, traditional men's clothiers since 1853. However do not just visit the shops, as the square's select hotels house some of the most opulent boutiques. The Westin St Francis is the square's upmarket landmark, offering the facilities and service demanded by its well-to-do guests, while the Chancellor Hotel on Powell is equally venerable, if less expensive.

The streets which delimit Union Square — Geary, Post, Powell, and Stockton — are lined with upmarket shops stocking goods with international trade marks like Gucci, Tiffany & Co, Cartier, Hermès and Jaeger. East on Post Street is the Galleria shopping and dining complex, topping its competitors with a rooftop garden. Maiden Lane, half a block south of Post, has the circular Frank Lloyd Wright Building, a prototype for New York City's Guggenheim Museum. Today it is hard to believe that Maiden Lane was formerly one of the Barbary Coast's most notorious red light districts.

Union Square received its name from vehement pro-Union demonstrations held at the onset of the Civil War. Parking was a problem even back in 1941, when the plaza was dismantled, a 1,000 space underground car park built, and the square reassembled overhead. Leave the car behind, as even illegal street-side spaces can be difficult to find (and expensive if used). Public transport is frequent and efficient, with taxis awaiting overburdened shoppers.

East from Union Square on Post is Crocker Galleria, a large glass-canopied shopping arcade inspired by Milan's Galleria Vittorio Emanuelle. Anyone interested in old telephones through to satellite message relay should detour to the **Telephone Pioneer Communications Museum** on New Montgomery Street before heading north to the Financial District. Montgomery, the district's main street, was dubbed 'Wall Street of the West.' The area is rich in architecture and

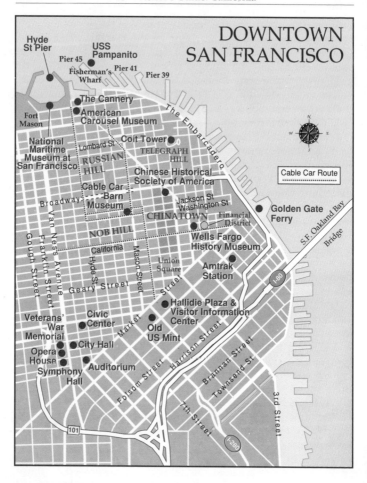

art, each structure trying to outdo its neighbours, especially with the decorative foyers.

 Although now a forward looking bank, the past is not forgotten at the delightful **Wells Fargo Bank History Museum** on Montgomery Street. Displays recapture the gold rush era and the part they played, including assay offices, telegraphs and stagecoach lines. Wells Fargo proudly recall their Pony Express days and exhibit a 130-year-old stage coach they have preserved. No part of The City would be complete without shopping and dining, and the Embarcadero Center offers both. The 27th floor observation area (closed on week-

The Cinco de Mayo parade celebrates San Francisco's Hispanic heritage

The skyline of Downtown San Francisco

ends and holidays) at the Transamerica Pyramid affords excellent views across to Coit Tower and the Golden Gate Bridge. To the north of the Transamerica Pyramid is Jackson Square, not an actual square but an old commercial area with 1850s buildings which have escaped the fire after the 1906 earthquake. Across Montgomery Street from the staid Financial District is the colourful Chinatown.

Chinatown to the Italian Quarter

Although San Francisco is famous for its cultural diversity, it is best known for its burgeoning Chinatown; the largest outside the Far East. In the nineteenth century this Oriental enclave segregated the Chinese from then intolerant San Francisco society. Today the city is proud of its Chinatown, rebuilt in classic Chinese style after the earthquake and fire of 1906, and this densely populated area welcomes all.

Down (east) from Portsmouth Square is the **Chinese Culture Center**, which offers changing exhibits of Oriental arts and artifacts. On selected days the centre takes guests through Chinatown, offering a Heritage Walk emphasizing Chinese culture and lifestyle, and a Culinary Walk. The lessons from this gastronomic tour of the markets is brought home by the grand finale, a Dim Sum lunch — reservations are strongly recommended. Those who prefer to explore Chinatown independently should still visit the centre, and perhaps utilize their list of authentic Dim Sum restaurants. Selecting from the plates of doughy delicacies requires no expertise, just a willingness to experiment — *do* try the lotus seed variety.

From Union Square the be-dragoned Gateway to Chinatown is found two blocks northeast on Grant Avenue. Shop-lined Grant offers electrical and photographic goods, tee shirt shops and bewildering bazaars offering Oriental curiosities. In general, those fancying a tasteful trinket or a 6ft-tall, thousand-armed Goddess of Mercy would do well to explore first, comparing prices, and then hone their bargaining skills. Old St Mary's Church is here on the corner of Grant and California, with cable cars running along the latter.

For the 'real' Chinatown, return east on Mason to Stockton Street, which is culturally closer to Hong Kong than San Francisco. Exploring an Oriental apothecary full of unidentifiable herbs and medicines is a fascinating experience. Beware that the Oriental love affair with ginseng makes that root incredibly expensive and often counterfeit. Shops and stalls sell fruit and vegetables, unfamiliar perhaps to Westerners but guaranteed ultra-fresh by the Chinese, who will not purchase anything which is not.

Just outside Chinatown, two blocks west of Stockton on Washington and Mason, is the **Cable Car Barn and Power House**. Incredibly, the entire cable car network is powered from this brick building. Although the underlying mechanism is very sophisticated, involving load sensors and cable fray detectors, the car operation is simplicity itself. Pull one lever to release the brakes, another to clamp onto the whizzing cable, and off the car goes. The free museum displays an 1873 cable car, an interesting film, and affords excellent views of the massive motors and wheels which propel the cables.

To see marathon mahjong and card games return east on Washington past Grant Avenue to Portsmouth Square. The clack of tiles is audible a block away, but do not expect to learn mahjong from watching their rapid-fire play. Also at the square are the newest generation of Chinese, brightly dressed for play and watched over by their proud grandparents.

The **Chinese Historical Society of America Museum** is a few blocks south of the culture centre on Commercial Street, offering a well balanced view of the Chinese community within the United States, and their contributions.

Grant Avenue continues north to the intersection with Columbus and Broadway, where tradition draws the border between Chinatown and North Beach. Looking down Broadway reveals the Chinese restaurants soon give way to neon nightclubs and sleazy strip joints — New York's 42nd Street without the underlying hint of menace. Columbus Avenue leads diagonally into **North Beach**, formerly the Italian quarter. Once barred from North Beach, the Chinese are making inroads on this erstwhile Italian stronghold; yet the Latin influence remains strong. Cafés serve such delights as *cappuccino, gelato* and *tira ma su*, and the occasional Italian neighbourhood store remains. Fine salamis and cheeses tempt the taste buds, while the shelves are stocked to the ceiling with bottles of Bardolino and Chianti — the makings of the perfect impromptu picnic.

From Washington Square drive or catch the eastbound number 39 bus up Telegraph Hill to give the feet a rest. Telegraph Hill affords one of San Francisco's most panoramic views of the bay and Golden Gate Bridge, especially from atop **Coit Tower**. Intended to resemble a fire hose, money for the tower was bequeathed by Lillie Hitchcock Coit, a wealthy, eccentric San Franciscan who would don protective gear and get to a blaze quicker than most firemen. Food is available at the base of the tower, as is limited parking. Once returned to Washington Square, continue north on Powell Street.

A schoolgirl in Chinatown

(opposite) At the Cable Car Barn visitors can see how the entire system is powered

Fish is always fresh at the Chinese market on Stockton Street

Fisherman's Wharf

Occupying prime San Francisco waterfront, Fisherman's Wharf is a continuous carnival. The fresh air carries the scent of steaming Dungeness crab; hawkers serve chowder in crusty sourdough rolls; buskers and mime artists compete with barking sea lions for the public's attention; while neon waxworks museums lure the passers-by away from the piers.

Pier 39 provides the essence of modern Fisherman's Wharf in one ※ renovated multi-storey boardwalk. Speciality shops and restaurants, cafes and bars, art galleries and entertainment — the pier even boasts its own motorized cable car trolley which tours San Francisco.

❋ Brash and breezy, the **San Francisco Experience** recalls the city's gold rush heyday, with a simulated earthquake to titillate the tourists. At times Pier 39 also hosts a California sea lion colony. The pinnipeds lounge along floating gangways, inured to the public's affections, free to come and go as they please. Another regular sighting is Pier 39's Blue & Gold Fleet, whose cruisers pass beneath the Golden Gate and Oakland Bay Bridges and near Alcatraz Island.

Strolling west along the waterfront leads to Pier 41, home of the Red & White Fleet. In conjunction with the National Park Service the
❋ Red & White offer an **Alcatraz Island** service. Guests may explore the island independently, with or without the park service's cassette tour. Within the notorious prison were America's most hardened criminals, where a long swim through cold, shark-filled waters awaited potential escapees (*officially*, no prisoners ever did). Infamous inmates include Al 'Scarface' Capone, George 'Machine Gun' Kelly, and Robert Stroud, who inspired the film *Birdman of Alcatraz*.

Other popular Red & White cruises include trips across the bay to the artist colonies of Sausalito and Tiburon, plus sailings to Vallejo, which offers Marine World Africa USA, a combined wildlife and marine mammal park: all described in the Northern Bay Area section
♣ of this chapter. Hikers and bikers love **Angel Island State Park**, reached by another Red & White cruise departing from Pier 41. A mostly paved road encircles the island, with trails up 781ft (238m) Mount Caroline Livermore. The island has been used variously as a Civil War fort, quarry, missile base, and an immigration station — use care when exploring and bring a picnic lunch. Red & White's 45-minute bay cruise departs from Pier 41 or nearby Pier 43 1/2. In evenings the bay cruise is extended to an hour, and includes hors d'oeuvres and a glass of champagne.

San Francisco offers various additional boating options. On weekends, Delta Riverboat Cruises journey up the Sacramento River to California's historic state capital, Sacramento. Leaving from Pier 43 1/2, the excursion can be round-trip or involve a bus ride in one direction. Going east (clockwise) along the waterfront away from Fisherman's Wharf, Hornblower Dining Yachts operate from Pier 33. Golden Gate Ferries operate an efficient service to Sausalito and Larkspur from the Ferry Building, which is further along the Embarcadero at the end of Market Street.

Fisherman's Wharf was named after the great fishing fleets which called San Francisco home, and while numbers have diminished some 200 boats are still moored just west of Pier 45. Surrounding the fleets are the seafood restaurants and sidewalk stalls which they supply. Steam rises from boiling pots while windows display fresh

Dungeness crabs (mid-November to May), mussels, *calimari*, and succulent shrimps to be cooked to order. Gold-seeking '49ers learned to make sourdough bread or went without, and at its best San Francisco sourdough is as crisp as French bread and twice as tasty. On cool days streetside vendors scoop out an oversized sourdough roll and fill the inside with west coast-style New England Clam Chowder. Just inland on Jefferson are **Ripley's Believe It or Not! Museum** and the **Wax Museum**.

Shoppers are well catered for at Fisherman's Wharf, with stores selling everything from nautically-oriented antiques to leather biker's jackets. Inland from Pier 39, Cost Plus Imports is a bargain hunter's paradise. The Cannery, a former Del Monte fruit-packing factory, and The Anchorage shopping and dining complexes are behind Fisherman's Wharf between Jefferson and Beach Streets. Just west of Hyde Street Pier and slightly uphill, a tall white sign proclaims Ghirardelli Square, previously a woolen mill then chocolate factory. Ghirardelli chocolate, still produced here using some of the original equipment, is amongst the finest, and the outlet store proffers specially packaged gift sets; the ideal choice for chocoholic friends. Apart from chocolate, this crenellated, white-edged red-brick complex with flower gardens and fountains offers specialty shops, art galleries, restaurants, bars and a fabulous view of the bay. Fisherman's Wharf, and especially these shopping complexes, attract buskers, mime artists, open air concerts and poetry readings, all adding to the colourful and vibrant atmosphere.

On Beach Street in Fisherman's Wharf is the **American Carousel Museum** where vintage photographs and two working carousel organs are supplemented by changing exhibitions of antique carved carousel animals.

Hyde Street plummets down from Russian Hill, coming to an abrupt end at the waterfront between Fisherman's Wharf and Ghirardelli Square. Hyde Street Pier is part of **San Francisco Maritime National Historical Park**, itself affiliated with Golden Gate National Recreation Area, considered the world's largest urban national park. Able-bodied visitors to the 'floating museum' at Hyde Street Pier tour several ships, including the *Balclutha*. This square-rigged three-masted Cape Horn sailing ship brought coal, wine, and manufactured goods to California in exchange for grain. Three-masted *C. A. Thayer* recalls the great fleets which brought Northwestern lumber to booming San Francisco. *Eureka* was, in her day, the world's largest passenger and auto ferry, losing her livelihood with the construction of the Golden Gate Bridge. The maritime national park shows films and gives displays of a seaman's skills. Nautical

Sea lions at Pier 39

books and gifts are sold in the Maritime Store, proceeds going to the park's interpretive and conservation programs.

The park also comprises the free and interesting **Maritime Museum** (just west of Hyde Street Pier and before Municipal Pier) with exhibits on Pacific maritime life from the 1800s to the present, an excellent collection of model ships and a huge photographic archive. At Pier 45 USS *Pampanito*, a World War II submarine ,offers a self-guided audio tour (stooping is required to get through the cramped passageways). Further west the *Jeremiah O'Brien*, thr last unaltered survivor of the Liberty Ships still in working order, is found by following the waterfront past the municipal pier. The desperate need for troop and supply ships during World War II engendered the Liberty Ship, with each of the 2,751 vessels assembled in 6-8 weeks.

Fisherman's Wharf attracts many streetside entertainers

The ship is open for tour and those visiting on 'steaming weekends' see the engines in operation.

The Holiday Inn and adjoining hotels at Fisherman's Wharf are conveniently located near the bus routes and not far from the cable car turntables — tourist attractions in their own right. Long queues build in the afternoon with visitors returning to Union Square hotels, so travellers may prefer to stay here and catch the cable car back to Fisherman's Wharf, reversing the trend. Those returning to Union Square in the afternoon would be advisable to return via cab or the bus from behind Ghirardelli Square. However, a trip on the Powell-Hyde line should not be missed as the cable car passes the top of 'the world's crookedest road' — hop off to photograph cars weaving to and fro to descend. While there remember to look back for the fantastic view across the bay to Alcatraz. The main 'photo opportunity' is as the cable cars ascend the hill, but do avoid being run over while taking that shot of a lifetime.

49-Mile Scenic Drive

The renowned 49-Mile Scenic Drive was opened in 1938 by President Franklin D. Roosevelt. Today San Francisco Convention and Visitors Bureau on Market Street produces an excellent free driving tour map covering the city's more widespread attractions. For convenience this narrative will follow the route for sights not yet described. Drivers will find the way marked by blue and white signs — alternatively take a Gray Line tour or use public transport to visit outlying sights of interest.

The drive starts at the **Civic Center**, a large complex southwest on Market Street from the Visitor Information Center. Bordered by Market, Hayes and Franklin streets and Golden Gate Avenue, the centre contains the fifth **City Hall**, an impressive domed French Revival building with a grand staircase and marble corridors. In front is the Civic Center Plaza bounded on the south by the **Civic Auditorium** which hosts conventions, sports and cultural events. To the east is the **Main Library**, a Beaux Arts structure housing over 1.2 million volumes and local history exhibits, including household items salvaged from the 1906 earthquake. Across Van Ness from City Hall is the **San Francisco War Memorial and Performing Arts Center** where opera, ballet dance, performing arts and symphony all take place. The second largest complex of its type in the USA, it comprises the Davies Symphony Hall, the War Memorial Opera House, and Herbst Theatre in the Veteran's Building. The United Nations Charter was signed in 1945 in the latter, while the third and fourth floors house the **San Francisco Museum of Modern Art**. 49-Mile Drive continues past Cathedral Hill, topped by the simple lines of the modern St Mary's Cathedral, and along Geary Boulevard.

Though the first Japanese arrived in the early 1860s, *Nihonmachi*, or **Japantown**, only began to form after the 1906 earthquake and fire. Today more than 12,000 Japanese-Americans call San Francisco home. **The Japan Center**, opened in 1968, is a 5-acre complex housing shops, art galleries, *sushi* bars, restaurants, Japanese baths, a hotel and eight cinemas. The central plaza contains the five-storey Peace Pagoda, a gift from the people of Japan. Visitors may browse the shops for a wide variety of interesting Japanese and Oriental products, sample artistically presented food floating past on small boats, or simply wander along Buchanan Mall past fountains and flowering plum and cherry trees. Japanese Cultural events are numerous, especially during the two weekends celebrating Cherry Blossom Festival (*Sakura Matsuri*), and throughout summer there is Japanese music and dance, flower arranging, origami, tea ceremonies and martial arts demonstrations.

California Historical Society is housed in the **Whittier Mansion**, one of the best examples of late nineteenth-century residential architecture in the city. The mansion on Jackson Street features changing exhibits on San Francisco before the 1906 earthquake. The 1886 Queen Anne style **Haas-Lilienthal House** is the only fully furnished Victorian house in the city open to the public (Wednesday and Sunday afternoons). The architecture is interesting — a tower, gables, dormers, art glass windows and each storey boasting a different shingle pattern.

Those who have thoroughly explored the downtown area by foot may wish to skip Union Square and Chinatown, instead heading straight for **Nob Hill**. Crisscrossed by cable car lines, it is a short hop west of Chinatown and affords views east down California Street across San Francisco Bay. Nob is short for the Hindi *nabob*, meaning Europeans of great wealth. The Big Four railroad barons and several Silver Kings who struck it rich with the Comstock Lode looked down upon San Francisco from Nob Hill. Their wooden palaces burned in the 1906 fire, making room for many others. **Grace Cathedral**, a fine example of Gothic architecture, is at California and Taylor atop the Crocker Mansion site. The main doors are exact replicas of Ghiberti's 'Gates of Paradise' at the Baptistry in Florence. Stanford Court Hotel, Fairmont Hotel and Mark Hopkins Hotel respectively replaced the Stanford, Fair and Hopkins homes, while Colton Hall became Huntington Park. Pause at Mark Hopkins Hotel for Sunday brunch or cocktails and a fantastic city vista from Top of the Mark.

The square-rigged sailing ship Balclutha *at Hythe Street Pier*

49-Mile Drive leads through Russian Hill with its small rural enclaves, and passes the top of **Lombard Street**, where nine hairpin bends in one block earned it the nickname 'the crookedest street in the world'. ❄

COW HOLLOW

The valley containing Union Street today was originally known as Cow Hollow. The first dairy was established in 1861, with numbers soon exceeding thirty in this rich grassland. Later as slaughter houses, tanneries and sausage factories invaded the valley the stench offended the affluent living atop Pacific Heights. By 1891 the Board of Health had evicted the cows and a residential and service district emerged. The regeneration of Victorian Union Street began in the late 1950s, producing an interesting area between Van Ness and Steiner. Passages lead to small courtyards, nooks and crannies best explored on foot, if time permits. Apart from an amazing variety of handicraft shops, fashion boutiques, restaurants and singles bars are two buildings of note. The **Octagon House** on Gough and Union 🏠 recalls the short-lived fashion for octagonal houses in the 1850s. The building is now headquarters of the National Society of Colonial Dames of America, and is a museum of colonial and Federal-period

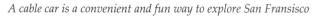

A cable car is a convenient and fun way to explore San Fransisco

antiques. **Vedanta Temple** (one block north of Union on Webster and Filbert) is a reflection of Vedanta belief that God can be reached through any religion and, one presumes, any style of architecture.

FORT MASON CENTER TO GOLDEN GATE BRIDGE

Starting one block west of Ghirardelli Square and lining San Francisco Bay, Fort Mason was once a military installation held by Spain, Mexico then America. Warehouses, piers, barracks and administration buildings have been turned into an entertaining national urban park. **Fort Mason Center**, in addition to an American Youth Hostel, houses a wide variety of small museums, theatres, studios, snack bars and restaurants, offering a lively melange of arts and recreational facilities. A large car park serves the complex.

The small but fascinating **Mexican Museum** is the first of its kind in the USA. Its permanent collection focuses on five main areas of Mexican art; pre-hispanic (including ceramic and stone artifacts), colonial (religious oil paintings, sculptures etc.), folk art, Mexican fine art and Mexican-American fine art (contemporary works in various media). The adjacent La Tienda sells authentic Mexican folk art, proceeds going to the museum. The **Museum of the San Francisco African-American Historical and Cultural Society** supplements a small permanent collection of African artifacts with changing art exhibits by African Americans and a gift shop. For a look at Italian art and culture visit the **Museo Italo-Americano**. The small permanent collection, library and gift shop are enhanced by changing art exhibitions, film, music and gastronomic events. Art of a different kind is displayed at the **San Francisco Craft and Folk Art Museum**. Here contemporary arts and crafts from diverse cultures can be appreciated through exhibitions and educational programs. Another athenaeum of note is the J. Porter Shaw Library, part of the National Maritime Museum, which focuses on commercial sail and steam ships of the Pacific. If hungry while at Fort Mason Center, try out Greens (gourmet vegetarian) Restaurant, owned and operated by the San Francisco Zen Center, or drop into Cooks & Company for soup and sandwiches. At Plowshares Coffeehouse the San Francisco Folk Music Center stages traditional music and entertainment.

Also located within the Fort Mason Center are the administrative headquarters for the **Golden Gate National Recreation Area**, offering maps, brochures and information on park events. Established in 1972, it is the World's largest urban park, covering an incredible 72,815 acres and including approximately 28 miles of coastline. Found on both sides of San Francisco Bay the area stretches from north of the Golden Gate Bridge, round the northern and western edges of the city down to Fort Funston, and includes Alcatraz Island. From Fort Mason the **Golden Gate Promenade** leads 3.5 miles (5.5 km) through Marina Green and Crissy Field to Fort Point below the Golden Gate Bridge. This walk offers spectacular bay views, but remember that windproof jacket.

Another major attraction on 49-Mile Drive is the **Palace of Fine Arts**. This plaster of Paris structure — the only surviving Beaux Arts structure of thirty-two palaces built for the 1915 Panama-Pacific Exhibition — was restored in 1967 and now houses a 1,000-seat theatre and the **Exploratorium**. This fascinating hands-on 'museum' offers unparalleled opportunity for children of *all* ages to investigate science, art and human perception, using their senses to the full. With over 650 experiments to perform, allow at least half a day. Those without children should borrow some or come on their own.

The Presidio, established in 1776 by the Spaniards, is one of the oldest military establishments in the USA. Currently its fate has not been decided, but many San Franciscans wish for the property to be added to the Golden Gate National Recreation Area.

The brick fortress at **Fort Point National Historic Site** sits beneath Golden Gate Bridge and contains displays of Civil War memorabilia. Above it towers the colossal orange-red **Golden Gate Bridge**, spanning the strait between San Francisco and Marin County to the north. The 49-Mile Drive suggests a convenient stop near the bridge, with a car park, restrooms, and shop.

The Golden Gate observation area provides excellent views of the bridge, but to really appreciate the enormity don a windproof and walk out onto the bridge (pedestrians and cyclists free, vehicular toll southbound only). The bridge affords excellent vistas to Sausalito, Alcatraz, San Francisco and on clear days beyond Berkeley to Mount Diablo.

The drive then leads south to 600ft (183m) long China Beach, offering a different perspective on the Golden Gate Bridge. Recreational includes picnicking, sunbathing and swimming in one of the bay areas safest beaches, with lifeguards on duty in summer.

Art lovers will appreciate the **California Palace of the Legion of Honor**, adapted from the original palace in Paris and commanding a hilltop in Lincoln Park. Donated to the city in 1924 as a museum of painting and sculpture, the twenty galleries and two courtyards house numerous masterpieces of European art. The museum is particularly strong in French works, dating from Medieval times to the twentieth century, with an outstanding collection of Rodin sculptures including *The Thinker*. Also here is the Achenbach Foundation for Graphic Arts — largest collection of prints and drawings (fifteenth century to present) in Western America. Visitors should note that admission includes same day entry to the de Young Museum and the Asian Art Museum, both found in Golden Gate Park.

49-Mile Drive next passes **Cliff House**, the third to occupy this picturesque site. To the cocktail lounge and restaurants are added spectacular views of the Marin coast, Seal Rocks and the Pacific

Follow the Golden Gate Bridge from San Francisco to Marin County

Ocean. Look for sea lions (September to June) and occasional schools of migrating whales in winter. Here too is a gift shop, Golden Gate National Recreation Area visitor centre and viewing platform. South is Ocean Beach, 4 miles (6.5km) of sand and surf, pleasant to stroll but too dangerous for swimming, even when it looks calm. Further south the road hugs the shoreline, paralleling the recreation area's coastal trail and passing the two windmills which mark the western entrance of Golden Gate Park. Further along is **San Francisco Zoo**, a popular outing for the locals.

A slight detour takes in the most southerly part of the Golden Gate Recreation Area and Fort Funston, where a wheelchair-accessible loop trail offers beautiful coastal views. The high cliffs and strong winds attract hang gliders so remember that windproof. Forty-nine mile drive then circles Harding Park where the 5 acres of freshwater **Lake Merced** offer boating and trout fishing. Those taking this route on summer Sundays can enjoy free musical entertainment at the Sigmund Stern Grove.

GOLDEN GATE PARK

Crown jewel of 49-Mile Drive is charming **Golden Gate Park**, 3 miles long and encompassing 1,017 acres of gardens, meadows, playgrounds, picnic areas, athletics fields, lakes and trees. This mammoth urban park also offers a taste of California culture, including some of the state's finest museums. 'Leisure' activities include traversing the 27 miles (43km) of footpaths, 7.5 miles (12km) of equestrian trails and 15 miles (24km) of roads; a number of the latter being closed on Sundays. Free guided walking tours are available weekends from May through October, with horse and buggy tours daily in fine weather. To enjoy Golden Gate Park to the maximum, the scenic drive meanders past the numerous attractions, including Buffalo Paddock where a small herd of bison graze.

From the southwest of scenic **Stow Lake** the pagoda from Taipei can be seen near Huntington Falls which grace Strawberry Hill. At over 400ft (122m) this is the highest point in the park. Further around is the Boat House, offering rentals for a pleasant jaunt across the lake. Golden Gate Band plays at the music concourse on Sundays at 1 pm, where stopping is definitely worthwhile despite the usual difficulty of parking.

California Academy of Sciences, the world-class natural history museum, was founded in 1853. Exhibits range from life-sized dioramas depicting the diversity of nature to hands-on learning using the latest video and computer technology. Within the Academy are the huge Steinhart aquarium, the Morrison Planetarium, and a gallery of humorous, biologically-orientated cartoons. Visitors can also feel the earth moving at 'Safequake', which simulates two San Franciscan tremors. If possible allow a half day for full exploration.

Across the Music Concourse the ever popular **M. H. de Young Memorial Museum**, started in 1894, features an outstanding and eclectic collection of paintings, sculpture, pottery, glass and textiles in some forty galleries. Of special note is the huge treasure of American art from colonial times to the mid-twentieth century. Included in the admission fee is entry to the adjacent west wing, which houses the excellent **Asian Art Museum**. Home to the largest collection of Asian art outside the Orient, the museum possesses over 10,000 items, of which only one tenth can be displayed at one time. The museum is especially strong on Chinese works with emphasis on Ming and Ching periods, though all Chinese periods and every major Asian country is represented.

Next to the Asian Art Museum is the **Japanese Tea Garden**, a serene 5 acres created in 1894 for the Midwinter International Exposition. Harmonious landscaping blends pools, waterfalls, streams, bridges, paths and pagodas. Watched over by the Buddha, the gardens are especially lovely in late March and early April, when cherry trees blossom and the azaleas are flowering. Waitresses in kimonos serve tea daily in the Tea Pavilion.

Budding naturalists can examine the world's varied vegetation at the free **Strybing Arboretum and Botanical Gardens**, where 6,000 plant species are arranged geographically or in specialized collections. The Strybing Store just outside the gates supply botanically-related gifts, while opposite is the large horticultural reference library, also open to the public.

On Kennedy Drive is the oldest building within Golden Gate Park, the **Conservatory of Flowers**, which in 1879 was shipped round Cape Horn from England. The conservatory has palms, cycads, two ponds containing water lilies and maintains a collection of 4,000 species. Of special note are the orchids, displayed in the west wing when in bloom. Before leaving the park those with youngsters may wish to take the winding Bowling Green Drive. The Children's Playground includes rides on the exquisitely restored Golden Gate Carrousel, built in 1912.

Next on 49-Mile Drive is the breathtaking climb up **Twin Peaks**. A road winds up to the 910ft (227m) summit and the panoramic view from atop is perhaps San Francisco's best. Coming back to earth and the roots of the city, the tour next visits Mission San Francisco de Asis, known locally as **Mission Dolores**. Father Serra established this, the sixth of his California missions in 1776. Completed in 1791, this adobe building is the oldest in San Francisco. The mission, basilica, cemetery and a small but interesting museum are open to the public, the latter containing the 1776 baptismal register and sacred items.

Candlestick Point State Recreation Area is a pleasant bayside park adjacent to Candlestick Park, home to the San Francisco '49ers football team and San Francisco Giants baseball team.

Northern Bay Area

Many delights lie across the bay, just a short drive or ferry-hop from The City. Tour operators cover these areas, which are also well serviced by BART and bay area public transport. Drivers should head north across the Golden Gate Bridge, stopping at the vista point for an excellent view of the bridge, boats on the bay, Alcatraz and the San Francisco skyline.

Marin Peninsula is a mixture of rugged, undeveloped coastline, panoramic hilltop views and the gentle bustle of the bay side communities. The peninsula also contains a large portion of Golden Gate National Recreation Area and **Mount Tamalpais State Park**, offering a natural respite from the excitement of San Francisco. For unparalleled views walk to Point Bonita Lighthouse on Marin Headlands State Park (open weekends in season) or hike to the top of 2,571ft (784m) Mount Tamalpais. Miwok Livery offers tuition and horses for a guided ride, while backcountry camping is available by permit. In Larkspur, Wheel Escapes provide rental cycles and offer cycle tours. Remember wind or fog is likely in the parks; dress accordingly.

Muir Woods National Monument is administered by the Golden Gate NRA. Preserving a great stand of massive coastal redwood, the world's tallest tree, Muir Woods is a pleasant day trip from San Francisco and the Bay Area. A bus tour is a sensible option as parking at Muir can be a problem, and a warm layer may be appreciated in the cool shadow of these giants, with old growth redwoods reaching up to 250tt (76m) high.

Bayside **Sausalito**, 8 miles (5km) north of San Francisco, is a picturesque community reminiscent of a small Mediterranean resort, complete with hillside homes and a fleet of yachts. Artists, writers and craftsmen attracted by the bohemian atmosphere inhabit a colony of houseboats moored along the waterfront. Visitors may purchase their works in the village markets and numerous galleries. Sausalito is a popular day trip from San Francisco, and the ferry ride involves an enjoyable cruise across the bay.

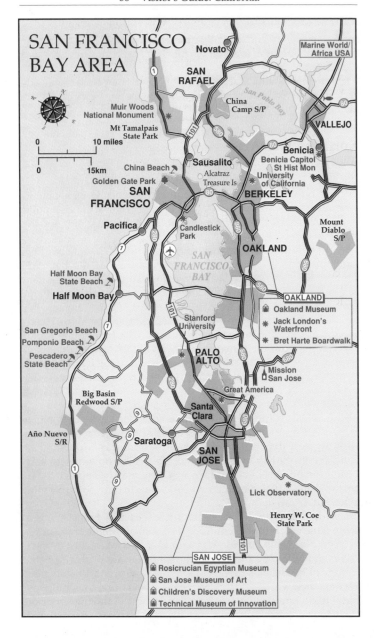

SAN FRANCISCO BAY AREA

Novato

SAN RAFAEL

China Camp S/P

San Pablo Bay

Marine World/ Africa USA

VALLEJO

Muir Woods National Monument

Mt Tamalpais State Park

0   10 miles

0   15km

Sausalito

China Beach

Golden Gate Park

Alcatraz
Treasure Is

Benicia

Benicia Capitol
St Hist Mon

University of California

BERKELEY

SAN FRANCISCO

Pacifica

Candlestick Park

OAKLAND

Mount Diablo S/P

SAN FRANCISCO BAY

Half Moon Bay State Beach

Half Moon Bay

Stanford University

OAKLAND

🏛 Oakland Museum

✴ Jack London's Waterfront

✴ Bret Harte Boardwalk

San Gregorio Beach

Pomponio Beach

Pescadero State Beach

PALO ALTO

Mission San Jose

Big Basin Redwood S/P

Great America

Santa Clara

Año Nuevo S/R

Saratoga

SAN JOSE

Lick Observatory

Henry W. Coe State Park

SAN JOSE

🏛 Rosicrucian Egyptian Museum

🏛 San Jose Museum of Art

🏛 Children's Discovery Museum

🏛 Technical Museum of Innovation

The **Bay Model Visitor Center** in the Marinship area houses a 2-acre hydraulic model of the bay and delta. This excellent overview is complimented by exhibits on the bay's cultural and natural history, an audio tour and a film. The **California Marine Mammal Center** rescues and rehabilitates sick and stranded animals, affording close-up views of the area's seals and sea lions.

Further round the bay is **San Rafael**, where Mission San Rafael Arcangel may be found just three blocks off US 101. This, the twentieth mission, was founded in 1817 to prevent encroachment by the Russians, and after being demolished in 1870 was rebuilt in 1949. While in the area check out current performances at the nearby **Marin Center**, which offers varied musical and theatrical productions. Four miles (6.5km) east of San Rafael is **China Camp State Park**, where rangers lead tours through the last of twenty such Chinese fishing villages. In addition to learning of the shrimping industry which once thrived there, visitors will find this natural area a good place for walking, swimming or bird watching. North at Novato the traveller can investigate early Native American artifacts and culture at the **Marin Museum of the American Indian**, located on a Coast Miwok archaeological site.

Moving clockwise around San Pablo Bay, the next stop is Vallejo.

Meet the dolphins at Marine World Africa USA, Vallejo

Capital of California for one brief week in 1852, Vallejo was site of the first Pacific naval station founded in 1854. The town's history, naval and otherwise, is examined at the **Vallejo Naval and Historical Museum** in the old City Hall. Vallejo is best known for its **Marine World Africa USA**, a combination natural habitat zoo and oceanarium. The crowds, many of whom travel up from San Francisco via ferry, are delighted by antics of dolphins and killer whales.

Further west is **Benicia**, which usurped Vallejo as state capital. **Benicia Capitol State Historic Park** preserves the state's third and oldest surviving capitol building. The 1852 structure has been lovingly restored and furnished in period, with park rangers on hand to answer questions about the state's early political history. Wrangling over the site of California's seat of government was fierce, with numerous towns making extravagant offers during the period dubbed 'The Capitol on Wheels'. Next to the capitol and also part of the park is the **Fischer Hanlon House**, a restored home which originated as a gold rush hotel. Although suffering an industrial periphery, downtown Benicia has numerous early buildings and the chamber of commerce leaflets outline walking and driving tours.

Oakland/Berkeley Area

The San Francisco-Oakland Bay Bridge (westbound toll) crosses San Francisco Bay, connecting Treasure Island to San Francisco and Oakland. Site of a large naval station, **Treasure Island** offers views across the bay back to the city and a naval history museum.

Oakland was first settled in 1850, the same year California achieved statehood, and was put on the map as terminus for the transcontinental railroad. The settlement further doubled in size after the 1906 earthquake and fire — far less severe in Oakland than across the bay, prompting many families to move there from San Francisco. Another population explosion occurred with the completion of the Oakland Bay Bridge in 1936, especially as Oakland overtook San Francisco as a major port.

Famous Oakland literary figures include Jack London and Bret Harte, the latter author of numerous gold rush stories and poems. Adjoining the site of his boyhood home, **Bret Harte Boardwalk** (5th Street) consists of a brick barn and renovated clapboard buildings from the 1870s, now housing shops and restaurants. At the bottom of Broadway on Oakland Estuary is **Jack London's Waterfront**, a revamped square with many restaurants overlooking the marina. While Jack London's Yukon log cabin has been moved here, the **First and Last Chance Saloon**, a favourite haunt of Jack London, remains in its original location a block from the square on Webster. Adjacent to the square is Jack London Village, a turn-of-the-century style shopping complex containing specialty shops, boutiques and restaurants.

To the northeast on 10th and Oak is the reknowned modern three-storey **Oakland Museum**, showing exhibits on Californian ecology, history and art. Further north is **Lake Merritt**, a large saltwater lake plied by a miniature sternwheeler. The surrounding **Lakeside Park** contains a botanical garden and the first wildfowl refuge in the USA. At the park's Grand Avenue entrance is the 7-acre **Children's Fairyland**, depicting various fairy tales and nursery rhymes. Resident animals are fed throughout the day.

On Bellvue Avenue is **Lakeside Park Garden Center**, offering a selection of gardens to enjoy. To the west on Broadway the Art Deco **Paramount Theatre of Arts**, home of the Oakland Symphony Orchestra, produces a varied selection of music, ballet, classic movies and a concert series on the theatre's Wurlitzer organ.

Oakland Zoo (5 miles east of downtown across MacArthur Freeway in **Knowland Park**) offers amusement and miniature train rides, a Skyride, playgrounds and picnic facilities in addition to animals. A children's petting zoo is included in the admission.

The freeway leads north towards lively and colourful Berkeley, best known for the long-established **University of California at Berkeley**, one of nine campuses throughout the state. The Information Center at the top of Telegraph Street and the Visitor Centre on Oxford Street give information and maps for self-guided walking tours while free guided tours leave from the Visitor Center. Take the lift up the popular 307ft (94m) Sather Tower (known as the Campanile) for views of campus and bay. Points of interest include Lowie Museum of Anthropology, the Museum of Paleontology, the University Art Gallery and Pacific Film Archives, Lawrence Hall of Science, a 30-acre botanical garden, theatres and a concert hall. The **Judah L. Magnes Museum** on Russell contains a large collection of Judaica, including ritual objects and fine arts.

Northeast in **Martinez**, across Carquinez Strait from Benicia, is the 1882 house which belonged to naturalist and author John Muir. This is now preserved along with the 1849 Martinez Adobe in **John Muir National Historic Site**. A self-guided tour, along with family memorabilia and a film, illustrate the life and work of the co-founder of Yosemite National Park.

South in **Danville** the **Behring Auto Museum** exhibits unique, custom-built cars, many worth over $1 million. The backdrop is **Mount Diablo State Park**, where views from the 3,849ft summit are said to take in more of the earth's surface than anywhere excepting the 19,000ft Mount Kilimanjaro. The panorama is certainly impressive, encompassing land between Golden Gate Bridge and the Sierra Nevada, and from Lassen Peak to Mount Whitney.

Southern Bay Area

There are two contrasting yet visually rewarding routes south from San Francisco. The inland choice, I-280, is an officially scenic highway while those wanting to leave civilization behind may pick up scenic Skyline Drive, which traverses a series of ridges overlooking the bay and ocean.

After the reservoirs I-280 passes **Filoli House and Gardens**, found to the right on Edgewood and right again on Canada. Book in advance for guided tours of the 1917 mansion and gardens (under 12 years old not admitted). I-280 continues south to high-tech Palo Alto and **Stanford University**. Attractions include a campus tour, Memorial Church, art gallery, Hoover Tower and the Stanford Linear Accelerator Center (SLAC). Silicon Valley, microcomputer capital of America, starts here and continues south past Palo Alto to San Jose, its self-styled capital.

Great America in **Santa Clara** offers the latest thrill rides (try the Vortex stand-up roller coaster), a huge IMAX cinema, and a special section for youngsters.

Mission Santa Clara de Asis was founded in 1777, and today the original gardens and a replica mission form part of the University of Santa Clara campus. The **de Saisset Museum** houses paintings, sculptures and a history of the missions. For nineteenth- and twentieth-century art visit **Triton Museum**'s 7-acre sculpture garden.

Greater San Jose

Pueblo de San Jose de Guadalupe, now **San Jose**, was founded in 1777 to provide food for San Francisco and Monterey. San Jose became first capital of the state of California, holding the title between 1849 and 1851. Situated in the fertile Santa Clara valley, agricultural land continues to do battle with the industrial estates of Silicon Valley. San Jose is still an important wine-producing area with three major wineries within the city limits (tours and tastings available).

The 1892 Romanesque post office now contains the excellent **San Jose Museum of Art**, supplemented by a new 45,000 square foot wing. The permanent collection contains contemporary paintings, photographs, sculptures and multimedia works, and international travelling exhibitions are often hosted. Youngsters will delight in the striking purple **Children's Discovery Museum** with its hands-on science, technology, and art exhibits, while all enjoy **Technology Center of Silicon Valley** ('The Garage'), supported by the valley's high-tech companies.

The fascinating **Rosicrucian Egyptian Museum** contains a diverse selection of mummies, Egyptian, Babylonian and Assyrian artifacts, and an extremely realistic full scale model of an Egyptian tomb. Included is the Rosicrucian Art Gallery, while opposite is the Rosicrucian Planetarium and Science Museum. Nearby Municipal Rose Gardens offer picnic facilities and a magnificent display of blooms in May and June.

Out on Winchester Boulevard, **Winchester Mystery House** has to be seen to be believed. A spiritualist told the wealthy Winchester rifle heiress she would achieve eternal life and appease spirits of those killed by the 'Gun that Won the West' only by continually adding to her house. The result — a 160-room house with over 10,000 windows, plus balconies, turrets, and staircases leading nowhere.

Kelly Park's 150 acres encompass **Happy Hollow Park and Zoo**,

Papyrus growing outside the Rosicrucian Egyptian Museum in San Jose

a creative children's playground, rides and a zoo; the tranquil **Japanese Friendship Gardens**, a place for quiet contemplation and refreshments at the tea house; and the **San Jose Historical Museum** with twenty-five buildings from San Jose's past. The more energetic may prefer Raging Waters Aquatic Theme Park, which offers thirty water attractions including slides, rivers and pools. Bargain-hunters must visit the San Jose Flea Market, billed the world's largest and covering 125 acres with a hodgepodge of goods, restaurants and free entertainment.

Located in **Fremont**, north of San Jose, Mission San Jose de Guadalupe was destroyed by an earthquake in 1868. The 1985 replica exhibits mission artifacts. Nearby Fremont Peak offers excellent views of the area. For longer views drive 19 miles (31km) east of San Jose to **Lick Observatory**, part of the University of California and found atop 4209ft (1,283m) Mount Hamilton. Alternatively, escape civilization completely at **Henry W. Coe State Park**, a rugged area of deep canyons and ridges with 125 miles (200km) of trails.

Southwest from San Jose on SR17 then west on SR9 leads to the resort town of **Saratoga**, where **Hakone Gardens** offer 15 tranquil acres of Japanese landscaping. An arboretum surrounds nearby **Villa Montalvo Center for the Arts**. The historic villa exhibits various works, while the performing arts are catered for in a 300-seat indoor and 800-seat outdoor theatre.

Big Basin Redwoods, California's oldest state park, offers 80 miles (130km) of hiking trails and an easy nature trail through redwood groves. Facilities support camping and picnicking, plus an excellent little interpretive centre. The coolness of the redwoods are especially popular on hot summer days.

SR9 continues south to Santa Cruz, covered in Chapter 5, and those returning to San Francisco may follow scenic SR1 north along the coast. Rugged **Ano Nuevo State Reserve** is renowned for its elephant seal population. Restrictions apply during the December through April breeding season, when rangers lead guided tours to view these huge creatures. Winter is also a good time for spotting migrating gray whales (call early for reservations). Outside breeding season trails are fully open for hiking with the chance of seeing harbor seals, sea lions, sea otters, and innumerable birds.

North of Ano Nuevo the coast offers picturesque state beaches where the surf pounds in — ideal for strolling but check locally before venturing into the water. Further north is **Half Moon Bay**, a quiet town overlooking 2 miles (3km) of crescent sandy beach. Civilization returns at the coastal resort of **Pacifica**, which offers a selection of seafood restaurants and its own series of beaches.

Additional Information

Regional Visitor Information

Marin County Visitor Bureau
30 N San Pedro Rd, Suite 150
San Rafael, CA 94903
☎ 415-472-7470

Oakland Visitors Bureau
1000 Broadway, Suite 200
Oakland, CA 94607
☎ 415-839-9000

San Francisco Visitors Bureau
201 Third St, Suite 900
San Francisco, CA 94103-3185
☎ 415-974-6900

San Jose Visitors Bureau
333 W San Carlos St, Suite 1000
San Jose, CA 95110
☎ 408-295-9600

Vallejo Visitors Bureau
Vallejo Ferry Terminal
495 Mare Island
Vallejo, CA 94590
☎ 707-642-3653

Visitor Information Center
Hallidie Plaza
Powell & Market Streets
San Francisco, CA 94101-6977
☎ 415-291-2000

The Missions

**Mission Dolores
(San Francisco De Asis)**
3321 16th St
San Francisco, CA 94114
☎ 415-621-8203
Open: 9am-4pm, except major
holidays
Basilica, museum, cemetery, gifts

Mission San Jose
43300 Mission Blvd, PO Box 3159
Fremont, CA 94539

☎ 415-657-1797
Open: 10am-5pm except major
holidays
Donation. Chapel, museum

Mission San Rafael Arcangel
1102 5th Ave
San Rafael, CA 94901
☎ 415-456-3016
Open: 11am-4pm Mon-Sat, 10am-
4pm Sun
Free; gift shop

Mission Santa Clara de Asis
920 Alviso St
Santa Clara University
Santa Clara, CA 95050
☎ 408-554-4023
Open: 10am-5pm Tue-Fri, 1pm-
5pm Sat & Sun
Free; museum, gifts, garden

Santa Cruz Mission
126 High St
Santa Cruz, CA 95060
☎ 408-426-5686
Open: chapel 9am-5pm

Places to Visit

Alcatraz Island
Pier 41, Fisherman's Wharf
San Francisco, CA
☎ 415-546-2896 (info)
415-392-7469 (reservations)
Times vary, book ahead. Admission
included with boat tour. Cassette
tour (extra), slide show, gifts

Angel Island State Park
Ferry from SF, Sausalito, or Vallejo
San Francisco, CA 94109
☎ 415-435-1915 (park)
415-546-2869 (ferry)
Open: 9am-sunset
Camp, hike, picnic

Ano Nuevo State Reserve
Highway 1
20 miles north of Santa Cruz, CA
☎ 415-879-0595
Open: 9am-3pm; guided tours mid-
Dec to Apr (book ahead)
Seal & bird watching, hiking, tide
pools

**Ansel Adams Center (Friends of
Photography Museum)**
250 4th St
San Francisco, CA 94103
☎ 415-495-7000
Open: 11am-6pm Tue-Sun
Gifts, exhibits of photography
including Ansel Adams

Asian Art Museum
Golden Gate Park
San Francisco, CA 94118
☎ 415-668-8921
Open: 10am-5pm Wed-Sun. Free
first Wed & Sat morning of month
Gifts, &

Benicia Capitol State Historic Park
831 First St
Benicia, CA 94506
☎ 707-745-3385
Open: 10am-5pm
Former capitol, restored home,
gardens, &

Cable Car Museum
Washington & Mason Streets
San Francisco, CA
☎ 415-474-1887
Open: 10am-5pm, -6pm Apr-Oct
Free; cable viewing room, film,
gifts, &

California Academy of Sciences
Golden Gate Park
San Francisco, CA 94118
☎ 415-750-7145
Open: 10am-5pm, extended summer
Natural history, aquarium,
planetarium, gifts, &

**California Historical Society/
Whittier Mansion**
2090 Jackson St
San Francisco, CA 94109
☎ 415-567-1848
Open: 1pm-4.30pm Tue-Sun, tours
1.30pm, also 3pm weekends.
Free on 1st Wed of month

**California Palace of the Legion of
Honor**
Lincoln Park
San Francisco, CA 94109
☎ 415-750-3659
Open: 10am-5pm Wed-Sun except
major holidays. Gifts

Cannery
2801 Leavenworth St.
San Francisco, CA 94133
☎ 415-771-3112
Free; shops, restaurants, galleries,
entertainment, &

Children's Discovery Museum
180 Woz Way
Guadalupe River Park
San Jose, CA
☎ 408-298-5437
Open: 10am-5pm Tue-Sat, noon-
5pm Sun
Hands-on learning, gifts, picnic (in
park)

Chinese Culture Center
750 Kearny St, Third Floor
San Francisco, CA 94108
☎ 415-986-1822
Open: 10am-4pm Tue-Sat except
holidays
Free; exhibits, events, cultural &
gastronomic tours by reservation

**Chinese Historical Society of
America Museum**
650 Commercial St (Basement)
San Francisco, CA 94111
☎ 415-391-1188
Open: Noon-4pm Wed-Sun except
major holidays. Gifts

Coit Tower
Telegraph Hill
San Francisco, CA 94133
☎ 415-362-8037
Open: 10am-5.30pm Jun-Sept, 9am-4.30pm Oct-May, except holidays
Views, gifts, restaurant

Conservatory of Flowers
Golden Gate Park
San Francisco, CA
☎ 415-558-3973
Open: 9am-6pm Apr-Oct, 10am-5pm Nov-Mar. Gifts

de Young Memorial Museum
Tea Garden Dr, Golden Gate Park
San Francisco, CA 94118
☎ 415-750-3659
Open: 10am-5pm Wed-Sun except major holidays
Free 1st Wed and Sat morning of month
Gifts, tours, &

Exploratorium
3601 Lyon St (Palace of Fine Arts)
San Francisco, CA 94123
☎ 415-561-0360
Open: hours vary but open late Wed. Closed Mon & Tue
Free on 1st Wed & after 6pm other Wed.
Hands-on learning, gifts, &

Fort Mason Center
Buchanan St & Marina Blvd
San Francisco, CA
☎ 415-441-5705
Open: hours vary
Art & cultural activities in former WW II warehouses

Ghirardelli Square
900 N Point St
San Francisco, CA 94133
☎ 415-775-5500
Free; shops, restaurants, entertainment, &

Golden Gate National Recreation Area
Park HQ, Building 201, Fort Mason
San Francisco, CA 94123
☎ 415-556-0560
Open: visitor centre 9.30am-4.30pm
Free; Beaches, hiking, Cliff House, seal watching, &

Golden Gate Park
McLaren Lodge Headquarters
Fell & Stanyan Streets
San Francisco, CA 94117
☎ 415-666-7200
Open: hours vary
Free; Walks, ponds, equestrian centre, gardens, museums, food, &

Great America Theme Park
Great American Highway
PO Box 1776
Santa Clara, CA 95052
☎ 408-988-1800
Open: 10-9 daily summers (-11 Sat), weekends in Spring & Autumn.
Amusement park rides, food & gifts, &

Hakone Gardens
21000 Big Basin Way
Saratoga, CA 95070
☎ 408-867-3438
Open: 10am-5pm Mon-Fri, 11am-5pm Sat & Sun
Donation. Gardens

Happy Hollow & Kelly Park
1300 Senter Rd
San Jose, CA 95112
☎ 408-277-4193
Open: hours vary
Children's park & petting zoo, Japanese gardens, history museum

Henry W. Coe State Park
Dunnie Ave, off Hwy 101
Morgan Hill, CA
☎ 408-779-2728

Open: 9am-Sunset
Camp, hike, mountain bike, ranch museum

Jack London's Waterfront
30 Jack London Square
Oakland, CA 94607
☎ 415-893-7956
Bayside shopping & restaurants, &

John Muir NHS
4202 Alhambra Ave
Martinez, CA 94533
☎ 415-228-8860
Open: 10am-4.30pm except major holidays
Victorian house, adobe house, orchards, gifts

Marine World Africa USA
Marine World Pkwy
Vallejo, CA 94589
☎ 707-644-4000
Open: 9.30am-5pm -6.30pm in summer
Zoo, marine mammal performances, food, gifts, ferry from SF, &

Mt. Diablo State Park
Diablo Rd, PO Box 250
Danville, CA 94528
☎ 415-837-2525
Open: 9am-Sunset
Views, camp, hike, picnic

Oakland Museum
1000 Oak St
Oakland, CA 94607
☎ 415-273-3401
Open: 10am-5pm Wed-Sat, Noon-7 Sun
Free; gardens, gifts, &

Old US Mint
Fifth & Mission Streets
San Francisco, CA 94103
☎ 415-744-6830
Open: 10am-4pm Mon-Fri except holidays
Free; gifts

Pier 39
PO Box 3730, Fisherman's Wharf
San Francisco, CA 94119
☎ 415-981-8030
Free; shops, restaurants, entertainment, SF Experience, &

Ripley's Believe It or Not! Museum
175 Jefferson St, Fisherman's Wharf
San Francisco, CA 94133
☎ 415-771-6188
Open: 10am-10pm, -midnight in Summer. Gifts

Rosicrucian Center
Park & Naglee Aves.
San Jose, CA 95191
☎ 408-287-2807 (Egyptian), 287-9171 (Science)
Open: 9am-5pm Tue-Sun, planetarium times vary.
Egyptian museum, science museum, art, gifts

SS Jeremiah O'Brien
Bldg A, Fort Mason Center
San Francisco, CA 94123
☎ 415-551-3101
Open: 9am-3pm
Tours of last unaltered Liberty Ship

San Francisco Experience
Pier 39, Fisherman's Wharf
San Francisco, CA 94119
☎ 415-982-7550
Open: shows from 10am
Gifts, &

San Francisco Maritime National Historical Park
Hyde Street Pier & Aquatic Park
San Francisco, CA 94123
☎ 415-556-3002
Open: 10am-5pm, -6pm Summer
Museum free; admission charge to ships
Maritime museum, sail & powered ships, gifts, part &

San Francisco Museum of Modern Art
401 Van Ness Ave.
San Francisco, CA 94102
☎ 415-863-8800
Open: 10am-5pm Tue-Fri (-9pm Thur), 11am-5pm Sat & Sun
Gifts, tours, ♿

San Francisco Performing Arts Center
401 Van Ness Ave.
San Francisco, CA 94102
☎ 415-621-6600
Open: tours 10am-2.30pm Mon, Performance times vary.
Davies Symphony Hall, War Memorial Opera House, Herbst Theater

San Francisco Zoo
Sloat Blvd & 45th Ave
San Francisco, CA
☎ 415-661-2023
Open: 10am-5pm
Admission (children under 12 free)
Gifts, food, children's section & tram extra, ♿

San Jose Museum of Art
110 S Market St
San Jose, CA 95113
☎ 408-294-2787
Open: 10am-6pm Tue-Fri, 10am-4pm Sat, Noon-4pm Sun. Gifts, ♿

San Mateo County Historical Museum
1700 W Hillsdale Blvd
San Mateo, CA 94402
☎ 415-574-6441
Open: 9.30am-4.30pm Mon-Thur, 12.30-4.30pm Sun
Donation. Research library

Technology Center of Silicon Valley ('The Garage')
145 West San Carlos
San Jose, CA

☎ 408-279-7160
Open: 10am-5pm Tue-Sun, except major holidays
Interactive exhibits, gifts, ♿

USS Pampanito
Pier 45, Fisherman's Wharf
San Francisco, CA 94133
☎ 415-929-0202
Open: 9am-6pm, -9pm weekends & summer
Tour restored submarine

Wells Fargo Bank History Museum
420 Montgomery St
San Francisco, CA 94101
☎ 415-396-2619
9am-5pm weekdays ex holidays
Free; gifts, books, placer gold

Winchester Mystery House, Gardens & Historical Museum
528 S Winchester Blvd
San Jose, CA 95128
☎ 408-247-2101
Open: 9am-5.30pm
Tour of estate, self-guided garden, gifts, cafe

Tours and Transportation

Airport Connection
100 B Produce Ave
South San Francisco, CA
☎ 800-247-7678
Airport-San Francisco shuttle

Airporter
923 Folsom St
San Francisco, CA
415-459-8404
Airport-San Francisco bus service

Amtrak Ticket Office
Transbay Terminal
First and Mission Streets
San Francisco, CA
☎ 800-USA-RAIL or 415-982-8512
Bus to Oakland Bay rail terminus

BART
800 Madison St
Oakland, CA
☎ 415-788-2278
Underground rail, &

Blue & Gold Fleet
Pier 39, Fisherman's Wharf
San Francisco, CA 94133
☎ 415-781-7877
Sailings vary
San Francisco Bay Tours

CalTrain
P.O. Box 7310, 4th & King Sts
San Francisco, CA
☎ 800-558-8661 or 415-557-8661
San Jose to San Francisco rail service

Golden Gate Ferries
Ferry Building, foot of Market St
San Francisco, CA
☎ 415-332-6600
Call for times. Ferries to Sausalito
and Larkspur, &

Good Neighbors Airport Shuttle
33 Harriet St, Suite 2
San Francisco, CA
415-777-4899
Airport-San Francisco shuttle

Great Pacific Tour Co
518 Octavia St
San Francisco, CA 94102
☎ 415-626-4499
Selection of van tours

Grey Line Tours
350 Eighth St
San Francisco, CA 94103
☎ 800-826-0202 or 415-558-7300
Selection of coach tours

Hornblower Dining Yachts
Pier 33
San Francisco CA, 94111
☎ 415-394-8900
Sailings vary
Lunch, brunch, & dinner-dance
cruises

MUNI
949 Presidio Avenue
San Francisco, CA
☎ 415-673-6684
Cable cars & bus service (some
buses &)

Red & White Fleet
Pier 41, Fisherman's Wharf
San Francisco, CA 94133
☎ 415-546-2655
Sailings vary
Ferry service, Bay tours

SuperShuttle
700 16th St
San Francisco, CA
☎ 415-558-8500 (to SFO airport)
415-871-7800 (from SFO airport)
Airport-San Francisco shuttle

2

GRAPES, GOVERNMENT AND GOLD

Grape vines were introduced into Northern California with the founding of the Sonoma Mission in 1823, some 25 years before the discovery of gold at Sutters Mill in 1848. Recognizing California's unique blend of traditional viticulture and modern technology, Sonoma and Napa Valleys still rank as *the* most important wine producing region in the USA.

But it was not grapes which brought California into the United States, nor did those sweet clusters of fruit convert an isolated region in the Sacramento Valley into the State Capitol. History tells us that Swiss immigrant John Augustus Sutter came into the valley in 1839, creating New Helvetia near the confluence of the Sacramento and American Rivers. Sutter's Fort required ready supplies of timber and, during construction of a lumber mill in 1848, an employee named Marshall discovered gold. When news leaked out fortune seekers invaded his land, stealing tools and trampling Sutter's crops. Despite being first on the scene, Marshall and Sutter were unable to capitalize on the discovery and both died asking for recompense.

Meanwhile, supplying the needs of the '49ers, New Helvetia grew into Sacramento which in 1854 was chosen as the final destination of the 'Capital on Wheels'. Despite floods the city prospered and today offers a glimpse into the days of 'Old Sacramento', and also affords easy touring of gold country. Would-be prospectors can still try their hand at panning — 'there's gold in them thar hills!'

Sonoma Valley

North of San Francisco on US101, Petaluma was the headquarters of the vast rancho owned by Mexican General Vallejo. Preserved today as **Petaluma Adobe State Historic Park**, this sprawling two-storey adobe and surrounding grounds exhibit furnishings and ranch life from the 1840s. Early breeds of Spanish livestock and demonstrations of cooking and craft add to the historic atmosphere. Turn-of-the-century Petaluma is the theme of **Petaluma Historical Museum and Library** while the **Great Petaluma Mill** encompasses four riverfront buildings including an 1854 warehouse. Brochures detailing a self-guided walking tour past 19th century and Victorian buildings are available from the Petaluma Chamber of Commerce.

East of Petaluma is historic **Sonoma**, where the local visitor's bureau delights in informing guests that **San Francisco Solano de Sonoma** was the last mission, and the only one founded under Mexican rule. Created in 1823 by a governor fearing Russian encroachment from Fort Ross, the padres' wing of the mission still remains. **Sonoma State Historic Park** embraces over a dozen buildings around the old plaza — including the mission — plus Sonoma Barracks, Blue Wing Inn and the Toscano Hotel. In 1846 the plaza was the scene of the famed Bear Flag Revolt when Mexican General Vallejo was taken prisoner and the short-lived Republic of California founded. Bear Flag Monument marks the spot where modern California was born out of the conflict between America and the fledgling Mexico, although today the park is used for quieter pursuits.

Also part of Sonoma State Historic Park is General Vallejo's home, Lachryma Montis, constructed during the 1850s and restored to its former lavish style. The **Sonoma Valley Historical Museum** in the old town depot recalls the California Republic through period clothing and furniture.

Nearby Sebastiani Vineyards still produce wine from the original mission vineyards. First planted in 1825, Sebastiani is one of California's oldest and largest, offering regular tours and tastings. Points of interest include an extensive collection of hand-carved casks and antique wine-making equipment. Found east of Sonoma, Buena Vista Winery was founded in 1857 by Agoston Haraszthy, known today as father of the Californian wine industry. Self-guided tours of early stone buildings and hand-hewn limestone cellars are offered, while the tasting room is in the restored stone press house.

North of Sonoma in **Glen Ellen**, **Jack London State Historic Park** preserves the estate of this celebrated author. London lived here from 1905 until his untimely death in 1916. The House of Happy Walls, now a museum containing photographs, exhibits and literary mementoes, was left to the state upon his wife's death in 1955. Outbuildings include their cottage, stables, barns, silos and the pig palace. The ruins of Wolf House, London's dream home destroyed by fire on its completion in 1913, and his grave site may also be seen. Nine miles of hiking and riding trails afford views of London's beloved 'Valley of the Moon' and surrounding countryside.

In **Santa Rosa** the former 1909 Post Office now houses the **Sonoma County Museum**, where their collection of photographs, artifacts and paintings recreates early Californian life and culture. Believe It or Not, the **Robert L. Ripley Memorial Museum** displays the much travelled cartoonist's life, plus an interesting look at Santa Rosa history. Famous horticulturist Luther Burbank made his home in Santa Rosa, and his house and gardens are today open to the public as **Luther Burbank Memorial Garden and Home**. Half hour tours of the house include the Carriage House, now a museum of his life and work, while many of his plant varieties are grown in the garden. Burbank is buried in the garden under the huge cedar of Lebanon.

The **Healdsburg Museum** north of Santa Rosa illustrates local history, including Pomo Indian basketry and antique firearms.

Napa Valley

East from Fulton leads to the northern end of Napa Valley and cordial **Calistoga**, established as a resort town due to its local hot springs. One manifestation of this thermal activity is **Old Faithful Geyser of California**, only a mile from the town and one of the world's few regularly erupting geysers. Every 40 minutes or so a fountain shoots 60ft into the air. En route is the **Petrified Forest**, a unique area where giant redwoods upturned by a volcanic eruption over 3 million years ago have been preserved. There is a museum and picnic area on the site.

Calistoga's **Sharpsteen Museum** depicts the heyday of this spa town through artifacts, photographs, dioramas and a restored 1860s resort cottage. Although the spas and mud baths are still popular, most visitors to Calistoga now come to sample vintages from the USA's premier wine-growing area.

This region was much loved by Robert Louis Stevenson, who spent his honeymoon in a cabin on the slopes of Mount St Helena (not to be confused with the St Helena in Washington State which erupted in 1980). Today the area forms **Robert Louis Stevenson State Park**, primarily a hikers' park with a 5 mile (8km) trail leading to the top of the mountain which affords excellent views on clear days of the Napa Valley, Mount Shasta, Lassen Peak and the Sierra Nevada. Clear Lake to the north is a popular recreational detour and the largest natural freshwater lake wholly within California, offering opportunities for fishing, swimming, boating and waterskiing. Clear Lake State Park on the south shore also offers a self-guided trail detailing the lives of the Pomo Indians, a pleasant visitor centre with interesting exhibits, and campgrounds.

Sonoma Mission is the most northerly and the only one founded under Mexican rule

Château and vineyard in the Napa Valley

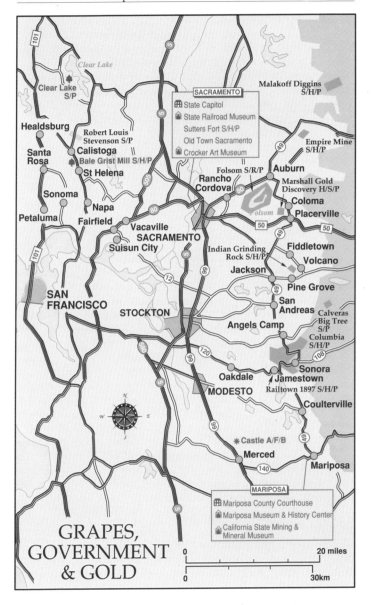

Clear Lake

Clear Lake
S/P

Malakoff Diggins
S/H/P

Healdsburg

Robert Louis
Stevenson S/P

Santa
Rosa

Calistoga

Bale Grist Mill S/H/P

St Helena

Empire Mine
S/H/P

Auburn

SACRAMENTO
- State Capitol
- State Railroad Museum
- Sutters Fort S/H/P
- Old Town Sacramento
- Crocker Art Museum

Folsom S/R/P

Rancho
Cordova

Marshall Gold
Discovery H/S/P

Coloma

Placerville

Sonoma

Napa

Folsom

Petaluma

Fairfield

Vacaville

SACRAMENTO

Fiddletown

Suisun City

Indian Grinding
Rock S/H/P

Volcano

Jackson

**SAN
FRANCISCO**

Pine Grove

San
Andreas

Calveras
Big Tree
S/P

Columbia
S/H/P

STOCKTON

Angels Camp

Oakdale

Sonora

Jamestown

MODESTO

Railtown 1897 S/H/P

Coulterville

Castle A/F/B

Merced

Mariposa

MARIPOSA
- Mariposa County Courthouse
- Mariposa Museum & History Center
- California State Mining &
  Mineral Museum

GRAPES,
GOVERNMENT
& GOLD

0   20 miles

0   30km

Scenic SR29 and the parallel Silverado Trail lead south through the valley past numerous vineyards to **Napa** itself. South of Calistoga, **Bale Grist Mill State Historic Park** recalls the first settlers of Napa Valley who used watermills to grind the grain they planted here.

In the important wine-producing town of **St Helena** the **Silverado Museum** is dedicated to the life and work of Robert Louis Stevenson, containing numerous first editions, manuscripts and Stevenson memorabilia. East of St. Helena the large, man-made Lake Berryessa offers campsites, a visitor centre and numerous watersports.

Converted from a winery and train station, Vintage 1870 in **Yountville** is a 22-acre complex containing specialty shops and restaurants. Within the complex is the Napa Valley Show, 15 minutes of slides and classical music depicting the seasons within the valley.

At the southern end of scenic SR29, Napa was originally a gold rush centre. Today there are 200 or so vineyards in the valley, with details of those offering tours and tastings available from the Napa Valley Chamber of Commerce. For luxury surroundings during a wine tasting try the Napa Valley Wine Train. Passengers enjoy a relaxing brunch, lunch or dinner (no smoking, jackets required for dinner) aboard restored turn-of-the-century Pullman cars. The train passes many famous vineyards on its 3-hour, 36-mile (58km) journey. Another popular way to view the vines is from the air — check with the Chamber of Commerce for companies offering Napa and Sonoma Valleys balloon trips.

To the southeast of Napa in **Fairfield** is **Travis Air Force Museum**, where high-fliers may view vintage aircraft. Nearby **Suisun City** houses the **Western Railway Museum** and its million dollar vintage railway collection, offering streetcar rides and picnic facilities. Beyond Suisun City on SR12, **Grizzly Island Wildlife Area** protects one of the USA's largest estuarine marshes, where visitors can see a variety of wildlife including otters, elk, wildfowl and birds of prey.

To the north **Vacaville** has preserved many Victorian houses and offers walking tours of the historic area courtesy of Vacaville Museum. Focusing on the history of Solano County, the museum has numerous photographs, artifacts and articles from daily life.

Sacramento

Sacramento Visitor Information Center is a good place to start a tour of California's capital, offering plenty of information and even some parking. Located in the 1864 California Steam Navigation Company Depot on Front Street in **Old Sacramento State Historic Park**, information and a walking tour map of the historic areas are available. Old Sacramento comprises several blocks of original buildings plus some modern ones in keeping with the 19th century style. Step back in time, soaking in the historic gold rush atmosphere while browsing the innumerable gift shops, restaurants, and cafés.

Eagle Theatre on Front Street was the first theatre on the West Coast, and today offers plays and musicals in this small reconstructed playhouse. The **Central Pacific Freight Depot** across Front Street re-creates its 1870 appearance, serving as boarding point for the weekend excursion train. Next door is the reconstructed **Central Pacific Passenger Depot**, which along with the Depot are parts of the excellent **California State Railroad Museum**. Another component of this world class treasure is the **Museum of Railroad History**, housed in a modern three-storey structure. The museum complex focuses on the history and cultural impact of the railroad on California and the West through an excellent selection of equipment, including restored engines from small steamers to massive diesels. The interpretive displays are exceptional, and admission includes a 30 minute film on railroad history. In front of the museum is the Big Four Building, named after the four entrepreneurs who founded the Central Pacific Railroad in 1863. Today the building houses the museum library, gift and bookstore, Standford Gallery and the Huntington Hopkins Hardware Store.

Next to the Big Four Building is the **Sacramento History Center**. A reconstruction of the 1854 original, the building housed the city water works, Mayor's office, council chambers and police office. The History Center follows California's fortunes with exhibits of a 1928 kitchen, a canning line, ethnic photographs, a print shop and an awe-inspiring display of gold. The brick **B. F. Hastings Building**, dating from 1853, was the western terminus of the famous Pony Express and housed a Wells Fargo office, the California State Telegraph offices and Supreme Court. Today it contains exhibits on Wells Fargo, the Pony Express and other forms of communication along with the reconstructed chambers of the Supreme Court.

On Second Street the California National Guard Historical Society run the **Citizen Soldier Museum** in what was the first home of the California National Guard during 1855 to 1874.

Back on Front Street the one-room Old Sacramento Schoolhouse is built in the style of the 1800s, while the riverboat *Delta King* is moored nearby in the Sacramento river. Now restored to her original splendour, the old lady now serves as a floating hotel with museums, shops and restaurants. For those who want to travel further along the Sacramento, M/V *Matthew McKinley*, an 80ft paddlewheeler, offers 90-minute sightseeing trips as well as lunch, dinner and happy hour cruises. Delta Cruises sail from the Port of Sacramento to the San

Francisco Embarcadero on 1- and 2-day excursions. Port of Sacramento, found in West Sacramento, is a deep water port capable of handling ocean-going vessels and is open for self-guided tours.

A few blocks southeast from Old Sacramento is the exceptional **Crocker Art Museum**. The first public art museum in the West, the collection was started by Edward Crocker, brother of 'Big Four' member Charles Crocker. Housed in the 1873 Victorian building is considerable European art, much collected during Crocker's tours of Europe, but also including superb works by Californian artists, plus Asian and contemporary art.

Car enthusiasts should make for the **Towe Ford Museum**, where Fords from every year between 1903 and 1953 are on display. Exhibits include vintage fire trucks and commercial vehicles.

No visitor to Sacramento should miss the beautifully restored Classic Revival California State Capitol. Free tours are offered — call for schedule — or pick up a self-guided tour leaflet from the basement. The **California State Capitol Museum** comprises a number of ground floor rooms furnished in early twentieth-century style to recreate the original elegance, while a film on the capitol's history is shown in the basement. When the Legislature is in session visitors may view the proceedings in the second floor chambers from the gallery. The California State Archives exhibit room displays government documents relating to California's history while murals in the State Library depict the history pictorially. Surrounding the capitol are 40 acres of park, boasting trees from around the world.

Near the capitol, the **Stanford House State Historic Park** preserves the mansion of Leland Stanford, member of the 'Big Four' and governor of California from 1862-3. To the northeast the **Old Governor's Mansion** became the official governor's residence in 1903, housing thirteen governors including Ronald Reagan. Now run by the state, the mansion is open for guided tours.

West of the State Capitol is **Sutter's Fort State Historic Park**, site of the area's first settlement and launching point for the California Gold Rush. Today the fort has been reconstructed to its 1846 appearance, offering an interesting walking tour with visitors guided back in time through the innovative use of acoustic wands. Next to Sutter's Fort, the **State Indian Museum** portrays the culture of the area's Native American tribes through comprehensive displays of Indian clothes, basketry and beadwork.

Nut lovers should visit Blue Diamond Growers, showing a film highlighting almond-growing and processing, with plant tours on offer and the latest batches of almonds to be sampled. To the east the Cal Expo grounds host the California State Fair from mid-August

Two aspects of Sacramento: relive the Gold Rush at Old Town (above); the Capitol Building (below)

until Labor Day. Celebrating the importance of Californian agriculture, the fair combines the best in homely arts and crafts with named entertainment and thrill. Should the California heat get too much in Summer, slide into the refreshing pools of **Waterworld USA**.

Out on Auburn Boulevard is the **Sacramento Science Center**, with a planetarium, nature trail, and picnic area. The natural history section is complimented by a live animal hall. To the southwest in William Land Park is **Sacramento Zoo** and the popular **Fairytale Town**, based on popular nursery rhymes.

The **Silver Wings Aviation Museum and Planetarium** in Rancho Cordova is west of Sacramento on SR50. Civilians should report to visitor control at the main gate of Mather Air Force Base before entering to see the aviation and space exhibits.

Gold Country

Found in the Sierra Nevada foothills, this rolling land of tree and rock set the world's imagination alight upon the discovery of gold in 1848. Although that rowdy heyday is long gone, every town has its story to tell, and numerous reminders remain of that golden era. Modern prospectors will find that considerable gold remains, whether panning for a special souvenir or seeking a long lost mother lode.

Folsom was one such mining boom town and picturesque Sutter Street retains its historic buildings and covered sidewalks. The Wells Fargo Assay Office, reconstructed on its original site, houses the interesting **Folsom History Museum** while the Old Train Depot displays vintage railroad cars, a blacksmith's shop and gold-panning exhibits in the railway yard. The **Powerhouse** in 1895 was the first in the world to provide long distance electricity transmission for commercial use — today it is open for guided tours. In summer the town attracts Independence Day crowds with one of California's favourite rodeos. The grey granite walls of **Folsom Prison** are a mile north of the town. One of America's first maximum security prisons, inmates man the gift shop while a sign in the small museum cheerfully proclaims 'No, Johnny Cash never did stay in Folsom Prison'.

To the north **Folsom Lake State Recreation Area** is one of the state's most popular recreation areas offering watersports, several campgrounds and 80 miles (129km) of trails. A 32-mile (51km) cycle trail leads to Old Sacramento while a section of the Western States Pioneer Express Trail links Folsom Lake with **Auburn State Recreation Area** to the north.

Historic **Auburn** boasts several interesting museums. The informative **Placer County Museum** features gold mining plus Indian artifacts, firearms and old photographs. An eighteenth-century farmhouse and winery buildings with displays on wine making comprise the **Bernhard Museum** while to the northeast the Foresthill Museum looks at the geography, geology and history of the area.

Auburn is on scenic SR49, numbered for the '49ers and running roughly north-south through the Mother Lode. SR49 leads north of Auburn to **Grass Valley**, where the world of hard rock mining can be explored at the exceptional **Empire Mine State Historic Park**. The visitor centre interprets mine history while various mine buildings further illustrate this huge enterprise. The park offers living history at the mine-owner's 'cottage' — call ahead for opening times.

Hidden behind the small, picturesque town of **Nevada City** is **Malakoff Diggins State Historic Park**, site of the areas largest hydraulic mining operation. Deeply scarring the land and filling the Sacramento Valley with mud, hydraulic mining was banned in 1884 and today nature is restoring the landscape. Main street has been preserved, where the former dance hall holds an enlightening museum on Malakoff Diggins, including an exhibit drawing attention to the many Chinese involved.

South of Auburn SR49 leads to **Marshall Gold Discovery State Historic Park**. Soon after gold was found the pioneering town of Coloma sprang up, much of it preserved within the park. Easy walks lead to the gold discovery site, reconstructed sawmill and an area for recreational gold panning. The comprehensive Gold Discovery Museum at the visitor centre features the gold rush era, including films highlighting the discovery and early mining techniques.

South of Coloma in a steep ravine is **Placerville**, originally named Old Dry Diggings and then Hangtown as the lawless got justice on its Main Street gallows. The boom town brought prosperity to a number of famous people: Mark Hopkins, one of the 'Big Four', had a store here; Philip Armour, meat processing magnate, ran a butcher's shop; and John Studebaker, a wheelwright on Main Street, subsequently manufactured cars in his native Indiana. Today few gold-era buildings remain but the town prospers as the crossroads of US50 and SR49, making it a good base for exploring gold country.

El Dorado County Fairgrounds west of Placerville hosts **El Dorado County Historical Museum** and its collection of gold-rush artifacts, period rooms and old mining equipment. **Hangtown's Gold Bug Park** to the north offers tours of various mine shafts and the remains of the quartz-crushing stamp mill, first step in this method of gold extraction.

South of Placerville, SR49 passes through pleasant countryside to the quiet town of **Plymouth** where a 6-mile drive leads to isolated

Fiddletown, a well preserved gold rush hamlet. Dating from 1850, the Chew Kee Store on Main Street was the herbalist shop serving the local Chinese community and contains original furnishings. Also set among the rolling hills is **Volcano**, where several stone buildings date back to the 1850s and the large St George Hotel bears witness to the boom which brought the population to a peak of 5,000.

On the Volcano to Pine Ridge road **Indian Grinding Rock State Historic Park** preserves a large limestone outcrop with over 1,000 mortar holes used by Miwok Indians when grinding acorns, their staple diet. The Chaw'se (Miwok for grinding rock) Regional Indian Museum features an outstanding collection of Native American crafts. The reconstructed Miwok village, including a large ceremonial roundhouse, is the venue of acorn harvest thanksgiving ceremonies in autumn. From May to September the Roaring Camp Mining Company in **Pine Grove** offers 4-hour guided tours into Mokelumne Canyon for gold panning, swimming, and to visit the Wildlife and Mining Artifacts Museum.

Jackson was first settled for its reliable spring, rather than gold, although rich deposits were later discovered. **Amador County Museum** in the 1859 Brown House contains original furnishings, working scale models of local mines and Miwok basketry.

Empire Mine State Historic Park offers realistic 'living history'

Nature has started to repair the mining damage at Malakoff Diggins

SR49 leads south to San Andreas, whose motto is 'It's not our fault!' (the San Andreas fault lies well to the west). Downtown retains its 19th century appearance, where **Calaveras County Historical Museum** occupies the original Courthouse, Jail and Hall of Records. The museum focuses on pioneer life with a special exhibit on notorious highwayman 'Black Bart' who was tried and convicted here. **Angels Camp** to the south was made famous by Mark Twain and his *Celebrated Jumping Frog of Calaveras County*, which is still celebrated at the Calaveras County Fair and Frog Jumping Jubilee. Angels Camp Museum features displays on the pioneers, Chinese, Native Americans, a blacksmith's shop and carriage house. A detailed 90-minute self-guided walking tour map of the town is produced by the Angels Camp Historic Committee.

Scenic SR4 leads to **Vallecito** where gold prospecting trips from 1 hour to several days are offered by Jensen's Pick & Shovel Ranch. Prospective spelunkers can visit nearby Moaning Cavern or California Caverns at **Cave City**, a California State Historic Landmark. Mercer Caverns can be found near the gold rush town of **Murphys**. East on SR4 is **Calaveras Big Trees State Park** where stately giant sequoias, the world's largest living things, tower in majestic groves. Hiking, fishing and camping are summertime pastimes while snowshoeing and cross-country skiing are favourites in winter.

To the south, just off SR49, boomtime **Columbia** was once second largest city in California. Today **Columbia State Historic Park** encompasses twelve square blocks of the town, giving one of the best impressions of the Gold Rush era. Activities in this lively ghost town include visiting the restored Wells Fargo office and browsing through the numerous shops, some museums and others selling mementos of yesteryear. The stagecoach tour passes the blacksmith's forge, a barn housing Conestoga wagons, Chinese temple, restaurants and hotels (spend a night in authentically restored Fallon Hotel and see a show at the Fallon Theatre). Gold fever is still alive with mine tours and gold panning on offer. The only drawback to the authenticity is restricted access to some buildings for handicapped visitors. Adventurers should book ahead for the river rafting excursions offered by Zephyr River Expeditions, based in Columbia.

The bustling community of **Sonora** is Tuolumne County seat, where **Tuolumne County Museum and History Center** is housed in the 1857 county jail, featuring Gold Rush era exhibits, oil paintings and vintage firearms. Sonora is the headquarters for **Stanislaus National Forest** where would-be prospectors can pan 800 miles (1,290km) of streams and rivers (maps showing campgrounds available from the Forest Supervisor's office on Greenley Road). Kennedy

Meadows Resort and Pack Station offers pack trips into the Emigrant Basin Wilderness and Yosemite National Park.

Jamestown hosts a range of gold prospecting, helicopter and whitewater rafting trips from the Old Livery Stable, Main Street. On 5th Avenue **Railtown 1897 State Historic Park** displays its collection ☀ of old-time steam locomotives. A walking tour includes the six-track Roundhouse and other authentic buildings, and various train trips are on offer in summer (book ahead).

Picturesque **Coulterville** suffered three fires but retains several Gold Rush structures, including the Jeffery Hotel, Magnolia Saloon and Sun Sun Wo Co Merchandise, last remnant of a once thriving Chinatown. Coulterville History Center and Museum displays his- 🏠 torical photographs and a working scale model of a stamp mill.

Mariposa resides at the southern end of the Mother Lode on one of the main routes into Yosemite (covered in Chapter 3). The 1854 wood-frame **Mariposa County Courthouse**, California's oldest, is still in use and offers tours. **Mariposa Museum and History Center** 🏠 combines a library with one of the best collections of Gold Rush memorabilia, augmented by period rooms, a working stamp mill and a reconstructed Miwok village. At the county fairgrounds the **California State Mining and Mineral Museum** has a gem and 🏠 mineral collection of more than 200,000 specimens. Exhibits include an assay office, stamp mill and mine tunnel.

To the west **Merced** is located in the fertile San Joaquin (Hwa-keen) Valley. The **Courthouse Museum** is housed in an Italianate 🏠 Renaissance building resembling the state capitol. Nature lovers will enjoy the full scale dioramas of North American wildlife at **Yosemite Wildlife Museum**. 🏠

North of Merced, adjacent to Castle Air Force Base, the **Castle Air Museum** shows the development of the US Air Force through an 🏠 collection of vintage aircraft and an indoor military museum.

Further north in the San Joaquin Valley, **Modesto** was named after the modesty of William Ralston, who declined to have the town named after him. Victorian **McHenry Mansion** is open for tours 🏠 while the **McHenry Museum** explores local history with re-crea-tions of doctor's and dentist's offices, blacksmith's shop, schoolroom and general store. The **Great Valley Museum of Natural History** 🏠 depicts the ecosystems of the Central Valley. Blue Diamond Growers provide tours, a film and almond tasting while in **Oakdale** Hershey ☀ Chocolate USA is a must for chocaholics.

If returning to San Francisco visit the Magnolia Historic District in Stockton and the San Joaquin Historical Museum in nearby Lodi. 🏠 Continue with Chapter 3 if pressing up into the higher Sierra Nevada.

Panned gold makes a great souvenir

Additional Information

Regional Visitor Information

Merced CVB
1880 N Street, PO Box 3107
Merced, CA 95344
☎ 209-384-3333 or 800-446-5353

Modesto CVB
1114 J St, PO Box 844
Modesto, CA 95353
☎ 209-577-5757

Sacramento CVB
1421 K St
Sacramento, CA 95814
☎ 916-449-6711

Sacramento Visitor Information Center
1104 Front St
Old Sacramento, CA 95814
☎ 916-442-7644

Stockton-San Joaquin County CVB
46 W Fremont St
Stockton, CA 94202
☎ 209-943-1987 or 800-888-8016

Auburn Area CVB
512 Auburn Ravine Rd
Auburn, CA 95603
☎ 916-885-5616 or 800-433-7575

Calistoga Chamber of Commerce
1458 Lincoln Ave
Calistoga, CA 94515
☎ 707-942-6333

Calaveras County Chamber of Commerce
1301 S Main St, PO Box 111
Angels Camp, CA 95222
☎ 209-736-4444 or 800-999-9039

Grass Valley & Nevada County Chamber of Commerce
248 Mill St
Grass Valley, CA 95495
☎ 916-273-4667 or 800-752-6222 (CA)

Mariposa County Chamber of Commerce
5158 Hwy 140, PO Box 425
Mariposa, CA 95338
☎ 209-966-2456

Napa Valley Chamber of Commerce
1556 First St, PO Box 636
Napa, CA 94559
☎ 707-226-7455

Placer County Information Center
661 Newcastle Rd
Newcastle, CA 95658
☎ 916-663-2061

Sonoma Valley Visitors Bureau
453 First St East
Sonoma, CA 95476
☎ 707-996-1090

Tuolumne County Visitors Bureau
55 W Stockton St, PO Box 4020
Sonora, CA 95370
☎ 209-533-4420

The Missions

Mission San Francisco Solano
Spain & First St East
Sonoma, CA 95476
☎ 707-938-1519 Open: 10am-5pm

Places to Visit

Amador County Museum
225 Church St
Jackson, CA 95642
☎ 209-223-6386
Open: 10am-4pm Mon & Tue. Free

Blue Diamond Growers
17th & C Streets
Sacramento, CA 95814
☎ 916-446-8409
Open: Tours 9am, 10am, 1pm, & 2pm Mon-Fri. Free
Film, gift shop, tastings, ᶑ

California State Capitol
10th St & Capitol Mall
Sacramento, CA 95814
☎ 916-324-0333
Open: 9am-4pm weekdays, 10am-4pm weekends
Free; gift shop, cafeteria, self tour, &

California State Railroad Museum
111 I St
Old Sacramento, CA 95814
☎ 916-448-4466
Open: 10am-5pm
Engines, gift shop, old station, film, &

Calaveras Big Trees State Park
1170 E Hwy 4
Arnold, CA 95223
☎ 209-795-2334
Hike, picnic, camp

Central Pacific Freight Depot
Front & K Streets
Old Sacramento, CA 95814
☎ 916-448-4466
Steam train, replica of 1867 depot

Columbia State Historic Park
P.O. Box 151
Columbia, CA 95310
☎ 209-532-4301
Free. Hotel, gifts, food, gold panning, tours

Crocker Art Museum
216 O St
Sacramento, CA 95814
☎ 916-449-5423
Open: 1pm-9pm Tue, 10am-5pm Wed-Sun
Art displayed in Crocker Mansion, gift shop, &

Delta Cruises
1450 West Capitol Ave
West Sacramento, CA 95691
☎ 916-372-3691
Sails weekends May-Oct.
500-passenger ship

Eagle Theatre
925 Front St
Old Sacramento, CA 95814
☎ 916-446-6761
Open: weekends May-Oct
Live plays & musicals

El Dorado County Historical Museum
100 Placerville Dr
Placerville, CA 95667
☎ 916-621-5865
Open: 10am-4pm Wed-Sat
Free

Empire Mine State Historic Park
10791 E Empire St
Grass Valley, CA 95945
☎ 916-273-8522
Open: 9am-5pm
Gifts, tours, living history, part &

Folsom Lake State Rec. Area
7806 Folsom-Auburn Rd
Folsom, CA 95630
☎ 916-988-0205
Swim, hike, picnic, camp

Hershey Chocolate USA
120 S Sierra
Oakdale, CA 95361
☎ 209-848-8126
Open: 8:30am-3pm weekdays
Free; tours & tastings

Indian Grinding Rock State Historic Park
14881 Pine Grove Volcano Rd
Pine Grove, CA 95665
☎ 209-296-7488
Open: 9am-5pm
Free; gifts, Miwok village

Jack London State Historic Park
2400 London Ranch Rd
Glen Ellen, CA 95442
☎ 707-938-5216
Open: 9am-5pm
Tours, gifts

**Luther Burbank Memorial Garden
& Home**
Santa Rosa Parks, 415 Steele Lane
Santa Rosa, CA 95402
☎ 707-576-5445
Open: grounds 8am-5pm, home
10am-4pm Wed-Sun in summer

**Malakoff Diggins State Historic
Park**
24579 N Bloomfield Rd.
Nevada City, CA 95959
☎ 916-265-2740
Open: 9am-5pm
Museum, gifts, hike, camp, picnic

Mariposa County Courthouse
10th & Bullions Streets
Mariposa, CA 95338
☎ 209-966-3222
Free, self-guided tours

**Mariposa Museum and History
Center**
12th & Jessie Streets, PO Box 606
Mariposa, CA 95338
☎ 209-966-2924
Free; self-guided tours

**Marshall Gold Discovery State
Historic Park**
Coloma, CA 95613
☎ 916-0622-3470
Open: 10am-5pm
Gifts, food, tours, raft

Napa Valley Wine Train
1275 McKinstry St
Napa, CA 94559
☎ 707-253-2111
Open: call for times

Old Faithful Geyser of California
1299 Tubbs Lane
Calistoga, CA 94515
☎ 707-942-6463
Open: 9am-5pm, -6pm summer
Gifts

Old Governor's Mansion
1526 H St
Sacramento, CA 95814
☎ 916-323-3047
Open: 10am-4pm
Tours, gifts

**Petaluma Adobe State Historic
Park**
3325 Adobe Rd
Petaluma, CA 94952
☎ 707-762-4871
Open: 10am-5pm
Living history, gifts, tours

**Petaluma Historical Museum and
Library**
20 4th St
Petaluma, CA 94952
☎ 707-778-4398
Open: 1pm-4pm Thu-Mon. Free

Petrified Forest
4100 Petrified Forest Rd
Calistoga, CA 94513
☎ 707-942-6667
Open: 9am-5pm, -5:45pm summer
Gifts, tours

Placer County Museum
1273 High St
Auburn, CA 95603
☎ 916-889-4155
Open: 10am-4pm Tue-Sun
Gifts, tours

Railtown 1897 State Historic Park
PO Box 1250
Jamestown, CA 95327
☎ 209-984-3953
Call for train times
Gifts, tours, part &

Riverboat Delta King
1000 Front St
Old Sacramento, CA 95814
☎ 916-444-KING
Stationary riverboat hotel, dining,
gift shop, &

Robert L. Ripley Memorial Museum
Juilliard Park, 492 Sonoma Ave
Santa Rosa, CA 95401
☎ 707-576-5233
Open: 11am-4pm Wed-Sun, closed Dec-Feb
Gifts, tours

Sacramento History Center
101 I St
Old Sacramento, CA 95814
☎ 916-449-2057
Open: 10am-5pm
Gifts, tours, &

Sacramento Science Center
3615 Auburn Blvd
Sacramento, CA 95821
☎ 916-449-8255
Open: 9:30am-5pm weekdays, noon-5pm weekends
Gifts, &

Sacramento Zoo
3930 W Land Park Dr
Sacramento, CA 95822
☎ 916-449-5885
Open: 9am-4pm, closed Xmas
Animals, food, gifts, part &

Silver Wings Aviation Museum
Mather Air Force Base
Rancho Cordova, CA 95670
☎ 916-364-2908
Open: 10am-4pm weekdays, noon-4pm weekends
Free; tours, exhibits

Silverado Museum
1490 Library Lane
St Helena, CA 94574
☎ 707-963-3757
Noon-4pm Tue-Sun
Free; Robert Louis Stevenson memorabilia

Sonoma County Museum
425 7th St
Santa Rosa, CA 95401
☎ 707-579-1500
Open: 11am-4pm Wed-Sun
Tours, gifts

State Indian Museum
2618 K St
Sacramento, CA 95816
☎ 916-324-0971
Open: 10am-5pm except major holidays
Gifts, books, exhibits

Sutter's Fort State Historic Park
2701 L St
Sacramento, CA 95816
☎ 916-445-4422
Open: 10am-5pm, last tour 4:15pm
Gifts, tours

Towe Ford Museum
2200 Front St
Sacramento, CA 96818
☎ 916-442-6802
Open: 10am-6pm except major holidays
Gifts

Vacaville Museum
213 Buck Ave
Vacaville, CA 95688
☎ 707-447-4513
Open: 1pm-4:30pm Wed-Sun
Free on Wed; gifts, walking tours

Vintage 1870
PO Box 2500
Yountville, CA 94599
☎ 707-944-2451
Shopping & dining complex, wine tours

Waterworld USA
1600 Exposition Blvd
Sacramento, CA 95815
☎ 916-924-0555
Open: Memorial Day-Labor Day
Food, gifts, children's area

3

THE HIGH SIERRAS

Combining unspoilt scenery, unparalleled skiing, and outstand ing hiking, the Sierra Nevada are a genuine natural high. Mile-high Lake Tahoe turns sunlight into an emerald oceanscape and, for those who demand more for their money, add the glamour of gambling in nearby Reno, 'The World's biggest little city'. America's crown jewels, Yosemite, Sequoia and Kings Canyon National Parks are here, connected via the extensive national forests and dotted with some fine California state parks and recreation areas. The focus here is on outdoor activities, whether taking a pack horse trip in summer or enjoying the diversity of the winter sports.

Also across the border in Nevada the state capital, Carson City, and fascinating Virginia City of Comstock Lode fame add historical insight to the 'Silver State'.

Yosemite National Park

Yosemite Valley was originally inhabited by the Ahwahneechee Indians who were considered a nuisance by gold-hungry miners. The Mariposa Battalion entered the valley in 1851 to enforce peace, and word of Yosemite's beauty soon spread. The Native Americans were soon removed and the first hotel opened in 1859. Worried about over development, conservationists urged Congress to act and in 1864 a land grant protected the area until the national park could be formed in 1890. Best known and most popular of California's national parks, Yosemite attracts over 3 million visitors annually.

The valley's stunning granite formations were produced some 2 million years ago, when ice carved mountain sides and left hanging valleys from which plunge Yosemite's magnificent waterfalls. The Merced and Tuolumne rivers produce tremendous flows in late spring and early summer, when the cascades are at their finest. It is

Reaching Yosemite

The main gateway is via SR140 from Merced, while SR120 east from Jamestown and SR41 north from Fresno offer the most scenic entrances. From the latter stop at the car park after the tunnel for perhaps the most famous view of Yosemite Valley. In winter these roads are normally open, but the Tioga Pass Road (SR 120 east through the park) is typically closed outside the June-September peak season; chose another route over the Sierra Nevada in winter. Tyre chains can be made mandatory between late autumn and early spring.

Amtrak provide daily train services from Oakland in the San Francisco Bay area to Merced and from Southern California to Fresno, or arrive by air at Fresno Air Terminal. Greyhound coaches have depots in both Merced and Fresno, while Yosemite Gray Line offer daily coach connections to the park from the airports, Amtrak stations and Greyhound depots in both Fresno and Merced.

GETTING AROUND YOSEMITE

Having arrived early in Yosemite Valley, park your car and avoid traffic jams by taking the free shuttle bus which circles points of interest, valley trailheads, lodgings and campgrounds. From July 1st to Labor Day a bus treks daily over the Tioga Pass past Tuolumne Meadows to Lee Vining, returning in the afternoon and allowing hikers access to trailheads en route.

The Valley Floor Tour departs several times daily, year round and a variety of sightseeing tours are offered from late spring to early autumn — book at Tour/Information Desks at Yosemite Lodge, the Ahwahnee Hotel, Camp Curry or the Village Store in Yosemite Village (advance reservations recommended). Glacier Point Hiker's Bus (weather permitting) is a one-way morning trip for those wishing to hike down into Yosemite Valley.

Walking is ever popular while Yosemite Valley Stables hire ponies for guided rides (advance reservation advised). Bicycle hire is available from Yosemite Lodge and Curry Village. Rented cycles can be used on the roads or on the 8 miles (13 km) of bike paths (map provided) but not outside Yosemite Valley. In winter skis or snowshoes can be hired and 1-hour snowcat tours are offered in the Badger Pass Ski Area.

claimed that a rainbow forms around Yosemite Falls during spring flows on nights when the moon is full, an experience not to be missed.

The most famous of the park's features, scenic Yosemite Valley, occupies only 7 of the park's 1,189 square miles. **Yosemite Village** offers full services year round including the visitor centre, Yosemite Museum, Indian Village of the Ahwahnee, the Ansel Adams Gallery, hotels, plus the sundry facilities which ensure a pleasant stay. **Curry Village** offers lodging, food, mountaineering and outdoor clothing shops, while between the two are the majority of campsites. For current events and the latest on park facilities read the *Yosemite Guide*, free at park entrance stations, visitor centres and hotel desks.

Walking is a popular pastime with scenic strolls or hikes for all abilities, although many trails are impassable from late autumn to early spring. Mirror Lake is a pleasant walk along Tenaya Creek, while the trails up to Vernal and Nevada Falls offer more challenge. The very fit can reach Half Dome, Upper Yosemite Falls, or Glacier Point, although the latter is attainable by road. Open to cars between June and October, **Glacier Point** offers a breathtaking vista across the High Sierra. The views down into Yosemite Valley and across Vernal and Nevada Falls to Half Dome definitely steal the show.

Rafts, paddles and life jackets may be hired at Curry Village for use on the Merced river between Yosemite Stables and El Capitan Bridge. Also at Curry Village Yosemite Mountaineering School offers a variety of rock climbing courses catering for all levels of experience. Guided backpacking is available and all necessary equipment for both activities can be rented.

With so much to do and see in Yosemite Valley most never get beyond its walls, leaving the back-country relatively serene. **Tuolumne Meadows** on the Tioga Pass is a delight of Alpine flowers in July and early August. An informative visitor centre is here and the High Sierra Camps are favourites with summer hikers.

The **Hetch Hetchy** area is quieter still, offering numerous back-country hikes including the trail along the Grand Canyon of the Tuolumne to Tuolumne Meadows. The latter part of this hike follows the Pacific Crest Trail, which starts in Canada and ends in Southern California, passing through Sequoia and Kings Canyon National Parks en route.

Wawona, west on SR41 from the valley offers the **Yosemite Pioneer History Centre**, a collection of historic buildings brought from various locations within the park. Near the SR41 entrance is **Mariposa Grove of Big Trees**, an impressive grove of giant sequoias including the 2,700-year-old Grizzly Giant.

Yosemite is open year round and **Badger Pass**, on the road to

Glacier Point, is the oldest established ski area in California. In winter Yosemite Cross-Country Ski School offers lessons in downhill and cross-country skiing. Beginner and intermediate slopes are there, plus 90 miles (145km) of cross-country skiing.

Fresno

South of the park Yosemite Mountain Sugar Pine Railroad offers narrow gauge steam locomotive trips on a 4-mile logging track. Passengers may picnic at Shady Slab Creek and return on a later train. **Millerton Lake State Recreation Area** offers camping and picnics, plus bird-watching for the magnificent bald and golden eagles.

Fresno is the financial and agricultural centre of the San Joaquin Valley, and sometimes known as the 'Raisin Capital of America'. A main gateway to Yosemite National Park, the city also offers **Fresno Metropolitan Museum of Art, History and Science**, which houses the Salzer collection of old masters, a selection of Ansel Adams' photographs, and exhibits on local history. Other points of interest include **Fresno Art Museum** and the **Discovery Center**.

Fort Miller Block House, built to protect settlers during the Mariposa Indian War, now houses a museum on life during the 1800s. Visitors may step back into Victorian times at the ornate **Meux**

(opposite) Yosemite Falls drop 2,425ft

Cathedral Rocks in Yosemite National Park

National Park Tips

Much of Yosemite Valley and/or Sequoia-Kings Canyon Parks can be seen in one day but allow as much time as possible and book well ahead. Summers are the busiest, and the park service must balance conservation efforts with rocketing attendance figures. Visitors risk being turned away on American holiday weekends between Memorial to Labor Day — check and book accommodation well ahead. Campers should make reservations through Ticketron eight weeks in advance (twelve weeks for group camps), and lodging is booked up to a year ahead.

Never feed animals — it is illegal and potentially dangerous. Even dainty looking mule deer can be lethal and always heed warnings about bears. Whilst the danger of large mammals is obvious, even cute ground squirrels can carry plague-infected fleas and rabies. Be aware that rattlesnakes and ticks share the parks — prevention is better than cure.

When hiking always treat lake and stream water for *Giardia* before drinking. Swimming in the Merced River is possible in late summer, but cold water and swift currents can be a hazard. Never swim above or near waterfalls or rapids and avoid slippery banks.

The park's altitude varies from 2,000ft to over 13,000ft (610-3,960m) and remember that altitude sickness can strike as low as

Home Museum, while 1903 **Kearney Mansion and Kearney Park** belonged to the 'famed' raisin baron. The French Renaissance-style structure contains many original furnishings including European wallpapers and art nouveau light fittings.

Also at Fresno is **Duncan Water Gardens**, 3.5 acres of brooks, waterfalls and artworks, and the 300-acre **Woodward Park**, home to the Japanese **Shin-Zen Friendship Garden**. **Roeding Park** contains **Chaffee Zoo**, numerous amusement rides and a series of lakes.

Sequoia and Kings Canyon National Parks

These adjoining parks were created to protect giant sequoias from overzealous loggers, and were extended in 1978 when a large ski resort complex threatened. Kings Canyon-Sequoia protects several important groves, including the Giant Forest and General Grant Grove, where the world's three largest living beings are preserved. With a height of 274ft (83.5m) and a circumference of 107.6ft (32.8m), General Sherman tree is only slightly shorter than the tallest coastal redwoods and yet boasts considerably larger girth. The free news-

8,000ft (2,500m). Symptoms include headache, nausea, shortness of breath and fatigue — contact the Yosemite Medical Clinic in Yosemite Valley immediately. Allow time to adjust to higher altitudes before hiking to avoid altitude sickness.

ABOUT SEQUOIA-KINGS CANYON

From Fresno take SR180 east to Kings Canyon, while SR198 leads from Visalia to Ash Mountain in Sequoia National Park. Both roads are open year round although the interconnecting Generals Highway may be closed in winter, when snow tyres or chains may be required. Public transport services to Fresno are detailed in the 'Reaching Yosemite' section while Visalia is served by major airlines and buses. Amtrak reaches Hanford with bus connections to Visalia. **No** public transport serves Sequoia-Kings Canyon, but car rental is available in Fresno and Visalia.

Lodging varies from deluxe motels to rustic cabins and a tent camp (advance reservations recommended). Nearby **Montecito-Sequoia** in Sequoia National Forest offers four rustic lodges at the Nordic Ski Resort. All campsites are on a first-come basis in winter — at other times reservations can be made for Lodgepole through Ticketron and for group sites apply in writing. Free backcountry permits are available at ranger stations for overnight camping.

paper *Sequoia Bark*, fortunately not made from that material, details current park information including facilities and services, ranger-led activities (campfire programs, nature walks, etc) and coach tours.

Sequoia-Kings Canyon extends from the edge of the San Joaquin Valley to the high Sierra, an area of outstanding beauty all the more desirable because most holidaymakers go to Yosemite. Mount Whitney, highest point in the contiguous USA, lies within Sequoia National Park. The complete absence of roads into the back country make this terrain ideal for hiking or horse-riding in warmer months, skiing and snowshoeing in winter. In addition to the western trails, the Inyo National Forest offers many trailheads — details available from the US Forest Service. The Pacific Crest Trail runs through the eastern section of the parks.

Grant Grove in Kings Canyon National Park offers a full range of facilities including visitor centre, shop, service station, food and lodging. A walk leads through the grove of Big Trees, past General Grant, the third largest sequoia and the nation's Christmas tree.

Past Grant Grove, SR180 is open only in summer. The road winds

Quincy

Portola

Pyramid Lake

Plumas N/F

Soda Springs

RENO

Virginia City

Truckee

Tahoe City

Lake Tahoe

CARSON CITY

South Lake Tahoe

Grover Hot Springs S/P

NEVADA

Markleeville

Toiyabe N/F

Toiyabe National Forest

Bridgeport

Mono Lake

Yosemite N/P

Mono Lake Tufa S/R

Lee Vining

June Lake

Inyo National Forest

Yosemite Village

Wawona

Mammoth Lakes

Mariposa Grove Of Big Trees

Ancient Bristlecone Pine Forest

Bishop

Inyo National Forest

FRESNO

Kings Canyon N/P

Kearney Mansion

Meux Home Museum

Fresno Museum of Art, History & Science

Roeding Park

Duncan Water Gardens

Fort Miller Blockhouse

FRESNO

Cedar Grove

Independence

Visalia

Sequoia N/P

Lone Pine

Hanford

Mineral King

Inyo National Forest

Sequoia National Forest

Kernville

BAKERSFIELD

Lake Isabella

| 0 | | 50 miles |
| 0 | | 80km |

THE HIGH SIERRAS

into the spectacular Kings Canyon, with peaks towering a mile overhead. The privately operated Boyden Cave is located in the Sequoia National Forest section of the canyon with daily tours in summer. The road follows the south fork of the Kings River to **Cedar Grove**, a popular trailhead between early July and October with a pack station for those wishing to ride. Current conditions and backcountry permits are obtained at the ranger station. Facilities include a shop, service station, food, lodging and camping.

From Grant Grove the Generals Highway leads south to **Lodgepole** in Sequoia National Park. Facilities include an informative visitor centre, shops, post office, service station and campground. Beyond the road leads south to another pack station and **Wolverton**, which offers downhill skiing and snow play areas from December through April. General Sherman tree is accessed via a well signposted trail just before **Giant Forest** village is reached. Shops, food and lodging are available at this excellent base for summer walkers and winter skiers.

A staircase climbs nearby Moro Rock for a breathtaking panorama of the High Sierra, and the road past Moro Rock ends at Crescent Meadow, a lush marshy area good for spotting wildlife. Beyond the car park and picnic area are several loop trails and longer walks —

Sequoia trees are the world's largest living things

pick up a map before setting out. Bearpaw Meadow is a popular 11-mile (18km) hike from Crescent Meadow and from late June until mid-September a tent camp is there (make reservations for accommodation and meals several months in advance).

✳ Generals Highway continues south past the Four Guardsmen, four magnificent sequoias, before the turnoff to **Crystal Cave**. The non-profit Sequoia Natural History Association operates trips into the marble cave, with tour schedules listed in *Sequoia Bark*.

Ash Mountain hosts the park headquarters and Foothills Visitor Center while further south the road to sub-alpine **Mineral King** allows easy access to higher altitudes in summer. Facilities here are rustic and limited but include a campsite, ranger station and pack station — acclimatize here before proceeding into the Sierra Nevada.

To the Eastern Sierra Nevada

West of Sequoia National Park, **Hanford** once boasted the largest Oriental population in California, an era recalled at the **Taoist Temple** in the historic China Alley district. The 1896 Courthouse Square now houses shops, restaurants and an art gallery while the **Hanford Fox Theater**, one of few surviving, offers tours, concerts, plays and films. Artifacts from early Hanford and Kings County are exhibited at the **Carnegie Museum**.

To the south, **Bakersfield** offers a look at native flora and fauna at the **California Living Museum** and at human inhabitants at **Kern County Museum**. SR178 follows the Kern River to Lake Isabella and on to scenic US395, which lies to the east of the Sierra Nevada; top up the fuel tank at Bakersfield before visiting this isolated area. The Eastern Sierra Visitor Center at US395 and SR136 junction provides information on the Owens Valley (along which US395 passes), the enormous Inyo National Forest, and Death Valley (see Chapter 8), plus Sequoia, Kings Canyon and Yosemite National Parks. The hardy should obtain a wilderness permit at the Lone Pine ranger station before taking the Whitney-Portal Road to climb the 11-mile (18km) trail to the summit of Mount Whitney.

The **Eastern California Museum** north in **Independence** illustrates the Inyo County heritage from Paiute-Shoshone basketry to pioneer farming equipment. Their Little Pine Village is a recreated pioneer settlement using relocated 1880s buildings.

The World's Oldest Living Things

♣ The **Ancient Bristlecone Pine Forest** high up in the Inyo National Forest is reached via SR168 from Big Pine (road open early June to late October). These fantastically gnarled trees are the oldest known living things on earth, the Methuselah tree being 4,700 years old. Schulman Grove has the oldest trees, an information centre and small picnic area, plus two self-guided trails through the grove. An unpaved road continues to the higher Patriarch Grove, affording spectacular views and a photographer's paradise.

Given the altitude and remote setting start early in the day with plenty of water, a full fuel tank, sun protection, and return to the valley below if shortness of breath, headache, fatigue, nausea or dizziness occurs.

Bishop is a popular base for hiking and riding, having access into remote sections of Kings Canyon National Park and Inyo National Forest. Packers offer the best of both worlds, with ponies to carry heavy items up the steep Sierra Nevada slopes. Bishop Chamber of Commerce has a list of registered packers and the excursions they offer. **Paiute Shoshone Indian Cultural Center Museum** illustrates the lifestyle, traditions and art of this Native American people while **Laws Railroad Museum and Historical Site** north on SR6 operates the *Slim Princess* narrow-gauge train and other railroad machinery.

Mammoth Lakes and **June Lake** is one of the USA's largest ski resorts with a season from late November to early July — details of the various resorts are available from Mammoth Lakes Resort Association. A four-seasons resort, Mammoth offers a variety of outdoor activities, plus the Mammoth Mountain Gondola, an ideal way to enjoy Sierra scenery with guided hikes from the top in summer.

Mammoth Lakes is gateway to **Devils Postpile National Monument**, open mid-June through October. During peak periods private vehicles (except for registered campers), are excluded and a shuttle bus brings visitors to the Devils Postpile. This 60ft (18m) high wall is one of the world's finest examples of columnar basalt.

North of the Postpile and east of Yosemite via Tioga Pass is **Mono Lake Tufa State Reserve**, an alien landscape of calcium carbonate formations created in the lake's mineral rich water and exposed when the water level receded. Activities include bird watching and a short trek to up Mono Craters, an interesting series of volcanoes which erupted just 600 years ago.

Bridgeport is another popular base for exploring the eastern Sierra Nevada; while there listen for the Italianate County Courthouse's carillon. **Mono County Historical Society & Museum**, housed in the 1880 school, contains a collection of Paiute basketry plus artifacts from the ghost town of Bodie, 19 miles (31km) to the southeast.

Once a sprawling, lawless 1880s gold town, today many fascinating buildings are preserved in a state of 'arrested decay' as **Bodie**

These gnarled bristlecone pines are the world's oldest living things

Tufa formations at Mono Lake

State Historic Park. This virtually intact ghost town affords a insight into the Gold Rush era, as many of the 170 buildings, including their interiors, have been left as they were. The Miners' Union Hall is now a museum, a self-guided tour leaflet is available, and rangers offer interesting guided history talks from Memorial through Labor Day. Weather is unpredictable outside summer — the town was named after a prospector who died during an early blizzard — but the site is extremely photogenic and well worth any detour.

Markleeville is the seat of the remote Alpine County, with the **Markleeville Museum** exhibiting old mining equipment and a reconstructed blacksmith's shop. **Grover Hot Springs State Park**, 3 miles west, are a series of springs and hot pools situated in a lovely Alpine valley. Hours depend on season but the pool is open year-round; even when the surrounding countryside is snow-clad.

In summer golfers can enjoy beautiful scenery while playing a round at the challenging 18-hole public golf course in **Lake Valley State Recreation Area**. During winter the area offers snowmobile and cross-country ski rentals.

Lake Tahoe

Picturesque **Lake Tahoe**, perched on the border of California and Nevada, is the largest Alpine lake in North America. This year-round

Bridgeport's Italianate County Courthouse dates from 1880

holiday destination offers camping, hiking and fishing in summer, while the area is a winter sports enthusiast's dream, with the surrounding mountains festooned with ski slopes.

South Lake Tahoe offers a selection of hotels, motels and restaurants, and a variety of outdoor activities including lake cruises year round on the paddlewheeler *Tahoe Queen*. **Lake Tahoe Historical Society Museum** presents an excellent collection of settlers' artifacts and memorabilia, while the self-guided Historic Sites Auto Tour takes in twenty historic landmarks.

The Lake Tahoe Visitor Center north of town is run by the US Forest Service and covers the area's human and natural history. Interpretation includes nature trails, naturalist-led walks, campfire programs and an underwater view of a creek where salmon spawn (open Memorial weekend to October).

At **Heavenly Valley Ski Resort** the Heavenly Tram operates from Memorial Day through September to transport visitors up 2,000ft (610m) above Lake Tahoe, with excellent views and a restaurant at the top. In winter Heavenly Valley offers skiing in two states, with miles of open countryside to chose from. Other South Lake Tahoe ski resorts include Sierra Ski Ranch south on US50 and Iron Mountain and Kirkwood, both found off SR88.

Clockwise along the western shore are three superscenic California state parks. In **Emerald Bay State Park** the Scandinavian-style Vikingsholm, accessible by boat or steep trail, is open for tours in summer. From there a beautiful lakeshore walk leads to adjacent **D. L. Bliss State Park**, with its sandy beach and summer naturalist programs. **Sugar Pine Point State Park** is the largest of these parks with a visitor centre and year-round camping. Many California and Nevada state park summer trails are groomed for skiing in winter.

In **Tahoe City**, another year-round resort, 2-hour long lake cruises are provided in summer by North Tahoe Cruises; check with them or North Lake Tahoe Visitors Bureau for sailing times. The **Gatekeeper's Log Cabin Museum** is set in a 3.5-acre park and depicts Tahoe's early history through Indian and pioneer artifacts. **Tahoe State Recreation Area** contains a small campsite and a picnic area, while 12 miles northeast of Tahoe City **Kings Beach State Recreation Area** is a scenic day-use park with a wide, gently sloping beach.

Squaw Valley USA in Olympic Valley, 7 miles (11km) northwest of Tahoe City, was the site of the 1960 Winter Olympics. Like many of California's premier resorts, this renowned area offers an excellent range of downhill and cross-country skiing plus the fast growing sport of snowboarding. Other resorts include Alpine Meadows, Homewood and the nursery slopes of Granlibakken.

To the north, I-80 follows a route across the Sierra Nevada used by early settlers. The 350-acre **Donner Memorial State Park** commemorates the ordeal of the pioneer Donner party who failed to cross the pass now named after them before heavy snows blocked their path. The park's Emigrant Trail Museum depicts how several struggled on to Sutter's Fort while the remainder made camp. By the time help arrived thirty-five of the eighty-two had died, the survivors having to resort to cannibalism. Today the park is popular in summer for hiking, swimming and fishing and in winter for cross-country skiing.

The quaint lumber town of **Truckee** to the west was founded in 1863 and boomed as the Central Pacific Railroad was routed this way. The area is blessed with numerous ski resorts, as evidenced at **Soda Springs** by the **Western American Ski Sport Museum**. Their exhibits trace the development of skiing from 1860 to the present. The Truckee-Donner area boasts **Sugar Bowl Ski Resort** and **Boreal**, the latter famed for night skiing, plus Donner Ski Ranch, Soda Springs, and Tahoe Donner.

A mile north of **Sierra City**, **Sierra County Historical Park** offers summer tours of a restored hard-rock gold mine and stamp mill. To the west, next to the Sierra County Courthouse in **Downieville**, are the original gallows erected in 1857. The **Sierra County Museum** on Main Street has a collection of pioneer artifacts and mining equipment while **Downieville Heritage Park**, in a pleasant riverside setting, displays yet more mining equipment. To the north, a little off the beaten track, **Plumas Eureka State Park** was once mined for gold but today offers miles of quiet trails for hiking or skiing.

Rail enthusiasts should head for **Feather River Railroad Museum** in Portola, where seventy items of rolling stock are held and train rides are available on summer weekends. North in **Quincy** the **Plumas County Museum** has an interesting collection of pioneer, logging and mining artifacts, plus an excellent selection of Maidu Indian basketry. **Beckwourth Cabin** recalls when its namesake mountain man made his home-cum-trading post here in 1852.

Reno, Nevada

Reno calls itself America's 'Biggest Little City', easily reached from San Francisco by travelling due east on I-80. The city offers a glittering array of 24-hour gambling, big name stars, cabaret lounges and nightclubs, with most of the gambling action south of the interstate on or near Virginia Street (Bally's Reno out on Glendale is the main exception). Bally's, Harrah's, the Flamingo Hilton and the Nugget have big time shows, while virtually all casinos have cabaret lounges. Many US Airlines operate from Reno Cannon International

Wintersports above Lake Tahoe at the Heavenly Valley ski resort

Reno, just over the Nevada border, offers nightlife and 24-hour gambling

Airport, and the city is also served by Amtrak and Greyhound.

Reno-Sparks Convention and Visitors Authority produces a comprehensive visitor guide listing accommodation, shopping, sightseeing and recreation. Beyond the air-conditioned casinos is the great outdoors, with ballooning, hiking, bicycle rental, boating, rafting, windsurfing, fishing, golf and horse riding in summer, whilst winter sports are equally well catered for. Check prices locally, as ski equipment is often less expensive to rent or buy in Reno than the resorts. Reno also offers a wide variety of cultural events from Shakespeare to grand opera, with details of current events available from the Sierra Arts Foundation.

Harrah Foundation National Automobile Museum houses over 200 cars in authentic scenes from the turn-of-the-century to the present, plus hands-on exhibits and a multimedia theatre presentation. At the north of the University of Nevada campus, **Fleischmann Planetarium** presents programs on astronomical phenomena while the **Mineral Museum** on North Center Street has metallurgical, geological and mining displays.

Lying south on SR341 off US395, **Virginia City** was founded as a gold rush town in 1859. Enterprising prospectors purchased a local gold mine blocked with blue clay. Assaying showed the troublesome material was in fact an ultra-rich vein of silver, thus giving birth to the extremely lucrative Comstock Lode.

This historic town's former opulence is still evident at 1868 **Castle** and the **Fourth Ward School Museum**, where gourmet European menus from the boom illustrate the high standard of living. C Street has interesting small museums including The Way It Was Museum, Mark Twain Museum of Memories and the Nevada State Fire Museum and Comstock Firemen's Museum. For an underground experience visit **Chollar Mine** while the Virginia and Truckee Railroad operates from Memorial Day through October. The 1880s Piper's Opera House offers guided tours.

Carson City, state capital of Nevada, was founded in 1858. The original silver-domed **State Capitol** is still in use and open for tours, while the old Mint Building houses the excellent **State Museum**. For Native American culture and art visit **Stewart Indian Museum**. **Nevada State Railroad Museum** preserves rolling stock from the Virginia and Truckee Railroad, offering weekend trips in summer.

One third of Lake Tahoe's shoreline lies within Nevada, with cruises by *MS Dixie* from Zephyr Cove. Incline Village on the northern shore is home to Ponderosa Ranch, as seen in TV's *Bonanza*. The town of **Stateline** which adjoins South Lake Tahoe offers big name casinos and one-armed bandits on the Nevada-California border.

Additional Information

Regional Visitor Information

Alpine County Chamber of Commerce
PO Box 265
Markleeville, CA 96120
☎ 916-694-2475

Bakersfield CVB
1033 Thruxton Ave, PO Box 192
Bakersfield, CA 93302
☎ 805-325-5051

Bishop Chamber of Commerce
690 N Main St
Bishop, CA 93514
☎ 619-873-8405

Central Valley Tourism Association
PO Box 1792
Fresno, CA 93717
☎ 209-233-0836

Fresno City & County CVB
808 M St
Fresno, CA 93721
☎ 209-233-0836 or 800-543-8488

Lake Tahoe Visitors Authority
1156 Ski Run Boulevard
PO Box 16299
South Lake Tahoe, CA 95706
☎ 916-544-5050 or 800-288-2463

Mammoth Lakes Resort Association
Village Center Mall
Main St, PO Box 48
Mammoth Lakes, CA 93546
☎ 619-934-2712 or 800-367-6752

North Lake Tahoe CVB
950 N Lake Boulevard
Suite 3, PO Box 884
Tahoe City, CA 95730
☎ 918-583-3494 or 800-824-6348

Truckee-Donner Visitors Center
10065 Donner Pass Rd, PO Box 2757
Truckee, CA 95734
☎ 916-587-2757 or 800-548-8388

Places to Visit

Bodie State Historic Park
PO Box 515
Bridgeport, CA 93517
☎ 619-647-6445
Open: 9am-5pm, roads closed in winter
Ghost mining town, tours

Boyden Cavern
Box 756
Kings Canyon National Park
CA 93633
☎ 209-736-2708
Open: 11am-4pm May & Oct,
10am-5pm Jun-Sep
Tours

California Living Museum
14000 Old Alfred Harrel Hwy
Bakersfield, CA 93386
☎ 805-872-CALM
Open: 10am-Sunset Tue-Sun
Botanical gardens, native wildlife

D. L. Bliss State Park
SR89, 19 miles south of Tahoe City
☎ 916-525-7277
Closed winter
Camp, picnic, hike, swim

Devils Postpile National Monument
c/o Sequoia/Kings Canyon NP
Three Rivers, CA 93271
(Situated near Mammoth, CA)
☎ 619-934-2289 (summer)
209-565-3341 (winter)
Bus & camping in summer

Discovery Center
1944 N Winery
Fresno, CA 93707
☎ 209-251-5531
Open: 11am-5pm Tue-Sun
Interactive exhibits, picnic, gifts

Donner Memorial State Park
PO Box 9210
Truckee, CA 96162
☎ 916-587-3841
Open: hours vary
Museum, camp in summer

Duncan Water Gardens
691 Temperance Ave
Fresno, CA 93727
☎ 209-255-7233
Open: 9am-5pm Tue-Sat, 10am-4pm Sun

Eastern California Museum
PO Box 206, 155 N. Grant St
Independence, CA 93526
☎ 619-878-2411
Open: 10m-4pm except Tue & holidays

Emerald Bay State Park
PO Drawer D
Tahoma, CA 96142
☎ 916-525-7277
Summer camping & tours of Vikingsholm

Fort Miller Block House
PO Box 2029
Fresno, CA 93718
☎ 209-441-0862
Open: 1pm-4pm weekends May-Sep; free

Fresno Metropolitan Museum of Art, History & Science
1555 Van Ness
Fresno, CA 93721
☎ 209-441-1444
Open: 11am-5pm Wed-Sun
Tours, gifts

Chaffee Zoo
894 W Belmont Ave, Roeding Park
Fresno, CA 93728
☎ 209-488-1111
Open: 10am-5pm, -6.30pm summer
Tours, food, gifts

Grover Hot Springs State Park
PO Box 188
Markleeville, CA 96120
☎ 916-694-2248
Open: year-round
Hot springs pool, camp, picnic

Heavenly Tram
PO Box 2180
Stateline, NV 89449
☎ 916-544-6263
Open: summer 10am-10pm, winter 9am-4pm
Aerial tram, restaurant, hike

Inyo National Forest HQ
873 N Main St
Bishop, CA 93514
☎ 619-873-5841
Free information

Kearney Mansion & Kearney Park
7160 W Kearney Blvd
Fresno, CA 93706
☎ 209-441-0862
Open: 1pm-4pm Fri-Sun
Tour mansion

Kern County Museum
3801 Chester Ave.
Bakersfield, CA 93301
☎ 805-861-2132
Open: 8am-5pm weekdays, 10am-5pm weekends
Tour sixty historic buildings

Lake Tahoe Cruises
PO Box 14292
South Lake Tahoe, CA 95702
☎ 916-541-3364 or 800-23-TAHOE
Call for times
Glass bottomed sternwheeler, ski shuttle

Laws Railroad Museum
PO Box 363 (north on SR6)
Bishop, CA 93514
☎ 619-873-5950
Open: 10am-4pm weather permitting

Mono Lake Tufa State Reserve
PO Box 99
Lee Vining, CA 93541
☎ 619-647-6331
Crusty tufa towers, tours. Free

**Paiute Shoshone Indian Cultural
   Center Museum**
2300 W Line St
Bishop, CA 93514
☎ 619-873-4478
Open: 9am-4pm weekdays, 10am-
4pm weekends, seasonal variations
Native art & traditions, free

Plumas Eureka State Park
310 Johnsville Rd
Blairsden, CA 96103
☎ 916-836-2380
Tours, camp, ski in winter

**Sequoia/Kings Canyon National
   Parks**
PO Box 789
Three Rivers, CA 93271
☎ 209-561-3314
Sequoia groves, hike, camp, ride,
picnic

Sugar Pine Point State Park
SR89 south of Tahoe City
Tahoma, CA 95733
☎ 916-525-7232
Hike, ski, camp year-round

**Western American Ski Sport
   Museum**
PO Box 729
Soda Springs, CA 95728
☎ 916-426-3313
Open: 11am-5pm, Tue-Sun winter,
Wed-Sun summer. Free

Yosemite Mt Sugar Pine Railroad
56001 Hwy. 41
Fish Camp, CA 93623
☎ 209-683-7273
Open: Apr-Oct
Narrow Gauge Railway

Yosemite National Park
Yosemite Park & Curry Co
CA 95389
☎ 209-372-0264 (info)
209-252-4848 (lodging)
Camp, hike, ride, picnic
Ahwahnee Hotel, Yosemite Lodge,
tent cabins. Book well ahead!

Ski Resorts

Heavenly Ski Resort
PO Box 2180
Stateline, NV 89449
☎ 916-541-1330
25 lifts, 3,600ft rise. 25% advanced,
50% intermediate, 25% beginners

June Mountain
PO Box 146
June Lake, CA 93529
☎ 619-648-7733
8 lifts, 2,500ft rise. 20% advanced,
45% intermediate, 35% beginners

Mammoth Mountain Ski Resort
PO Box 24
Mammoth Lakes, CA 93546
☎ 619-934-2571
30 lifts, 3,100 ft rise. 30% advanced,
40% intermediate, 30% beginners

Squaw Valley USA
PO Box 2007
Olympic Valley, CA 96146
☎ 916-583-6985
32 lifts, 2,900 ft rise. 30% advanced,
45% intermediate, 25% beginners

Sugar Bowl
PO Box 5
Norden, CA 95724
☎ 916-426-3651
9 lifts, 1,500 ft rise. 50% advanced,
30% intermediate, 20% beginners

4

NORTHERN CALIFORNIA

Welcome to Northern California, home of the towering redwood and the soaring eagle. Some of the state's best preserved Victorian architecture is found here, but large towns are few and attractions are 100 per cent natural. Northern California's geology is distinctly volcanic, evidenced by Lava Beds National Monument and sugar-coated Mount Shasta, which dominates the skyline for hundreds of miles.

The former Russian colony at Fort Ross

San Francisco is the popular starting point, and before leaving obtain a copy of *Redwood Empire* which covers the 400 miles north to the Oregon border. Scenic SR1 follows the coast, passing such interesting places as the former Russian colony of Fort Ross and the artists' colony of Mendocino. US101 is a faster inland route which eventually overtakes SR1.

Scenic SR1 North

SR1 north from San Francisco leads to **Olema**, gateway to the 65,303 acre **Point Reyes National Seashore**. Start with Bear Valley Visitor Center for maps, camping permits, a 20-minute introductory film, and exhibits covering local weather, geology, flora and fauna. Short walks lead to Kule Loklo, a reconstructed Miwok village, and the Earthquake Trail which follows the San Andreas fault.

Point Reyes offers considerable outdoor pursuits, from an extensive trail network to whale watching between November and April. Other coastal activities include beachcombing and tidepooling (swimming is generally unsafe), while horse riding is popular (stables near the Bear Valley Visitor Centre). Birdwatching is best from the observatory at the park's southern end, while the Tule Elk reservation is north. Point Reyes itself is a lighthouse some 300 steps beneath the cliff edge. Topside is an ideal spot for whale-watching, with nearby Sea Lion Overlook offering views of these and harbour seals.

Tomales Bay State Park lies along the San Andreas fault, an area marked by the long, narrow gulf edged with tidal marshes. Protected from the surf, the beaches at Tomales are popular for swimming while the informative Indian Nature Trail details the uses the Miwok put to the region's plants. Further north **Sonoma Coast State Beach** preserves a rugged 10 mile stretch of shoreline, where Bodega Head at southern end offers coastal views and excellent whale-watching in winter.

Fort Ross State Historic Park was constructed in 1812 to supply and protect Russian trappers who engaged in the lucrative sea otter pelt trade. The Russians were recalled in 1841, selling the fort to John Sutter before it eventually becoming a ranch. Amazingly one of the original structures remains, and the reconstructed blockhouses, palisade walls, and Russian Orthodox chapel give a good idea of the original fort. Interpretive Specialists dressed in Russian clothes answer questions and during peak season historical presentations are given at 11am and 2pm. Some thirty miles north of Fort Ross is **Point Arena Lighthouse and Museum**, which is open for tours.

Allow plenty of time for picturesque **Mendocino**, an arty New

England-style coastal village boasting numerous galleries and antique shops within the town's well-preserved nineteenth-century gingerbread buildings. The 1861 Kelley House hosts a small museum and library relating to Mendocino's history while the nearby 1854 Ford House serves as visitor centre for Mendocino Headlands State Park. Exhibits include natural history, logging and Pomo Indian artifacts and the grounds offer a picnic area. At the heart of Mendocino, the modern Art Center is a focus for art and craft classes, concerts and theatrical productions. Surrounding Mendocino are no less than six state parks, beaches and reserves protecting the rugged coastline. Continuing north leads to **Mendocino Coast Botanical Gardens**, 17 acres of woods and gardens.

Next comes **Fort Bragg**, whose main attraction is California Western Railroad's Skunk Trains. The scenic Skunk line, built for logging, runs inland for 40 miles (64km) through mountains and redwood groves. Steam power gave way to the Skunk trains, small self-powered cars smelt before they were seen. Today the service takes Skunks and 'Super Skunks' historic diesel and steam locomotives on full and half day trips to Willits, with reduced schedules in winter. Noyo Harbour in Fort Bragg is home to the commercial fishing fleet with 'catch of the day' sold at seafood markets or served in local fish restaurants.

Beyond Rockport SR1 heads inland, threading its way through wooded hills to Leggett. Those travelling further should pick up the narrative in the Redwood Country section of this chapter.

Alternate US101 North

Sights off US101 include **Hendy Woods State Park** north of **Boonville** on scenic SR128. This inland park offers a warmer, less foggy climate in summer than its coastal brethren. One of the old-growth redwood stands has a wheelchair-accessible nature trail and the parks campgrounds are a good base for exploring the Anderson Valley wine district. Artists' colony Mendocino is a short detour north on SR128.

Next on US101 comes **Ukiah**, regional information available from Mendocino County CVB. For Native American culture visit **Grace Hudson Museum and Sun House**, which contains a collection of Pomo artifacts and oil paintings of Pomo Indians by Grace Hudson. Man-made **Lake Mendocino** to the north offers swimming, fishing, boating, hiking and camping. The Pomo Visitor Center at the lake's north end contains exhibits, films and demonstrations on Pomo culture and local natural history.

A scenic section of US101 leads to **Willits**, the other terminus for

There are 300 steps down to the lighthouse at Point Reyes

The Skunk railroad to Fort Bragg. Willits' **Mendocino County Museum** displays Pomo and Yuki Indian basketry, exhibits on Mendocino county and their collection of art.

Redwood Country

In **Leggett** the Chandelier Tree is focus of a 200-acre redwood grove in **Drive-Thru Tree Park**. Further north the quieter **Standish-Hickey State Recreation Area** straddles the South Fork of the Eel River. Popular for nature-loving campers, miles of park trails lead through the redwood groves while swimming holes provide old-fashioned family fun.

North of Leggett lie most of the redwood groves, plus the inevitable tourist shops selling carved redwood gifts and statues of bears and lumberjacks. For the ultimate tourist experience, visit the 'World Famous' Tree House, partially housed in a living redwood trunk.

US101 passes through the 51,000-acre **Humboldt Redwoods State Park**, most of which lies west of the highway. High point of the park is the popular Avenue of the Giants, a scenic route along the Eel River beneath the redwood canopy. Scenic turnouts, picnic areas and a

The Skunk Line is a 40-mile scenic route using historic steam or diesel trains

visitor centre are along the route, which runs parallel to US101. Founders Grove in the park's north offers a popular self-guided nature trail past the 362ft (110m) Dyerville Giant. Walking along the Giant, which sadly fell in 1991, gives an insight into the heights redwoods attain. Humboldt Redwoods, boasting a hundred miles (160km) of hiking trails and a selection of campgrounds, is one of California's premier state parks; ideal for both casual visitor and outdoor enthusiast alike. Adventurous drivers may pass through Bull Creek and the heart of Humboldt to pick up SR211, which leads north to Ferndale, skirting the California coast en route.

North on US101 from Humboldt is the company town of **Scotia**, where the **Pacific Lumber Company Museum** tells of the timber industry. Passes are available here for self-guided tours of the world's largest redwood mill. **Fortuna Depot Museum** to the north is housed in an old railway station.

A 5-mile detour off US101 leads visitors to the picturesque village of **Ferndale**, which despite earthquakes continues to preserve many Victorian homes. Owned by local dairy barons, the houses were known as 'butterfat palaces'. A walking tour map of Main Street is available, while **Ferndale Museum** recreates local history through room-like settings.

Eureka on the Humboldt Bay is the largest Californian port north of San Francisco. Founded in 1850 as a gold rush town, Eureka developed with the lumber and shipping industries and lumber is still important. Many splendid buildings were Victorian lumber magnates' mansions, including much photographed Carson Mansion on 2nd and M Streets (now a private club). The nearby Eureka/ Humboldt County Visitors Bureau offers guided 'Discover Eureka' tours (reserve in advance) and provide an excellent city map which highlights much of the Victorian architecture for which this area is famous. Beyond Carson Mansion, **Humboldt Bay Maritime Museum** examines Eureka's seafaring history. A large fishing fleet is still based here, providing fresh seafood for local shops and restaurants.

The renovated Old Town lies along the city's waterfront with harbour cruises and carriage rides available. The interesting **Clarke Memorial Museum** (3rd and E Streets) has an excellent collection of Native American basketry and pioneer memorabilia. Also in Old Town, real ale fans will find that micro-breweries have gained a significant following in Northern California.

Just off US101 in the south of Eureka, **Fort Humboldt State Historic Park** was the site of an outpost established in 1854 to protect gold miners and settlers from displaced Native Americans. The fort's hospital has survived in the form of a museum. Wheelchair-accessible grounds display logging equipment, including locomotives and the revolutionary steam donkeys used to haul logs out of the forests. Railroad enthusiasts can take the 10-hour trip between Willits and Eureka along the scenic Eel River on North Coast Daylight: Redwoods by Rail.

North of Eureka and halfway across Samoa Bridge, Woodley Island Marina affords a panorama of the city's waterfront. The large fisherman's statue commemorates those lost at sea. Across Humboldt Bay the **Samoa Cookhouse** is the last surviving lumber-camp cookhouse in the West. Hearty breakfasts, lunches and dinners are served and a museum looks at the logging industry.

Samoa Road (SR255) offers a scenic alternate route to **Arcata**, formerly a supply centre for nearby gold fields and lumber camps. This is a pleasant town built around a traditional town square. **Jacoby's Storehouse** was built of local stone and bricks to guard against fire, and is today a California State Historical Landmark. G Street has the local chamber of commerce, which offers a self-guided architectural tour of Arcata, and the **Humboldt State University Natural History Museum**. The **Arcata Marsh and Wildlife Sanctuary** on I Street offers nature trails and picnic areas, while the **Mad River Slough and Dunes** nature preserve is west off SR255.

Those with limited time or who have seen enough redwoods can take scenic SR299 inland to Redding before returning south. Sights along the way include a short detour north for the Hoopa Valley Indian Reservation. Experience tribal culture at **Hoopa Tribal Museum**, where details of special tours of Hoopa Indian villages can be obtained. Joss House State Park in Weaverville is covered in the Inland Options section of this chapter.

Those travelling north on US101 will find **Patrick's Point State Park** offers a lovely beach backed by rugged cliffs and bejewelled with wave-polished agates. The park boasts a museum, Yurok Indian Village, picnic facilities and campgrounds.

Several pristine redwood forests await to the north, commencing with **Redwood National Park**. The Redwood Information Center just before Orick orientates the visitor with a short slide presentation and offers a summer shuttle bus service to the Tall Trees Trailhead, where the world's tallest tree is found (allow 4.5 hours for the round trip and wear comfortable walking shoes). Detailed trail maps are available for longer hikes, while Lady Bird Johnson nature loop trail offers a pleasant short walk through old growth redwoods.

To the north US101 leads through **Prairie Creek Redwoods State Park** with 70 miles (113km) of hiking trails, including jogging and

Ferndale preserves many of its picturesque buildings

Many of Eureka's spendid Victorian mansions were built for lumber magnates

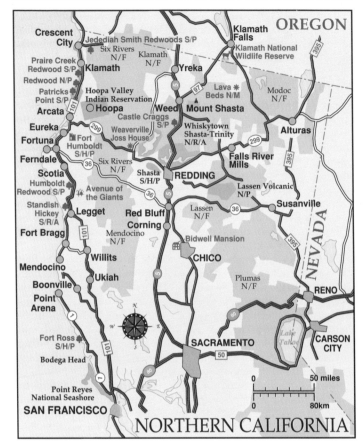

NORTHERN CALIFORNIA

mountain bike trails. An interesting feature is the short nature trail for the blind or disabled (tape recorders provided at the visitor centre). Prairie Creek is the natural habitat of Roosevelt elk, normally visible from US101, and a population of black bears. Further up US101 **Klamath** is home to Trees of Mystery, with giant statues depicting the life of Paul Bunyan and the End of the Trail Museum.

Another section of Redwood National Park is encountered before **Del Norte Coast Redwoods State Park** is reached, which features dense old growth redwoods combined with particularly scenic coastline. **Crescent City** houses the Redwood National Park Headquarters in an unusual bridge-shaped structure designed to withstand tidal waves, while more general regional information is available from Crescent City-Del Norte County CVB. Museums of note include the small but well stocked **Del Norte County Historical Society Museum** and **Battery Point Lighthouse Museum**, a working lighthouse containing nautical artifacts and photographs.

Inland Options

From Crescent City travellers must chose whether to return south on US101 or continue on to central California by taking US199 north into Oregon before returning south. Those opting for the latter first reach **Jedediah Smith Redwoods State Park**. From the banks of the clear, green Smith River it is much easier to appreciate the enormous height coastal redwoods attain. Named after the famous mountain man and explorer, the park offers 18 miles (29km) of hiking trails and camping amongst redwoods. While in Oregon, consider enjoying an exhilarating boat ride on the Rogue River at Grants Pass, followed by a detour to Oregon Caves National Monument or spectacular Crater Lake National Park.

The fastest route south is I-5, but nature lovers may wish to first take a scenic detour. From Medford (Oregon) take SR140 east then SR39 south to the California border. This wild and scenic country is a birdwatchers paradise, where spring and autumn bring sky-fulls of migratory waterfowl. **Klamath Basin National Wildlife Refuge Visitor Center** near **Tulelake** has information on self-guided auto tour routes and a canoe trail. In summer Klamath is a breeding ground for waterfowl and marsh birds, while the basin is a wintering ground for birds of prey, including the bald eagle.

Nearby **Lava Beds National Monument** occupies 46,500 acres of volcanic land sporting defunct cinder cones, spatter cones, lava flows and interconnecting lava tubes; some containing permanent ice. Originally inhabited by a Modoc Indian tribe forced onto this inhospitable land, the area became a battle ground when the Modocs refused relocation to a reservation. Outnumbered twenty to one, the Modocs and leader Captain Jack held off the US Army for five months in 1872-3, and today Captain Jack's Stronghold, a natural fortification, can be visited by interpretive loop trail.

Another favourite park pastime is exploring the lava tubes. Mushpot Cave at the visitor centre is illuminated; for the others join a ranger-led tour or obtain maps, protective hard hats and flashlights from the visitor centre (do follow park safety rules). Return to Klamath Falls, Oregon then take US97 south to Weed, picking up the narrative from there.

Those following I-5 south from Oregon will find a California Welcome Center, followed by the town of **Yreka**. Founded in 1851 upon the discovery of that precious yellow metal, **Siskiyou County Courthouse** displays gold nuggets from the area. **Siskiyou County Museum** covers Indian, gold rush and pioneer periods, combining the latter two with a restored pioneer village containing mining equipment. Self-guided tours commence either here or from the information centre on Main Street. For more information on the surrounding countryside visit **Klamath National Forest Interpretive Museum**, while railroad enthusiasts should consider the 3-hour steam trip to **Montague** on the Blue Goose Excursion Train.

South of Yreka SR3 offers an alternative, scenic route south. This meandering road first passes **Fort Jones Museum** and its displays of Indian and pioneer artifacts before reaching Clair Engle Lake, part of **Whiskeytown-Shasta-Trinity National Recreation Area**. The three areas covered by the recreation area offer swimming, boating (houseboats are popular), fishing and hiking some 1,400 miles (2,250km) of trails, including a portion of the Pacific Crest Trail.

SR3 leads to **Weaverville**, a former gold mining community employing numerous Chinese. Their Taoist temple is preserved as **Weaverville Joss House State Historic Park**. Entitled 'Temple of the Forest Beneath the Clouds', this is the oldest Californian Chinese temple still in use (call for guided tour schedules). **J. J. Jackson Memorial Museum** examines the history of Trinity County while **Scotts Museum** looks at local nineteenth-century ranching.

Those following I-5 south from Yreka will find the countryside dominated by Mount Shasta. The quaint town of **Mount Shasta** offers regional information at the national forest ranger station and the chamber of commerce. Before climbing 14,162ft (4,317m) Mount Shasta visit the town's sports shop for detailed topographical maps, necessary equipment and useful local knowledge. Also ideal for winter sports enthusiasts, the mountain challenges downhill skiers and snowmobilers at **Mount Shasta Ski Park**, while 30 miles (50km) of groomed trails are accessible from **Castle Lake Cross Country Ski Area**. For local geology and history visit **Sisson Hatchery Museum**.

Just south of Dunsmuir is the popular **Castle Crags State Park**, a series of dramatic rock outcrops with views across to Mount Shasta. Nearby Railroad Park Resort is an unusual motel utilising cabooses and antique railroad dining cars.

I-5 also passes through Whiskeytown-Shasta-Trinity National Recreation Area, and from Shasta Lake a combined boat and bus tour visits **Lake Shasta Caverns** (wear comfortable shoes and be prepared to tackle stairs). From the huge Shasta Dam and associated visitor centre a vista point looks across the dam and lake to the ubiquitous Mount Shasta.

Bald eagles may often be seen in Northern California

Shasta Dam with Mount Shasta in the background

Redding serves as a base for many visitors to north-central California. **Carter House Natural Science Museum** features local natural history while **Redding Museum of Art and History** offers well presented exhibits on Shasta County. The historic **Old City Hall Gallery & Performing Arts Center** has exhibits and a 100-seat theatre presenting plays and musical productions. During the hot summers cool off at popular Waterworks Park. Nearby **Shasta State Historic Park** preserves the ruins of the Shasta, a prosperous mining supply centre usurped when the railroad came to Redding. A self-guided walking tour leads through the remains, including a restored courthouse doubling as a museum.

Those wishing to experience the remoteness of northeastern California can follow a 300-mile triangle starting with SR299 west from Redding to Alturas, then US395 south to Susanville, followed by SR44 west to Redding. En route drivers may visit the popular **McArthur-Burney Falls Memorial State Park** and **Ahjumawi Lava Springs State Park**. The latter preserves an unusual area of springs and porous lava flows rich in bird life (remember insect repellant). At **Fall River Mills** the **Fort Crook Museum** boasts a one-room schoolhouse, log cabin and jail, while in **Alturas** the **Modoc County Museum** features well displayed Indian artifacts, a collection of firearms and considerable pioneer relics. **Roop's Fort and William Pratt Memorial Museum** in **Susanville** exhibits early Lassen County history while the **William H. Pratt Museum** displays local artifacts including lumbering equipment and tools.

The area's most popular attraction, **Lassen Volcanic National Park**, is accessible from Redding via SR44 east. Dominated by 10,457ft (3,187m) Lassen Peak, the park also offers boardwalks overlooking colourful hot springs, fumaroles and boiling mud pots (stay on the path!). The park's headquarters are on SR36 west of Mineral, while visitor centres are at the northern and southern entrances. Park roads are generally impassable between late October and early June, excepting the southern entrance which provides access to **Lassen Park Ski Area & Ski Touring Center**.

From Lassen follow SR36 west to the I-5 at **Red Bluff**. Their **Kelly-Griggs House Museum** is an elegantly restored 1880s Victorian building furnished in style. Pioneer artifacts, photographs and an exhibit on Ishi 'the last wild Indian' are also on display. **William. B. Ide Adobe State Historic Park** occupies an idyllic setting on the banks of the Sacramento River (bring a picnic). After being the first and only president of the Bear Flag Republic, an office he held for twenty-two days in 1846, William Ide returned to Red Bluff to live in this small adobe house.

South in **Corning** is **Woodson Bridge State Recreation Area**, also situated on the banks of the Sacramento River. Before returning south consider a short detour to **Chico** for another state-run attraction, the elegant **Bidwell Mansion**. Built in the 1860s, this fascinating three-storey Italian villa features what in Victorian times were innovative advances in the art of domestic science.

Additional Information

Regional Visitor Information

Crescent City-Del Norte County CVB
1001 Front St, PO Box 246
Crescent City, CA 95531
☎ 707-464-3174

Eureka/Humboldt County CVB
1034 Second St
Eureka, CA 95501
☎ 707-443-5097 or 800-346-3482

Lassen County Chamber of Commerce
720 Main St, PO Box 338
Susanville, CA 96130
☎ 916-257-4323

Mendocino County CVB
320 S State St, PO Box 244
Ukiah, CA 95482
☎ 707-462-3091

Modoc County Chamber of Commerce
522 S Main St
Alturas, CA 96101
☎ 916-233-2819 or 800-34-MODOC

Redding CVB
777 Auditorium Dr
Redding, CA 96001
☎ 916-225-4100

Redwood Empire Association
One Market Plaza, Spear Street
Tower, Suite 1001
San Francisco, CA 94105
☎ 415-543-8334

Yreka Chamber of Commerce
1000 S Main St
Yreka, CA 96097
☎ 916-842-1649

Places to Visit

Battery Point Lighthouse Museum
End of A Street
Crescent City, CA 95531
☎ 707-464-3089
Open: Apr-Sept 10am-4pm Wed-Sun
Tours (tide permitting)

California Western Railroad's Skunk Trains
PO Box 907
Fort Bragg, CA 95437
☎ 707-964-6371
Train tours — call for times

Castle Crags State Park
PO Box 80
(South of Dunsmuir off I-5)
Castella, CA 96017
☎ 916-235-2684
Views, picnic, camp

Clarke Memorial Museum
3rd & E St
Eureka, CA 95501
☎ 707-443-1947
Open: noon-4pm Tue-Sat
Tours

Del Norte Coast Redwoods State Park
US 101
South of Crescent City, CA
☎ 707-445-6547
Redwoods, camp, hike

Del Norte County Historical Society Museum
577 H St
Crescent City, CA 95531
☎ 707-464-3922
Open: 10am-4pm Mon-Fri May-Sep

Ferndale Museum
3rd & Shaw Streets
Ferndale, CA 95536
☎ 707-786-4466
Open: 11am-4pm Wed-Sat, 1pm-4pm Sun

Fort Humboldt State Historic Park
3431 Fort Ave
Eureka, CA 95501
☎ 707-445-6567
Free; museum, logging equipment

Fort Ross State Park
SR1
12 miles north of Jenner, CA
☎ 707-847-3286
Reconstructed 1812 Russian fort

Grace Hudson Museum and Sun House
431 S Main St
Ukiah, CA 95482
☎ 707-462-3370
Open: 10am-4.30pm Tue-Sat, Noon-4.30pm Sun, 4th July to Labor Day
Tour, museum, park, Pomo artifacts

Humboldt Redwoods State Park
PO Box 100
Weott, CA 95571
☎ 707-946-2311
Camp, picnic, hike, Avenue of the Giants drive

Klamath National Forest Interpretive Museum
1312 Fairlane Rd
Yreka, CA 96097
☎ 916-842-6131
Open: 8am-4.30pm Mon-Fri
Free; tours

Lake Shasta Caverns
PO Box 801
O'Brien, CA 96070
☎ 916-238-2341
Call for opening times
Boat & bus to caverns, tours

Lassen Volcanic National Park
PO Box 100
Mineral, CA 96063
☎ 916-594-4444
Mud pots, hot springs, hike, camp

Lava Beds National Monument
PO Box 867
Tulelake, CA 96134
☎ 916-667-2282
Explore lava tubes, Modoc War site

Mendocino Coast Botanical Gardens
18220 N Hwy 1, PO Box 1143
Fort Bragg, CA 95437
☎ 707-965-4352
Open: 9am-5pm Mar-Oct, 10am-4pm Nov-Feb
Gardens & woods, food

Modoc Museum
600 S. Main St
Alturas, CA 96101
☎ 916-233-2944
Open: 9am-4pm Mon-Fri, 10am-4.30pm Sat, Sun & Holidays
Free; firearms & Native artifacts

North Coast Daylight: Redwoods by Rail
PO Box 3666
Eureka, CA 95502
☎ 707-442-7705
Train operates May-Oct

**Old City Hall Gallery &
  Performing Arts Center**
1313 Market St
Redding, CA 96001
☎ 916-241-7232
Open: 9am-4pm Mon-Fri
Free; tours, gifts

Pacific Lumber Company Museum
Main St
Scotia, CA 95565
☎ 707-764-2222
Open: 7.30am-10.30am & 12.30pm-
2.30pm Mon-Fri
Museum summers only

Point Reyes National Seashore
SR 1
Point Reyes, CA 94956
☎ 415-662-1092
Lighthouse, Miwok village, hike,
wildlife

Prairie Creek Redwoods State Park
US101
6 miles north of Orick, CA
☎ 707-488-2171
Redwoods, elk, hike, camp, fern
canyon

**Redding Museum of Art and
  History**
Caldwell Park, 56 Quartz Hill Rd
Redding, CA 96003
☎ 916-225-4155
Open: hours vary, closed Monday.
Local & Native history, changing art

Redwood Information Center
PO Box 7
Orick, CA 95555
☎ 707-488-3461
Open: 9am-5pm, -6pm summers,
except major holidays
Shuttle bus, info, books, slide show

Redwood National Park HQ
1111 Second St
Crescent City, CA 95531
☎ 707-464-6101
Info for southbound drivers

Shasta State Historic Park
PO Box 2430 (Route 299)
Redding, CA 96087
☎ 916-225-2065
10am-5pm, closed Tue-Wed winter
Museum, tours

Siskiyou County Museum
910 S Main St
Yreka, CA 96097
☎ 916-842-3836
Open: 9am-5pm Mon-Sat, 1pm-
5pm Sun, closed Sun-Mon winter
Free

**Weaverville Joss House State
  Historic Park**
PO Drawer 1217
Weaverville, CA 96093
☎ 916-623-5258
Open: 10am-5pm except major
holidays
Tour oldest Chinese temple in use

**William B. Ide Adobe State
  Historic Park**
21695 Adobe Rd
Red Bluff, CA 96080
☎ 916-527-5927
Open: 8am-sunset, home noon-
4pm
Tour, picnic

5

COASTING SOUTH FROM SANTA CRUZ

Hugging much of the twisting California coastline, SR1 offers a super-scenic route from Santa Cruz and the Bay Area south to Los Angeles. Follow serpentine SR1 south past numerous beaches to historic Monterey, capital of Spanish Alta (Upper) California, before visiting San Simeon's monument to wealth — Hearst Castle.

Those who find SR1 too curvacious may opt for US101, which follows the Spanish 'El Camino Real' past numerous missions. The two routes converge at San Luis Obispo, so drivers could follow SR1 down the coast and return on US101. Those pressing south from San Luis Obispo will find more missions and plenty of wineries, plus the red-tiled roofs of beautiful Santa Barbara. The California coast is ideal for historians, holidaymakers, and outdoor enthusiasts alike, but don't rush it. If travelling down from San Francisco plan for several stops, and allow days rather than hours.

Santa Cruz

Sunny Santa Cruz is a melange of contrasts; from its university upon redwood-covered mountain slopes past downtown's New Age shops to a beachside amusement park straight out of some 1960s beach movie. Found just past the municipal pier, Santa Cruz Beach Boardwalk was actually established in 1868. The 1900 casino now houses the entertainment centre, while the 1911 carrousel and 1924 Giant Dipper roller coaster still attract the crowds. The mile wide stretch of sand in front is a free attraction, perfect for volleyball or sunbathing.

Follow the beach west or drive along West Cliff Drive for the **Surfing Museum**, found occupying the ground floor of picturesque **Mark Abbot Memorial Lighthouse**. A collection of surfboards and photographs illustrate surfing from the 1930s, while agile surfers in

Steamer Lane compete for spectators' attention. Those with binoculars can also watch the antics of barking sea lions on Seal Rock. Further west is **Natural Bridges State Beach**, a secluded sandy cove backed by a eucalyptus grove populated with migrating monarch butterflies in autumn. The interesting eroded rock formations lie just off the bluffs near the car park.

The **Santa Cruz Mission** is in from the beach and just west of the river. Badly hit by earthquakes, remnants include stone foundations, the ruins of the soldiers' barracks and Santa Cruz Mission Adobe, a one-storey structure located in Santa Cruz Mission State Park. In the grounds of Holy Cross church, near the original site, a half-scale mission replica was built in 1931. The nearby **Santa Cruz County Historical Trust Museum**, occupying an 1882 octagonal building, offers information on walking tours of the historic area. Just north of Santa Cruz, straddling SR1, **Wilder Ranch State Historic Park** was the main rancho supplying the Santa Cruz Mission. Visitors may explore barns, Victorian houses, the gardens and a historic adobe, with tours of the blacksmith's shop and Wilder home available.

Across the San Lorenzo River on East Cliff Drive, **Santa Cruz City Museum of Natural History** has artifacts and information on the Ohlone Indians native to Monterey Bay and local natural history exhibits including a hands-on (or in) tidepool. **Twin Lakes State Beach** stretches along East Cliff Drive, offering another mile of sandy shore for swimming and picnicking, while the lagoons attract bird-watchers. **Antonelli Begonia Gardens** to the northeast are a feast of begonias and tropical flowers, reaching a colourful peak in August and September.

The **University of California at Santa Cruz (UCSC)** was founded in 1965 on a hillside overlooking Santa Cruz and Monterey Bay — self-guiding tour maps are available from the main entrance information booth. Their Barn Theatre and Performing Arts Centre offer a wide selection of programs. UCSC's **Joseph M. Long Marine Laboratory** (found at the end of Delaware Avenue) offers a touch tank, aquarium, 85ft blue whale skeleton, and exhibits on present research. Adjacent to the main campus or inland on SR9 is **Henry Cowell Redwoods State Park**, where a short self-guided trail leads through an impressive redwood grove. A nature centre, picnic area, campground and 15 miles (24km) of hiking and horse trails make this a popular park.

North in **Felton** is one of California's rare covered bridges, built in 1892 and now a State Historical Landmark. Felton is a rail enthusiast's dream, where an 1880 steam train makes a 75-minute trip up through the redwoods at Roaring Camp and Big Trees Narrow

Gauge Railroad. Alternatively take the scenic 2.5-hour excursion on the Santa Cruz Big Trees and Pacific Railway down through Henry Cowell Redwoods State Park along the San Lorenzo River Canyon, roughly paralleling SR9 to Santa Cruz.

Those following SR1 south should continue with the Monterey Bay section, while those who opt for the faster inland route past the missions may skip ahead to the US101 section.

Monterey Bay

From Santa Cruz, nestled at the northern end of Monterey Bay, scenic SR1 follows a stretch of coast boasting nine state beaches. New Brighton State Beach in **Capitola** and Seacliff State Beach in **Aptos** are both popular seaside areas with sandy beaches and campsites (book well ahead). Manresa State Beach offers limited facilities while Sunset State Beach's miles of sand are very popular for day use and camping.

Moss Landing offers a quaint fishing harbour stocked with a mixture of pleasure craft and commercial vessels. The fresh catch of the day is sold direct from the quayside or served in Moss Landing's unpresumptuous cafes and restaurants. Behind the harbour is Elkhorn Slough Reserve, 1,340 acres of near pristine coastal estuarine wetland. A visitor centre provides information on this important waterfowl habitat, with its observation hides and nature walks.

Zmudowski and **Salinas River State Beaches** are good for fishing, and horse riding is allowed on both beaches (not the dunes). The prevalent sea breeze at **Marina State Beach** is perfect for the hang-gliding lessons offered there, but swimmers should avoid the area's very rough sea. Just beyond Seaside, Sand Dunes Road leads to **Monterey State Beach**, where the calmer water offers safer swimming. Hikers may follow the 18 mile (29km) recreation coastal trail from Castroville, artichoke capital of the world, to Asilomar State Beach in Pacific Grove.

Monterey

This historic town, former military and ecclesiastical capital of Alta California, is today as lively and colourful as ever. Monterey Peninsula Visitors Bureau on Alvarado Street produces an excellent road map highlighting points of interest along Monterey Peninsular. The *Path of History* booklet is available from Pacific House, Cooper Store and Colton Hall, giving a self-guided walking tour past historic adobe structures, many being museums within **Monterey State Historic Park**.

Santa Cruz beach and boardwalk

Colton Hall, Monterey, where California's first constitution was signed in 1849

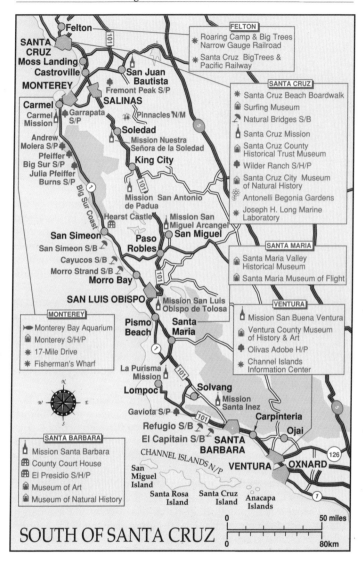

SOUTH OF SANTA CRUZ

Felton

SANTA CRUZ
Moss Landing
Castroville
MONTEREY

Carmel
Carmel
Mission

Andrew
Molera S/P
Pfeiffer
Big Sur S/P
Julia Pfeiffer
Burns S/P

Garrapata
S/P

San Juan
Bautista
Fremont Peak S/P

SALINAS

Pinnacles N/M

Soledad
Mission Nuestra
Señora de la Soledad

King City

Mission San Antonio
de Padua

Hearst Castle

San Simeon
San Simeon S/B
Cayucos S/B
Morro Strand S/B
Morro Bay

Paso
Robles

Mission San
Miguel Arcangel
San Miguel

Big Sur Coast

SAN LUIS OBISPO

MONTEREY
- Monterey Bay Aquarium
- Monterey S/H/P
- 17-Mile Drive
- Fisherman's Wharf

Pismo
Beach

Santa
Maria

Mission San Luis
Obispo de Tolosa

La Purisma
Mission

Lompoc

Gaviota S/P

Refugio S/B
El Capitain S/B

SANTA BARBARA
- Mission Santa Barbara
- County Court House
- El Presidio S/H/P
- Museum of Art
- Museum of Natural History

Solvang
Mission
Santa Inez

Carpinteria

SANTA
BARBARA

CHANNEL ISLANDS N/P

San
Miguel
Island

Santa Rosa
Island

Santa Cruz
Island

Anacapa
Islands

VENTURA

OXNARD

Ojai

FELTON
- Roaring Camp & Big Trees
  Narrow Gauge Railroad
- Santa Cruz BigTrees &
  Pacific Railway

SANTA CRUZ
- Santa Cruz Beach Boardwalk
- Surfing Museum
- Natural Bridges S/B
- Santa Cruz Mission
- Santa Cruz County
  Historical Trust Museum
- Wilder Ranch S/H/P
- Santa Cruz City Museum
  of Natural History
- Antonelli Begonia Gardens
- Joseph H. Long Marine
  Laboratory

SANTA MARIA
- Santa Maria Valley
  Historical Museum
- Santa Maria Museum of Flight

VENTURA
- Mission San Buena Ventura
- Ventura County Museum
  of History & Art
- Olivas Adobe H/P
- Channel Islands
  Information Center

0   50 miles
0   80km

First stop on this 3-mile (5km) tour is **Pacific House**, offering exhibits on Californian history and a collection of Indian artifacts. The American Stars and Stripes was first raised in California on 7 July

1846 just north of nearby **Custom House**. Today the building displays the cargo of a typical 1830s trading ship. California's First Theater, built in 1846-7, was a lodging house and tavern until 1850 when a stage was added. Re-opened as a theatre in 1937, visitors can enjoy ninteenth-century melodramas in an atmospheric setting.

Restored to its original appearance as an 1845 grocery store, **Casa del Oro** still contains the original safe reputedly used to store miners' gold. The stone **Colton Hall Museum** was opened in 1849 as a school and public meeting hall. Today the second floor has been restored to its 1849 appearance when California's first constitution was signed here. Added to the hall when it served as the county courthouse, the 1854 **Old Monterey Jail** has granite walls and iron bars and was mentioned in John Steinbeck's *Tortilla Flat*.

The two-storey adobe **Larkin House** was the forerunner of the Monterey Colonial style, combining features from New England and Mexico. Now beautifully restored it contains antiques, some having belonged to Larkin himself. **Stevenson House** began as a simple adobe structure, later extended into the boarding house where Robert Louis Stevenson lodged in 1879. Among Stevenson memorabilia is the desk at which he wrote *Treasure Island*.

Royal Presidio Chapel (San Carlos Cathedral) was completed in 1795, last remnant of the original Spanish presidio and amazingly still in use today. Just off the main walking route, north on Pacific, is the present army **Presidio** where the Defense Language Institute exhibits dioramas and artifacts highlighting local army life since the 1840s. Centrally located on Pacific Street is the **Monterey Peninsula Museum of Art**.

The new **Stanton Center** in the historic Custom House Plaza houses **The Maritime Museum of Monterey**. Seven major themed areas explore Monterey's maritime history through artifacts, pictures and graphics, while the centre's theatre offers a short orientation film on Monterey's past and visitors should not miss the museum gift shop.

Adjacent to the Stanton Center is **Fisherman's Wharf**. Built in 1846 as a pier for Cape Horn schooners, later it was used to unload the famed Monterey fishing fleet. Fish markets operate on the wharf to this day, although the commercial fleet has since moved to Municipal Wharf. Now boats at the old wooden wharf offer sight-seeing cruises, whale-watching and sport fishing. Landlubbers may browse the art galleries and gift shops lining the wharf, or watch the antics of seals, sea lions and otters. Although not nearly as commercialized as San Francisco's Fisherman Wharf, seafood lovers can still opt to sample the day's catch.

John Steinbeck immortalized **Cannery Row**, but his raunchy characters and the sardine factories have long gone, replaced by gift shops, boutiques, galleries, wine tasting rooms and restaurants. In the Monterey Cannery Building the **Spirit of Monterey Wax Museum** exhibits life-sized replicas of local historical figures.

Save time for the acclaimed **Monterey Bay Aquarium**. This world-class complex dives into the fascinating diversity of sea-life found within the twenty-three major habitats of Monterey Bay. The massive kelp forest exhibit and sea otter pool with its entertaining inhabitants are so deep they require multilevel access. Reefs, shore-line and tide pools are all revealed, while closer contact with sea creatures is positively encouraged at the touch pool. Food and drink, books and gifts are available too, so allow several hours for a visit (to re-enter the same day have your hand stamped).

Ocean View Boulevard leads north from Cannery Row to Pacific Grove. The road (and a recreation trail) follow the picturesque rocky coast, passing a sheltered sandy cove at Lovers Point Park — perfect for a quick dip in warmer weather. Beyond Point Pinos Lighthouse, operational since 1855, the boulevard becomes Sunset Drive. The recreation trail ends at Asilomar Conference Center and State Beach, occupying a prime position overlooking the Pacific. Beach and tide pools may be accessed via a boardwalk across the dunes from the conference grounds.

Pacific Grove museums worth visiting include the **John Steinbeck Memorial Museum**, situated in his grandparents' Victorian house and containing memorabilia from his youth, plus the local **Museum of Natural History**.

Sunset Drive leads to the scenic **17-Mile Drive** of Pebble Beach, popular with tourists and locals since the 1880s. This toll road (no motorbikes and restrictions on cyclists) passes through privately owned Del Monte Forest, and a map detailing points of interest is provided at the entrance stations; allow at least an hour. The area offers many facilities including hotels, restaurants, up-market shopping, horse-riding, and picnic facilities, all in a beautiful setting which includes those world famous golf courses. Enjoy the drive but do *not* venture out onto rocks, as the surf and currents are extremely hazardous. In clear weather **Cypress Point Lookout** affords a panorama as far as Point Sur lighthouse 20 miles (32km) south, in addition to views of basking seals, barking sea lions and playful sea otters. **Crocker Grove** contains the oldest and largest stand of Monterey Cypress while photographers and artists rush to capture the Lone Cypress, a famous Californian landmark.

Carmel

Originally an artists' colony, zoning restrictions outlawing high-rise developments have preserved a pleasant village-like atmosphere with delightfully tree-shaded streets. Tourism, given a boost when Clint Eastwood was elected mayor in 1986, is catered for by a wealth of top class boutiques, art galleries and antique stores, while the local market is a gourmet's delight. Fast-food outlets are banned, but restaurants cater to every taste.

The unique **Tor House and Hawk Tower** on Carmel point celebrate the life and works of poet Robinson Jeffers. However, the main attraction in Carmel must be Mission San Carlos Borromeo del Rio Carmela. Better known as **Carmel Mission**, this was the second of the missions founded by Father Junipero Serra. This famed founder of the California missions lived here from 1770 to 1784, and was interred beneath the alter. The picturesque restoration with gardens and a fountain is a photographer's delight, while the museum includes a replica of the mission kitchen. The nearby Carmel River opens out into a small lagoon at **Carmel River State Beach**, perfect for bird-watching and walking, albeit unsafe for swimming or wading.

The Lone Cypress at Pebble Beach is a well-known Californian landmark

Found 3 miles (5km) south of Carmel, **Point Lobos State Reserve** encompasses a dramatically eroded coastline crisscrossed by numerous trails. Bring binoculars for spotting sea lions, harbor seals, grey whales, sea otters and countless birds. Spring produces a profusion of wildflowers and seal pups whereas whales pass as close as 500yd offshore between December and May with January the peak. Various guided tours are offered on a regular basis; for comfort and safety wear sturdy shoes or boots. The number of visitors to the reserve is restricted to minimize environmental impact so arrive early during peak season.

Southbound SR1 hugs the **Big Sur** coastline, where the Santa Lucia range plunges into the Pacific Ocean, forming one of the world's most spectacular coastal drives. Start with a full fuel tank and take Big Sur southbound, as this presents the best views and access to scenic turnouts. Allow plenty of time, especially in winter when monarch butterflies and whales are an added attraction.

Carmel Mission, the second to be founded and the resting place of Father Junipero Serro

The California state parks, some with campsites, offer opportunities for peaceful exploration of this incomparable area. Garrapata State Park is largely undeveloped and accessed from roadside turnouts, while further south the 4,800-acre **Andrew Molera State Park** has miles of trails, beaches and the Big Sur River. A private stable offers guided horse rides, offering those panoramic views without having to hike up the mountain, while the primitive trail camp is a popular stopover for cyclists.

Pfeiffer Big Sur State Park is a well developed site. The excellent facilities include stores, restaurant, laundromat, and an information centre. The Big Sur Lodge offers rooms and cabins, while the family campsite stretches along 2 miles (3km) of the redwood edged Big Sur River. Swimming holes and hiking trails offer leisurely recreation, while the park is also a major trailhead for the Ventana Wilderness area. **Julia Pfeiffer Burns State Park**, 12 miles (19km) south of Pfeiffer Big Sur, is set amidst rugged terrain and offers good hiking and, for the experienced only, unparalleled scuba diving. While there visit the beautiful little cove backed by cliffs where a 50ft (15m) waterfall drops straight into the ocean.

Eventually the most spectacular scenery is left behind, and the mountains gradually recede from the coast. All the surrounding countryside was once part of the William Randolf Hearst empire, comprising an epic cattle ranch, the world's largest private zoo, and *La Cuesta Encantada*, the enchanted hill, home of **Hearst Castle**. Now officially known as Hearst San Simeon State Historical Monument and owned and operated by the state, the castle attracts over a million visitors each year. The only way to view this architectural extravaganza is by ranger-led guided tours: book tours and accommodation ahead or arrive early.

The visitor centre offers a large gift shop and cafeteria with a patio dining area, from which telescopes allow a sneak preview of the site. The excellent free museum highlights the life of newspaper magnate and media mogul William Randolph Hearst, and introduces architect Julia Morgan. She worked with Hearst for three decades to produce this Mediterranean Revival complex, home to Hearst's priceless art and antique collection.

As the castle (Casa Grande), guest houses and grounds are so extensive there are four daytime tours to choose from, each lasting about 1 hour 45 minutes, plus a 100-minute living history evening tour. Each tour includes the scenic bus drive up to the 'Enchanted Hill', plus the opulent outdoor Neptune Pool, impressive indoor Roman Pool, and sections of the extensive gardens with their rich statuary and fountains. Note that all are walking tours of at least half a mile which include steps — special arrangements are made for disabled visitors who must make advanced bookings. Comfortable shoes and suitable outdoor clothing are recommended for the tours.

Tour 1, recommended for first-time visitors, gives an overall feel for la Cuesta Encantada, one guest house, the lower floor of the Casa Grande including the rich tapestry-hung assembly room, mock medieval refectory, morning room, billiard room and theatre. A 6-minute movie highlights life at the castle during the 1920s and 1930s.

Tour 2 visits the upper floors of the Castle, comprising guest bedrooms, a library boasting 5,000 books and ancient Greek pottery, the Gothic Suite (Hearst's private quarters occupying the entire third floor), and the huge, well-equipped kitchen.

Tour 3 encompasses the smallest guest house (Casa del Monte), the new wing's three floors of guest bedrooms, each with magnificent marble bathroom, plus a Hearst home movie of celebrity guests.

Tour 4 available spring, summer and autumn emphasizes the grounds and gardens. The tour includes Casa del Mar, the largest guest house, the wine cellar, 'hidden terrace' (a network of stairs) and the Neptune Pool dressing rooms.

Across SR1 within **Old San Simeon** just north of Hearst Castle is Sebastian's Store, built in 1852, which serves breakfast and lunch in addition to selling gifts. Purchase picnic supplies before heading to William Randolph Hearst State Beach, a pleasant protected cove ideal for a cooling swim. Fishermen can rent equipment here for use on the pier or book a sport fishing trip. A short drive south to San Simeon State Beach offers 2 miles (3km) of surf-splashed shoreline and a congenial campsite.

Continuing south affords a scenic drive to **Morro Bay**. State beaches include **Cayucos** and **Morro Strand**, the latter including a campsite looking out towards Morro Rock. This large local landmark is formed of volcanic rock jutting 578ft (176m) from the ocean, and the top is a nesting site for the endangered peregrine falcon. Morro Bay has a quiet seaside feel, with a good sized commercial fishing fleet in its picturesque harbour. The **Embarcadero** houses gift shops and galleries, plus an aquarium offering views of the local marine life. A variety of indoor and outdoor restaurants offer excellent seafood in this waterfront setting, or stock up for a barbecue at the local fish market. Harbour cruises past Morro Rock depart from the Embarcadero every few hours.

Just south of the town **Morro Bay State Park** encompasses an 18 hole golf course, marina and the informative Museum of Natural History. Exhibits include local wildlife, geology, and life of the Chumash Indians, plus a touch tank, videos and views across the

The spectacular Big Sur coastline

The sumptuous Neptune Pool at Hearst Castle

Tours of Hearst Castle include 'Casa Grande'

harbour to Morro Rock. Budding naturalists should not miss **Montana de Oro State Park**, found south of Morro Bay and encompassing 8,066 acres, over 3.5 miles (5.6km) of rugged rocky coastline, and an extensive network of trails.

Drivers following SR1 south should continue the text at San Luis Obispo.

US101 South

Those who opted for the inland route south from Santa Cruz will find a multiplicity of missions to choose from. The first mission town, **San Juan Bautista**, is a delightful little place saved from over-development when bypassed by the railroad in 1876. Despite straddling the San Andreas Fault, Mission San Juan Bautista has survived every disaster since the epic earthquake of 1812. Boasting three aisles, this was the largest of the mission churches and is still used today. The paint of the original 1818 reredos is still beautifully bright and several rooms are preserved in period as a small museum.

The buildings around the mission plaza have been conserved as **San Juan Bautista State Historic Park**. This includes the old Plaza Hotel and the Monterey-style Castro-Breen adobe, which is decorated in period and open for self-guided tours. Other attractions include the historic park's gardens, a Spanish orchard, and carriages and coaches on display in the stable. **Fremont Peak State Park** is a popular side-trip south of San Juan Bautista, affording spectacular views of the countryside from its 3,169ft (966m) summit. On selected evenings the astronomical observatory opens for public programs.

Continuing south on US101, **Salinas** is famous as birthplace of John Steinbeck and was the setting for several of his novels. The John Steinbeck Public Library dedicates a room to his memorabilia while the turreted Victorian **Steinbeck House**, the author's birthplace, is now a restaurant. **Borondo Adobe**, the town's oldest structure, has been restored and contains exhibits on life in Monterey County.

Mission Nuestra Senora de la Soledad, the thirteenth founded, crumbled into ruin before being rebuilt in 1954. Today a chapel and small museum in the padres' wing have been completed, with a full reconstruction planned.

Pinnacles National Monument is accessed from US101 via SR146 or from its eastern slopes by SR25 then SR146. No road pierces the heart of this colourful area of steep bluffs and crags; 16,000 volcanic acres of paradise for geologists and hikers alike. Many interesting formations can be seen from a car, especially on the west side, while hiking information can be obtained from the western ranger station or the eastern visitor centre.

Boasting the furthest mission from a present day highway, **Mission San Antonio de Padua** is one of the best restored sites and benefits from an unspoilt setting on land formerly part of William Randolph Hearst's ranch. The nearby Mission Revival building was designed by architect Julia Morgan for Hearst. Currently an army headquarters, the structure is often mistaken for the mission itself. San Antonio de Padua was the third mission, founded in 1771, and is once again used by brown-robed Franciscans. The tour includes the flour mill, blacksmith's forge, wine vats and the padres' garden. Remaining original features include a well, tannery and a remnant of the aqueduct, while the excellent museum uses unearthed artifacts to illustrate mission life.

Located further south in Salinas Valley, **Mission San Miguel Arcangel** was founded in 1797 and its colonnaded outbuildings with irregularly sized arches still survive, having been spared earthquake damage. The present church with 6ft-thick walls has the best preserved and one of the most ornate interiors of the mission churches. Much of the painting and decoration dates from the 1820s, carried out by Indian converts. A self-guided tour brochure is available from the gift shop. The nearby **Rios Caledonia Adobe**, an inn and stagecoach stop built in the two-storey Monterey style, has been restored and furnished in period.

Paso Robles is an attractive town surrounded by almond orchards, grain fields, stands of oak (for which the town was named) and a number of wineries which offer tours and tastings. On US101, **Helen Moe's Antique Doll Museum** is home to a collection of some 700 dolls, along with dolls' houses and other antique toys.

San Luis Obispo

SR1 and US101 rejoin at the pleasant little city of San Luis Obispo, best know for **Mission San Luis Obispo de Tolosa**. Long known as 'The Prince of Missions', San Luis Obispo was one of the first to use the red curved roof tiles which are synonymous with the Mission style. Now surrounded by a small city, the statue of a grizzly bear at the plaza fountain recalls the hazards found when the mission was established in 1772. A self-guided tour takes in the unusual L-shaped chapel, a lovely peaceful garden and a museum displaying native Chumash craftsmanship and early settlers' memorabilia.

The **San Luis Obispo County Historical Museum** opposite Mission Plaza is found in the old Carnegie Library. The nearby San Luis Obispo County Visitors Bureau offer information and brochures on San Luis Obispo County, including a visitors guide book detailing a 2-hour 'Path of History' stroll through downtown San Luis.

On Thursday nights Higuera Street is closed to vehicles from 6.30-9.00pm for the Farmers' Market. This colourful weekly festival attracts visitors and locals alike — do sample offerings from the various barbecues and food stalls. Planned and spontaneous entertainment such as bands, puppet shows and jugglers add to the carnival atmosphere.

South of San Luis Obispo US101 becomes the main coastal route, passing through **Pismo Beach**, once famous for its abundance of tasty clams. Unrestricted clamming led to a great decline and today the area is better known for the Butterfly Trees, a grove of Monterey pine and eucalyptus which attract millions of migrating monarch butterflies from late November through March. The 1,200ft (365m) long Pismo Beach Pier is a popular fishing spot while the lovely wide sandy beaches offer a variety of recreational facilities. **Pismo State Beach** stretches along the coast for about 8 miles (13km), where activities include camping, swimming, surfing, beachcombing, fishing and bird-watching. **Pismo Dunes State Vehicle Recreation Area** to the south provides an area of high dunes where vehicles are allowed, with beach campsites a popular attraction. For a quieter appreciation of California coastline, visit **Pismo Dunes Preserve**, where plants and animals are protected and such birds as the peregrine falcon and bald eagle have been sighted.

SR227 is a shorter route from San Luis Obispo to Arroyo Grande, bypassing Pismo Beach. Local wineries offer tours and tastings, making this detour off US101 worthwhile. Return to the main highway south for **Santa Maria**, where the **Santa Maria Valley Historical Museum** displays artifacts dating from Chumash Indian through the mission, rancho and pioneer periods. At the airport the **Santa Maria Museum of Flight** looks at local aviation history.

If time is short press south on US101 for Santa Barbara — otherwise take SR1 through **Lompoc**. This major flower seed producing area is especially colourful from May to September, with local history well presented at the Lompoc Museum. Those who enjoy experiencing the past must not miss **La Purisima Mission State Historic Park**, perhaps California's finest reconstruction Spanish mission. Still in its original rural setting with old-fashioned breeds of livestock and gardens stocked with traditional plants (labelled), La Purisima gives an excellent impressions of mission life. Allow two or more hours to fully explore the visitor centre and museum in the old infirmaries, church, chapel, workshops, padres' and general living quarters, and perhaps make use of the picnic area. It is worth writing ahead for living history days and other special events.

Return to US101 via SR246, which leads into the heart of the rural

Santa Ynez Valley. **Buellton** is known as 'the home of split pea soup' after Pea Soup Andersen's Restaurant which opened in 1924. A short hop west from Buellton is **Solvang**. Established in 1911 by Danish settlers from the Midwest, today this picturesque town is a major tourist attraction boasting four working windmills, nineteenth-century Danish architecture, authentic Danish gifts and delightful cuisine. The **Bethania Lutheran Church** is an excellent reproduction of fourteenth-century architecture, with a hand-carved pulpit and traditional miniature fully rigged sailing ship representing God guiding the soul on life's sea. In a replica eighteenth-century farmhouse with some period rooms the **Elverhoy Danish Heritage & Fine Arts Museum** combines an art gallery with displays of artifacts and memorabilia relating to Solvang and its heritage.

The Visitors Bureau on Mission Drive offers details of accommodation, eateries and current events. Ask here for the schedule of the Honen, a horse-drawn streetcar modelled on early twentieth-century ones used in Copenhagen. The third weekend in September heads the Solvang calendar with the Danish Days celebration, while the outdoor Theaterfest features a wide range of productions. Solvang is well situated to tour the surrounding wineries, many being open to the public.

If the commercialism of Solvang becomes too much, retreat to the quiet sanctuary of **Mission Santa Ines**, tucked away at the edge of town just off Mission Drive. Step back into the peaceful precincts of the tranquil garden and beautifully restored mission, which still serves as the parish church. The interesting museum contains vestments, parchment music books, mission furnishings and other artifacts dating back to the early nineteenth century.

Take either US101 along the coast or follow scenic SR154 inland through the heart of the Santa Ines Wine District and past Lake Cachuma. US101 passes a string of state beaches, starting with **Gaviota State Park**, which combines a sandy cove popular for swimming, a store, campsite and an upland area with a warm sulphur spring and trail up 2,458ft (749m) Gaviota Peak. The view from the summit encompasses the coastline and the Channel Islands. The palm trees at **Refugio State Beach** add a tropical feel, and both Refugio and **El Capitan State Beach** offer swimming, surfing and camping, with a 2.5 mile (4km) blufftop bikeway to connect the parks.

Just before Santa Barbara, the small community of Goleta offers family recreation and the Goleta Depot Railroad Museum which contains railroad memorabilia, photographs and hands-on exhibits.

Santa Barbara

This charming city lies on a small plain bounded by the Santa Ynez Mountains and palm-fringed beaches. Famous for its attractive red-roofed, white-walled Spanish Revival buildings, Santa Barbara is a popular up-market resort. The city first began with the establishment of the presidio in 1782 and portions have been restored or reconstructed as **El Presidio de Santa Barbara State Park**.

The nearby **Santa Barbara Historical Museum** offers an interesting overview of the city's Spanish, Mexican and American heritage through documents, furniture, costumes and the arts. The museum grounds house the Covarrubias Adobe, built here in 1817, and an 1837 Historic Adobe relocated to this site. Four blocks up Santa Barbara Street is the 1929 **County Courthouse**, an elaborate Spanish Revival building with balconies, turrets and archways. First take in the murals depicting Santa Barbara's history then take the lift up to El Mirador tower for a panoramic view of the city's rooftops. Maps for the aptly named Red Tile Tour are available from the Santa Barbara Visitor Center.

Probably the city's most famous historic landmark is **Mission Santa Barbara**, 'Queen of the Missions', situated on a knoll a mile north of the presidio. Santa Barbara is the only mission continuously owned by the brown-robed Franciscans, being used by them since its foundation in 1786. The self-guided tour encompasses the twin-towered church, museum, garden and cemetery. Those interested in needlework with a biblical bent should ask to view Brother Antonine's studio. His varied art works include tapestries, religious figures and vestments which are prized worldwide.

Santa Barbara also has much to offer in the way of the arts. Well worth a visit, the small **Santa Barbara Museum of Art** contains a permanent collection including Asian, European and American paintings, classical antiquities, photographs, prints and drawings; all augmented by touring exhibits. **Arlington Center for the Performing Arts** is home to the Santa Barbara Symphony Orchestra and the **Lobero Theatre**.

Other points of interest include the **Andree Clark Bird Refuge**, with over 40 acres of gardens including a lagoon whose islands provide shelter for migratory and indigenous species. Well situated in the foothills of the Santa Ynez Mountains, the 65 acre **Santa Barbara Botanic Garden** displays a diverse selection of native Californian plants which can be enjoyed alongside the 5 miles (8km) of trails. Of further botanical interest is the **Santa Barbara Orchid Estate**, with thousands of species from around the world.

Santa Barbara Zoological Gardens has an interesting botanical collection as well as 500 animals, a picnic area, snack bar, playground and miniature train. Those feeling the heat may prefer the shady wooded setting of the excellent **Santa Barbara Museum of Natural History**, where visitors are greeted by the huge skeleton of a blue whale. Apart from all aspects of natural history, this comprehensive museum covers the Chumash Indian culture, includes a planetarium, and offers a large reference library.

Stearns Wharf at the wet end of State Street boasts the interesting little **Sea Center**, featuring species native to the Santa Barbara Channel. Exhibits include a life-sized model of a California grey whale and calf, aquaria, sea birds, and marine archaeology. The **Nature Conservancy** centre on the wharf offers information and video programs on their current projects. Stearns Wharf was originally built in 1872 for cargo and passenger ships, but today offers restaurants, specialty boutiques, fresh fish shops and a good view of the harbour and city.

Good shopping and a wide variety of restaurants abound downtown. One of the most popular malls is the picturesque Spanish style El Paseo which incorporates Casa de la Guerra, a restored U-shaped adobe now housing a number of shops. Once El Paseo's many specialty stores have been explored, dine *al fresco* in a sunny courtyard. La Arcada Court also boasts a courtyard and fountains while Brinkerhoff Avenue retains its original houses, many now antique stores or specialty shops. The largest mall is La Cumbre Plaza and the two newest are The Galleria and Paseo Nuevo; all offer a wide variety of shops and restaurants. Closer to the beach, Santa Barbara Winery is open daily for tours and tastings.

For those in need of a rest, the city's Parks and Recreation Department publishes a map detailing the multitude of parks and facilities in 'Tree City, USA'. The nautical will find boats may be hired from Santa Barbara Sailing Center at the public boat ramp, while boats at Stearns Wharf offer fishing trips and charter cruises to the Channel Islands National Park. Whale watching excursions are also available in season.

Continuing along the coast, scenic US101 leads to **Carpinteria**, which lies between the Santa Ynez Mountains and the Pacific. The sandy shore here is protected by a natural reef, making Carpinteria State Beach one of California's safest, and with its large campground very popular for families. The small **Carpinteria Valley Museum of History** displays turn-of-the-century memorabilia, agricultural, oil-boom and Chumash Indian artifacts.

Inland on SR150 **Ojai** (pronounced Oo-hi), from the Chumash for moon, was chosen as the setting for Shangri-La in the 1937 film *Lost Horizon*. This tranquil little town today houses the **Ojai Valley Museum** exhibiting Native American history and crafts, pioneer photographs and a collection of stuffed animals.

Ventura is short for San Buenaventura, named after the city's Spanish mission. Albinger Archaeological Museum is located on part of the mission's site, exhibiting Chumash artifacts as well as Spanish, Chinese and Mexican objects. Across the street is the excellent **Ventura County Museum of History and Art** with collections of Native American, Spanish and pioneer artifacts and an assortment of agricultural equipment. One of their more unusual exhibits is the George Stuart Historical Figures, miniatures of world famous historical people from the Renaissance to the Russian Revolution. For those requiring more history the **Olivas Adobe Historical Park** and the **Ortega Adobe** both offer restored and reconstructed adobes while anyone on the mission trail should visit **Mission San Buenaventura**. The attractive church, dating from 1809, is the only surviving building from the large mission complex founded in 1782. The 200-year-old paintings of the Stations of the Cross have been expertly restored and the museum in the gift shop features the mission's two original wooden bells.

Dine al fresco at Harbor Landings, Oxnard

Nature lovers will find camping at **Emma Wood State Beach** along with a pebble beach good for swimming, surfing, dolphin spotting and views to Anacapa Island. **San Buenaventura State Beach** also offers swimming and surfing, while **McGrath State Beach** is best enjoyed by bird watchers — the current is too dangerous for bathing.

Channel Islands National Park Information Center in Ventura Harbor offers wildlife exhibits and an enlightening video on the **Channel Islands**, five of the eight being part of the national park. Sizes vary from tiny Anacapa to large sandy-beached Santa Rosa and rugged Santa Barbara. Half-day cruises (no landing), one- and two-day trips (combined with whale watching December to March) are offered by the park's concessionaire, Island Packers, located near the information centre. Crossings may be rough and weather changes are often encountered, so visitors should be well prepared with proper footwear and rain- and wind-proof clothing. The Channel Islands are popular spots to play Robinson Crusoe and, as numbers are restricted, advanced booking is especially recommended for weekends. Primitive camping (bring everything including water) is available for longer stays — camping permits are free of charge. Confirmed landlubbers can still enjoy the sight of Ventura Harbor whilst browsing the shops or dining in its waterfront restaurants.

South on scenic SR1, **Oxnard** boasts a busy harbour and 7 miles (11km) of beaches. Channel Islands Harbor is a shopper's paradise with waterfront stores as well as restaurants at Harbor Landing, and specialty shops and restaurants in a New England style waterfront setting named Fishermans Wharf. This complex includes nine marinas, a resort hotel and **Ventura County Maritime Museum**, where local nautical history is augmented by ship models and an excellent maritime art collection. **Carnegie Art Museum** housed in the old Carnegie Library and town hall, displays works of art, historical and archaeological exhibits.

From Oxnard scenic SR1 continues to follow the California coastline, skirting the Santa Monica Mountains en route to Malibu, Santa Monica, and Greater Los Angeles.

Additional Information

Regional Visitor Information

Morro Bay Chamber of Commerce
895 Napa St, Suite A-1
Morro Bay, CA 93442
☎ 805-772-4467

Monterey Peninsula Visitors Bureau
380 Alverado St,
PO Box 1770
Monterey, CA 93942
☎ 408-649-1770

San Luis Obispo County Visitors Bureau
1041 Chorro Street, Suite E
San Luis Obispo, CA 93401
☎ 805-541-8000

Santa Barbara Visitors Bureau
510 State St, Suite A
Santa Barbara, CA 93101
☎ 805-966-9222

Ventura Visitors Bureau
California & Santa Clara Sts.
Ventura, CA 93001
☎ 805-648-2075

The Missions

Carmel Mission
3080 Rio Rd
Carmel, CA 93923
☎ 408-624-3600
Open: 9.30am-4.30pm Mon-Sat,
from 10.30am Sun, except major
holidays. Donation
Father Serra's resting place, gardens

Mission Nuestra Senora de la Soledad
Fort Romie Rd
Soledad, CA
☎ 408-678-2586
Open: 10am-4pm Wed-Mon
Donations. Museum, chapel

Mission San Antonio de Padua
Jolan Rd
Hunter Ligget Military Reserve, nr
King City, CA
☎ 408-385-4478
Open: 10am-4.30pm
Donations. Museum

Mission San Buenaventura
211 E Main St
Ventura, CA 93001
☎ 805-643-4318
Open: 10am-5pm Mon-Sat, 10am-
4pm Sun, call for service times
Gifts, museum

Mission San Juan Bautista
408 Second St
San Juan Bautista, CA 95045
☎ 408-623-2127
Open: 9am-4.30pm Nov-Feb,
9.30am-5pm Mar-Oct
Chapel, museum, gifts

Mission San Luis Obispo de Tolosa
782 Monterey St
San Luis Obispo, CA 93401
☎ 805-543-6850
Open: 9am-5pm, except Thanksgiving Day, Xmas, 1 Jan
Donations. Museum, garden, gifts

Mission San Miguel
801 Mission St, PO Box 69
San Miguel, CA 93451
☎ 805-467-3256
Open: 9.30am-4.30pm except major
holidays. Gifts

Mission Santa Barbara
Laguna & Los Olivos Streets
Santa Barbara, CA 93101
☎ 805-682-4149
Open: 9am-5pm except major
holidays. Museum, garden,
cemetery, monastery, gifts, studio

Mission Santa Ines
1760 Mission Dr, PO Box 408
Solvang, CA
☎ 805-688-4815
Open: 9.30am-4.30pm Mon-Sat,
noon-4.30pm, except Easter,
Thanksgiving Day, Xmas
Museum, gifts

Places to Visit

Andrew Molera State Park
Hwy 1
Big Sur, CA
☎ 408-667-2315
Open: 8am-sunset
Hike, beach, horse trails, walk-in
camping

Antonelli Begonia Gardens
2545 Capitola Rd
Santa Cruz, CA 95010
☎ 408-475-5222
Opening hours vary
Free. Garden best Aug-Sep

Arlington Center for Performing Arts
1317 State St
Santa Barbara, CA 93101
☎ 805-963-4408
Santa Barbara Symphony & many others, &

Asilomar Conference Center & State Beach
800 Asilomar Blvd, PO Box 537
Pacific Grove, CA 93950
☎ 408-372-8016
Meeting rooms, accommodation, heated pool, beach, &

Bethania Lutheran Church
603 Atterdag Rd
Solvang, CA 93463
☎ 805-688-4637
Danish style church

Big Basin Redwoods State Park
Hwy 9, Near Boulder Creek, CA
☎ 408-338-6132
Open: 8am-sunset
Interpretive centre, picnic, hike, camp, gifts, &

Carnegie Art Museum
424 South C St
Oxnard, CA 93030
☎ 805-984-4649
Open: 10am-5pm Tue-Fri, Noon-5pm Sat & Sun. Free
Former Carnegie Library, art exhibits

Carpinteria State Beach
5361 6th St
Carpinteria, CA 93013
☎ 805-684-2811
Open: 8am-sunset
Swim, picnic, camp, tide pools, &

Channel Islands National Park Information Center
1901 Spinnaker Dr, Ventura Harbor
Ventura, CA 93001
☎ 805-644-8262
Open: 8am-5pm. Free
Film, exhibits, books (tour via Island Packers), &

El Presidio de Santa Barbara State Park
122 E Canon Perdidio St
Santa Barbara, CA 93101
☎ 805-966-9719
Open: 10.30am-4.pm
Reconstructed Presidio, exhibits, gifts

Elkhorn Slough Reserve
Hwy 1
Moss Landing, CA
☎ 408-7228-2822
Visitor center, waking trails, observation blinds

Embarcadero
895 Napa St, #A-1
Morro Bay, CA 93442
☎ 805-772-4467
Restaurants, galleries, gifts, aquarium, &

Fisherman's Wharf
885 Abrego St
Monterey, CA 93940
☎ 408-373-3720
Opening hours vary. Free
Restaurants, fish stalls, boats (whale watching & fishing), &

Fremont Peak State Park
San Juan Canyon Rd
San Juan Bautista, CA
☎ 408-623-4255
Open: 9am-sunset
Picnic, views, primitive camp, observatory

Hearst Castle (State Historical Monument)
PO Box 8
San Simeon, CA 93452
Reservations ☎ 800-444-7275
Opening hours vary, book ahead
Interpretive exhibits free
Tours, gifts, food, tour 1 is & if pre-booked

Henry Cowell Redwoods State Park
Hwy 9 (day use)
Graham Hill Rd (camp)
Felton, CA
☎ 408-335-4598 (day use)
408-438-2396 (camp)
Open: 9am-sunset
Picnic, hike, camp

Island Packers
1867 Spinnaker Dr, Ventura Harbor
Ventura, CA 93001
☎ 805-642-7688
Departures vary
Channel Island tours, whale spotting (Jan-Mar)

La Purisima Mission
2295 Purisima Rd
Lompoc, CA 93436
☎ 805-733-3713
Open: 9am-4.30pm, -5.30pm summer
Restored mission, living history, gifts, trails, part &

Lobero Theatre
33 E. Canon Perdido
Santa Barbara, CA 93101
☎ 805-963-0761
Show times vary

Long Marine Laboratory
100 Shaffer Rd
Santa Cruz, CA 95060
☎ 408-429-4308
Open: 1-4pm Tue-Sun except holidays
Donations
Extension of UCSC

Montana de Oro State Park
Off Los Osos Valley Rd
Los Osos, CA
☎ 805-772-2560
Open: 9am-sunset
Picnic, camp, hike, beach, trails

Monterey Bay Aquarium
886 Cannery Row
Monterey, CA 93940
☎ 408-648-4888
Open: 10am-6pm except Xmas
World-class aquarium, gifts, restaurant, &

Monterey Peninsula Museum of Art
559 Pacific St
Monterey, CA 93940
☎ 408-372-7591
Open: 10am-4pm Tue-Sat, 1-4pm Sun
Gifts

Monterey State Historic park
20 Custom House Plaza
Monterey, CA
☎ 408-649-7118
Opening times vary
Historic buildings, gifts, tours, sections &

New Brighton State Beach
New Brighton/Park Ave Exit, Hwy 1
Capitola, CA
☎ 408-475-4850
Open: 9am-sunset
Beach, picnic, camp, &

Pfeiffer Big Sur State Park
Hwy 1, Big Sur, CA 93920
☎ 408-667-2315
Open: 8am-10pm
Lodge, camping, restaurant, gift & general stores, picnic, trails, &

Pinnacles National Monument
Paicines, CA
☎ 408-389-4485
Open: 8am-sunset
Camping, picnic, hike

Point Lobos State Reserve
Route 1 (3 miles south)
Carmel, CA
☎ 408-624-4909
Open: 9am-5pm, -7pm spring &
autumn
Guided walks, hiking, picnic, seal
& sea otter spotting

**Roaring Camp & Big Trees
    Narrow-Gauge Railroad**
Graham Hill Rd, PO Box G-1
Felton, CA 95108
☎ 408-335-4400 or 4484
Train times vary. Ride to moun-
tains or beach; store, BBQ, picnic

**San Juan Bautista State Historic
    Park**
PO Box 1110
San Juan Bautista, CA 95045
☎ 408-623-4881
Open: 10am-4.30pm except
Thanksgiving Day, Xmas, 1 Jan
Historic buildings, plaza, slide
show, tours

**San Luis Obispo County
    Historical Museum**
696 Monterey St
San Luis Obispo, CA 93401
☎ 805-543-0638
Open: 10am-4pm Wed-Sun. Free

Santa Barbara Botanic Gardens
1212 Mission Canyon Rd
Santa Barbara, CA 93105
☎ 805-682-4726
Open: 8am-sunset
Native plants, gifts, nursery,
library, walks

Santa Barbara County Courthouse
1100 Anacapa St
Santa Barbara, CA 93101
☎ 805-962-6464
Open: 8am-5pm Mon-Fri, 9am-5pm
Sat & Sun. Free
Moorish architecture, views, ♿
except tower

Santa Barbara Historical Museum
136 E De la Guerra St
☎ Santa Barbara, CA 93101
805-966-1601
Open: 11am-5pm Tue-Sat (-9pm
Thur), noon-5pm Sun. Donations
Mission/Mexican/Early American
periods, gifts, ♿

Santa Barbara Museum of Art
1130 State St
Santa Barbara, CA 93101
☎ 805-963-4364
Open: 11am-5pm Tue-Sat (-9pm
Thur), Noon-5pm Sun. Free
Gifts

**Santa Barbara Museum of Natural
    History**
2559 Puesta del Sol Rd
Santa Barbara, CA 93105
☎ 805-682-4711
Open: 9am-5pm Mon-Sat, 10am-
5pm Sun
Chumash Indians & natural
history, gifts, planetarium, ♿

Santa Barbara Zoological Gardens
500 Ninos Dr
Santa Barbara, CA 93103
☎ 805-962-6310
Open: 10am-5pm, extended
summer, except Thanksgiving Day
& Xmas
Zoo, picnic, playground, mini-
train, ♿

Santa Cruz Boardwalk
400 Beach St
Santa Cruz, CA 95060
☎ 408-423-5590
Open: from 11am daily in summer,
weekends spring & fall
Free admission, pay for rides
Beachside amusement park, rides,
games, restaurants, food

Santa Cruz City Museum
1305 E. Cliff Dr
Santa Cruz, CA 95062
☎ 408-429-3773
Open: 10am-5pm Tue-Sat, noon-
5pm Sun except holidays. Donations
Natural history & Indian exhibits

Santa Cruz Lighthouse
1305 E Cliff Drive (Lighthouse Point)
Santa Cruz, CA 95062
☎ 408-429-3429
Open: noon-4pm except Tue
Donations. Surf museum, gifts

**Santa Maria Valley Historical
    Museum**
616 S Broadway, PO Box 584
Santa Maria, CA 93456
☎ 805-922-3130
Open: 1-5pm Tue-Sat, 1-4pm Sun,
except holidays. Free
Chumash artifacts, local history, &

**Santa Ynez Valley Historical
    Museum**
3592 Sagunto St, PO Box 181
Santa Ynez, CA 93460
☎ 805-688-7889
Open: Fri-Sun 1-4pm. Free
Chumash & local history, carriage
house

Sea Center
211 Stearns Wharf
Santa Barbara, CA 93101
☎ 805-962-0885
Open: noon-5pm, extended
Saturdays & summer
Aquarium, oil rig exhibit, &

Seventeen Mile Drive
PO Box 967
Pebble Beach, CA 93593
Coastal drive, no motorcycles

Spirit of Monterey Wax Museum
700 Cannery Row
Monterey, CA 93940
☎ 408-375-3770
Open: 9am-10pm
Waxwork history of Monterey

Steinbeck House
132 Central Ave
Salinas, CA 93901
☎ 408-424-2735
Restaurant & gifts

Tor House
Carmel Point, PO Box 1887
Carmel, CA 93922
☎ 408-824-1813
Open: 10am-3pm Fri & Sat, by
prior reservation. Tours

**University of California at Santa
    Cruz (UCSC)**
Bay & High Streets
Santa Cruz, CA
☎ 408-459-4008
Open: pre-booked tours 10.30am
and 1.30pm weekdays
Barn theatre, arboretum, perform-
ing arts

**Ventura County Museum of
    History & Art**
100 E Main St
Ventura, CA 93001
☎ 805-653-0323
Open: 10am-5pm Tue-Sun except
major holidays
Stuart collection, artifacts, library,
part &

Ventura Harbor
1603 Anchors Way Dr
Ventura, CA 93001
☎ 805-642-8538
Shops, restaurants, charter boats,
hotel, &

6

GREATER LOS ANGELES

Home to Hollywood, Beverly Hills, Malibu and all that glitters in Southern California, Los Angeles exceeds expectations and often exceeds definition. Other attractions are across the Los Angeles County border, and millions visit Disneyland and Knott's Berry Farm each year not realizing they are next door in Orange County.

Los Angeles

Called a collection of suburbs in search of a city, Los Angeles *is* a diverse collection of neighbourhoods, but with a heart. The present day metropolis traces its routes back to a small and picturesque Spanish settlement preserved as **El Pueblo de Los Angeles Historic** ✳ **Park**. The central feature, colourful Olvera Street, is a tapestry of street vendors selling Mexican gifts, clothing, snacks and delicacies, while al fresco dining may include an impromptu *mariachi* band.

The park is a colourful introduction to Los Angeles and its Hispanic heritage with the Visitor Information Center in Sepulveda House showing an orientation film. Certain historic buildings now house shops while others, like Avila Adobe, re-create Spanish Alta 🏛 (Upper) California. An interesting reconstruction of an 1818 one-storey house damaged in the 1971 earthquake, Avila Adobe is furnished in the style of a prosperous 1840s family.

Southwest across Santa Ana Freeway are the **Los Angeles Children's Museum**, which provides youngsters with a TV studio to 🏠 explore in addition to more usual fare, and the **Wells Fargo History Center**. Found off Grand Avenue, the centre boasts a brace of stagecoaches and a reconstructed Wells Fargo office, plus an impressive display of gold samples. Just east of downtown the flashy **Museum of Neon Art** collection is electric and kinetic, while the 🏠 **Museum of Contemporary Art** and the **Temporary Contemporary**

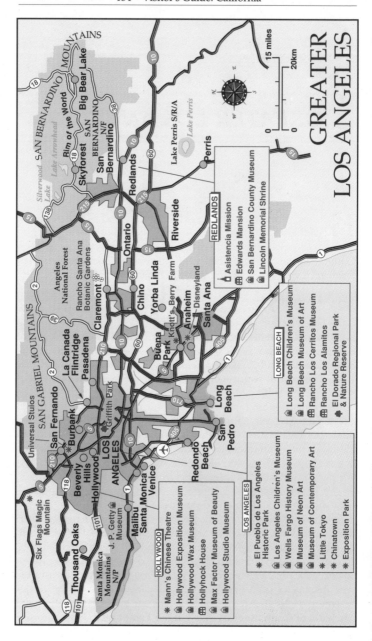

GREATER LOS ANGELES

0 — 15 miles
0 — 20km

HOLLYWOOD
* Mann's Chinese Theatre
* Hollywood Exposition Museum
* Hollywood Wax Museum
* Hollyhock House
* Max Factor Museum of Beauty
* Hollywood Studio Museum

LOS ANGELES
* El Pueblo de Los Angeles Historic Park
* Los Angeles Children's Museum
* Wells Fargo History Museum
* Museum of Neon Art
* Museum of Contemporary Art
* Little Tokyo
* Chinatown
* Exposition Park

LONG BEACH
* Long Beach Children's Museum
* Long Beach Museum of Art
* Rancho Los Cerritos Museum
* Rancho Los Alamitos
* El Dorado Regional Park & Nature Reserve

REDLANDS
* Asistencia Mission
* Edwards Mansion
* San Bernardino County Museum
* Lincoln Memorial Shrine

Little Tokyo's Japanese Friendship Garden, Los Angeles

Into and Around Los Angeles

Los Angeles International Airport (LAX) was extended for the 1884 Olympics, and still seems impossibly busy. For door to door transportation throughout Los Angeles and Orange Counties take Super Shuttle and Prime Time coaches, while Airport Coach has connections to local and Anaheim (Disneyland) hotels.

Amtrak operates from Union Passenger Terminal, just across Alameda Street from El Pueblo Historic Park, while the Greyhound and Trailways Transportation Center is southwest on Los Angeles between 6th and 7th Streets. Los Angeles Metro Rail system is a 300-mile long light rail system planned for the 1990s. The Blue Line links downtown Los Angeles with Long Beach while the first leg of the Red Line is due for completion in 1993 and the Green Line in 1994.

Pick up taxis at airports, train and bus terminals and major hotels or telephone, as passing cabs often do not stop. DASH shuttle bus services offer low-cost transportation within several communities and the exact 25 cent fare is required (see the *Los Angeles Visitor Guide* for routes).

Because of distances the car is the most popular mode of transport. Interstates form a major part of the sometimes frantic freeway system, linking outlying areas and acting as traffic arteries within greater Los Angeles. I-5 is the busy major north-south route through the heart of Los Angeles supplemented by the equally heavily travelled I-405. East running I-10 links downtown Los Angeles to Florida and points between with connections to I-15 and Las Vegas. A good map is essential, and drivers should orientate themselves before setting off and always follow freeway numbers en route, not their names.

Los Angeles Convention and Visitor Bureau produces *Datelines*, a free quarterly listing the city's wide range of events, museum exhibitions and sports. The bureau operates Visitor Information Centers in Los Angeles and Hollywood, where free maps and guides, listings of hotels and restaurants, plus free tickets for live TV recordings are available. The *Los Angeles Visitor Guide* lists an interesting selection of walking tours.

Hotel location should be considered as Greater Los Angeles covers a very large area. Those wishing to visit Disneyland as well as Hollywood and Universal Studios might opt for a two-centre holiday, choosing hotels with free shuttles to major attractions.

are devoted to art from 1940 to the present. The large international collection includes painting and sculpture, environmental works and live performances. Admission includes both museums with a free shuttle between the two.

The Hispanic heritage is indisputable, but many other cultures have contributed. **Little Tokyo** surrounds San Pedro and 2nd Streets and boasts fine shopping and dining. The tranquil **Japanese Garden** is adjacent to the **Japanese American Cultural and Community Center**'s varied exhibits on Japanese culture and art. Other highlights include **Japan America Theatre** productions and **The Japanese American National Museum**. West and north of Little Tokyo are respectively the major centres for Los Angeles finance and government, while the city's **Chinatown** is north of El Pueblo Historic Park along North Broadway. Although eclipsed by publicity for San Francisco's Oriental enclave, the Los Angeles Chinatown offers exceptional cuisine and nooks and crannies to explore.

Music Center and associated theatres bring numerous productions into the city — read the Sunday *Los Angeles Times* calendar supplement for details of events there. Also listed are productions at **LA Theatre Centre** near Little Tokyo and happenings at Universal and Century Cities. Tours of the Los Angeles Times building are offered on weekdays.

Southwest at University of Southern California (USC) visitors may take a free hour-long walking tour of the campus. Allow longer for **Exposition Park** and its excellent collection of museums. **California Museum of Science and Industry** comprises an IMAX theatre and halls filled with interactive exhibits at Technology Hall, Aerospace Hall, Kinsey Hall of Health and Mark Taper Hall of Economics and Finance. Each offers hands-on experiments in its relevant field, and would be a fully fledged museum anywhere else. Nearby **California Afro-American Museum** focuses on the history, culture and achievements of Afro-Americans while the **Natural History Museum of Los Angeles County** houses informative displays on animal life, present and prehistoric, an excellent mineral and gem collection and the history of California from 1540 to 1940. A 7-acre rose garden and sports facility also grace Exposition Park, while Dodger Stadium to the north hosts LA's major league baseball team.

Wilshire Boulevard is home to several excellent museums, not least of which is **Armand Hammer Museum of Art and Cultural Center**. Highlights of the eclectic collection include the unique *Leonardo da Vinci Codex*, while two galleries are dedicated to changing exhibitions. The nearby **Craft and Folk Art Museum** examines works from around the world while the exceptional **George C. Page**

Museum of La Brea Discoveries offers a fascinating glimpse into the animals and plants of the Ice Age. The tar pits trapped and preserved prehistoric creatures, and today form one of the world's most famous fossil sites. The paleontology research laboratory is in public view, as are the summer excavations in the museum grounds.

Not far away is the exceptionally comprehensive **Los Angeles County Museum of Art**, encompassing five buildings and virtually every artistic period. Start at the Times Mirror Central Court visitor centre where helpful volunteers aid art lovers and from which tours are given daily. A block north is the Farmers Market with its distinctive white clock tower. Look here for fresh Californian produce, clothing, gifts and outdoor cafés.

Hollywood

The famous sign on the Santa Monica mountainside proclaiming **Hollywood** was originally erected as a real estate gimmick. Today Hollywood Boulevard sports T-shirt and memorabilia vendors, but is still paved with the names of stars along the Walk of Fame. Not to be missed are the hand, foot and hoof prints of Hollywood greats immortalized in concrete outside **Mann's Chinese Theatre** (formerly Grauman's). The adjacent Hollywood Promenade complex chronicles achievements of the entertainment industry at **Hollywood Exposition Museum** while nearby **Hollywood Wax Museum** displays celebrities from 1927 to the present. On Hollywood Boulevard is also Frank Lloyd Wright's distinctive **Hollyhock House**.

Glamorous Hollywood is the theme of **Max Factor Museum of Beauty**, combining developments in cosmetics with Hollywood memorabilia. **Hollywood Studio Museum** is situated in the original barn used for *The Squaw Man*, the first full length feature shot entirely in Hollywood. Many experience the glamour of Hollywood by taking a guided tour past homes once owned by the movie stars.

To the north is the **Hollywood Bowl**, hosting Los Angeles Philharmonic and Hollywood Bowl Orchestra Concerts plus top jazz and pop musicians in its natural amphitheatre. The grounds contain picnic areas and the interesting **Hollywood Bowl Museum**. Above Hollywood amid the Santa Monica Mountains is Mulholland Drive, pleasantly above the heaviest smog and ideal to see how the other half live. Waysides along this scenic route afford views of Hollywood Bowl and Universal Studios.

San Fernando Valley

While Hollywood is synonymous with movies, major studios are

The Hollywood stars immortalised outside Mann's Chinese Theatre

Universal Studios stage spectacular shows

mostly located in the San Fernando Valley at **Universal City** or **Burbank**. Established in 1915, **Universal Studios** now incorporates an action-packed theme park into the working studios and sets. To the many thrill rides set in blockbuster movies are added live stunt shows and original movie sets — keep an eye out for famous stars when filming is in progress. Free tickets for live TV shows are available on a first-come, first-served basis.

The **Warner Brothers Studios** VIP Tour is more composed, giving guests behind the scenes views of studio life and taking in whatever is happening that day. Whenever possible live filming is included and tours may include recording studios and prop shops as well as indoor and outdoor sets. Book a table in the Commissary Dining Room for a chance to dine alongside celebrities and producers, but make reservations well in advance. Children under 10-years-old and photography or recording equipment are not permitted.

Situated just north of Hollywood, **Griffith Park** offers something for everyone. The entertaining and informative **Gene Autry Western Heritage Museum** compares the 'real' Wild West with Hollywood's rendition. Seven galleries of permanent displays give insight into the 'Spirits of the West' including a large firearms collection, paintings and sculpture by Remington, and a museum complex theatre which presents films old and new.

Also within the park is the 113 acre **Los Angeles Zoo**, one of California's largest with a cast of thousands of animals. A miniature train runs between the zoo and **Travel Town**, a transportation museum with an outdoor collection of locomotives and rolling stock. Summer concerts by famous singers, light opera and ballet regularly take place at the 6,000-seat **Greek Theatre**, while the star-struck should visit nearby **Griffith Observatory, Planetarium and Laserium**. The Hall of Science examines the universe and astronomical phenomena while on clear evenings the twin-refracting telescope is operational. The 600-seat theatre features astronomical shows and laser light presentations against a background of stars.

Activities within Griffith Park include picnicking, golf courses, tennis courts, and extensive hiking (Sierra Club provides information at the Crystal Springs Drive visitor centre). Horse rentals are available across Ventura Freeway at the **Equestrian Center**.

North in San Fernando, **Mission San Fernando Rey de Espana** has been restored and opened to the public. After the bustle of Los Angeles and Burbank, this historic setting is decidedly peaceful. South in Encino off Ventura Boulevard, **Los Encinos State Historic Park** contains the warm water spring which first attracted humans to this site. Historic adobe buildings are preserved here and tours of ranch house and outbuildings are offered.

Ever popular Six Flags Magic Mountain, a 260-acre family theme park, offers monster roller coasters and water rides, plus Bugs Bunny World and an animal farm for the youngsters. Nearby **William S. Hart County Park** incorporates this Hollywood star's ranch house and Spanish mansion, with its original furnishings and paintings by famous Western artist Charles Russell.

East Los Angeles and Pasadena

Northeast of downtown, Lawry's California Center offers free tours of their seasoned salt and spice blending rooms and test kitchens, plus a restaurant and specialty shops.

Heritage Square Museum contains relocated buildings from Greater Los Angeles, illustrating life here from 1865 to 1914. Those interested in Native American cultures from Alaska to South America *must* visit the exceptional **Southwest Museum**. Founded in 1907, the four main halls focus respectively on native cultures from the southwest, California, Great Plains and northwest coast, plus a gift shop crammed with unusual gifts and souvenirs.

North at **Forest Lawn Memorial Park** many famous actors and personalities are buried in a park-like atmosphere heightened by marble and bronze statuary, memorials, a temple and reproduction churches. Attractions include a large stained-glass version of Leonardo's *The Last Supper*, huge paintings of the Crucifixion and the Resurrection and a replica of the Liberty Bell.

Pasadena is famed for its annual Rose Bowl football contest and Tournament of Roses Parade. Purchase tickets for the game and seats for the parade well ahead. **Tournament House and Wrigley Gardens** were built for chewing-gum magnate William Wrigley, Junior. Tours include Rose Bowl and Parade memorabilia, as the mansion is headquarters for the Tournament of Roses Association.

Art lovers will enjoy Pasadena's **Norton Simon Museum of Art**, which focuses on European masterpieces from the Renaissance to the mid-twentieth century including an outstanding collection of French paintings. Also exhibited are stone and bronze sculptures from India and Southeast Asia. **Huntington Library and Art Gallery** was built as a palatial Neoclassical mansion and is surrounded by a diversity of gardens. Collections include American, English and French works, while the library houses rare manuscripts including a Gutenberg Bible. Also in Pasadena, the **Pacific Asia Museum** is a replica Chinese Treasure House surrounded by a courtyard.

Los Angeles State & County Arboretum in **Arcadia** comprises 127 acres of exotic flora — a favourite location for movie-makers.

Explore a steam locomotive at Travel Town in Griffith Park

Historic buildings include an 1839 adobe house, Queen Anne Cottage and coach barn and an 1890s Santa Fe Railroad Station. **Mission San Gabriel** was badly damaged by the 1987 earthquake, but the gardens remain open to the public.

Beverly Hills and Malibu

Although totally surrounded by Los Angeles, **Beverly Hills** is a city in its own right. This upmarket area boomed when the fabulous Beverly Hills Hotel was built, attracting movie stars and becoming the focus for the Hollywood social scene. Today magnificent mansions may be seen and **Rodeo Drive**, a few blocks south of famed Sunset Boulevard, offers the ultimate shopping experience. Further west on Sunset is Bel Air and UCLA, **University of California, Los Angeles**. A 90-minute walking tour is offered by the university's visitor centre, or obtain a self-guided tour map.

Malibu conjures images of beautiful people experiencing that perfect sunset, cocktails in hand. This upmarket neighbourhood also has limited parking and restricted beach access because of the exclusive homes towering over the sand. Fortunately state-run beach parks offer public access, swimming, surfing and fishing. In addition the **Malibu Lagoon State Beach** museum explores local

The Getty Museum at Malibu is based on a Roman villa

history from Indian times to advent of the movie stars.

The **J. Paul Getty Museum** houses his amassed collection of Greek and Roman antiquities and other priceless artwork in a replica Roman villa. Advance parking reservations (1-2 weeks ahead) are required for this free museum. However, visitors without reservations may arrive by taxi, bicycle or motorcycle, while pedestrians *must* show a museum pass obtainable only from the Rapid Transit District (RTD) route 434 bus driver. In other words do *not* park outside and attempt to walk in.

Santa Monica Mountains

Santa Monica Mountains National Recreation Area is a collection of national, state and regional parks abutting Malibu, Santa Monica and Los Angeles. Covering 150,000 acres of hills and canyons, beaches and lagoons, it offers diverse outdoor activities and protects the area from over-development.

North of Malibu, Malibu Canyon Road leads to **Malibu Creek State Park**, used for many years by Twentieth Century Fox for movies and television programs including MASH. Nearby but within Los Angeles city limits is **Topanga State Park**. Both parks offer miles of trails for hiking, biking or horse-riding, while trails lead from Topanga State Park into the adjacent **Will Rogers State Historic Park**. Also reachable by car, today the estate and retreat of this famous actor-writer from the 1920s and '30s are open to the public. The grounds included a golf course, stables and polo field, but since there was no swimming pool a beachside site was purchased and is now operated as **Will Rogers State Beach**. Seaside activities include volleyball courts, a playground, gymnastic equipment and the South Bay Bicycle Trail.

A network of roads wind through Santa Monica National Recreation Area, which resides between coastal SR1 and US101, the Ventura Freeway. **Satwiwa Native American Indian Culture Center** is set in the mountains above **Thousand Oaks**, the centre's aim being to enlighten the general public to the heritage of Native Americans against a backdrop that their forebears would have recognized.

In Thousand Oaks itself is the reconstructed **Stagecoach Inn Museum**, which contains furnished period rooms and a stagecoach, and nearby **R. P. Strathearn Historical Park**. Between Simi Valley and Thousand Oaks is the **Ronald Reagan Presidential Library and Center for Public Affairs**, featuring a life-sized replica of his oval office, a section of the Berlin Wall, and displays of thousands of gifts of state received during his presidency.

Santa Monica Bay

Oceanside **Santa Monica** is a popular resort town, boasting the wide stretch of sand at Santa Monica State Beach and Santa Monica Pier, a local landmark since 1908. The pier is most famous for its turn-of-the-century carousel featured in *The Sting*. Places of interest include **Angels Attic** with its seven galleries of antique toys, plus the period rooms and exhibits of **Santa Monica Heritage Museum**; both occu- pying restored Victorian houses. The **Museum of Flying** at Santa Monica Airport displays vintage aircraft, models and exhibits on flying in a high-tech building overlooking the airport.

Venice Beach is especially popular with the younger set and an ideal place for people-watching, while wealthy Marina del Rey residents to the south overlook their yachts from towering condominiums. Fisherman's Village, a replica New England coastal community, is a shopping, dining and entertainment complex overlooking Marina del Rey Harbour. Narrated harbour cruises are available as are free jazz concerts on Sunday afternoons.

South of Los Angeles Airport SR1 goes through the oceanside communities of Manhattan and Redondo Beaches, which hosts the International Surf Festival each August. King Harbour proffers a waterfront restaurant, plus fishing trips, boat cruises, and a seasonal ferry to Catalina Island.

Palos Verdes Drive follows the rocky coast south with views across to Catalina island. In **San Pedro** the Port of Los Angeles is one of America's largest deepwater ports, from which cruise ships to Mexico set sail. **Los Angeles Maritime Museum** boasts a collection of 700 model ships while the adjacent Ports O'Call Village offers a full range of shops and some fifteen restaurants in a New England-style setting. Harbour and dinner trips depart from here and the Catalina Island Ferry leaves from its terminal nearby. **Cabrillo Marine Museum** focuses on the underwater life of Southern California, with whale watching in season.

Inland SR1 passes **South Coast Botanical Garden** with native Californian plants and the **General Phineas Banning Museum**, a Greek Revival home with exhibits on nineteenth-century Los Angeles.

Long Beach

Formerly a nineteenth-century seaside resort, **Long Beach** is now California's fifth largest city. Apart from tourism, the area thrives on a busy shipping harbour and rich oil reserves — look for 'nodding donkeys' on land and palm-fringed islands offshore. Planet Ocean, which covers Long Beach Arena, depicts life-sized whales and other

Native Americans share their heritage at Satwiwa in the Santa Monica Mountains

See the Los Angeles Rams play American football at Anaheim Stadium

marine life in the world's largest mural (122,000 square feet).

When sun and sand become overpowering sample the local culture at **Long Beach Museum of Art**. History buffs will enjoy the 1844 adobe **Rancho Los Cerritos Museum**, furnished in period, and **Rancho Los Alamitos**, an 1806 ranch house examining early life in the west. **Long Beach Children's Museum** encourages youngsters through interactive and imaginative exhibits.

Currently the ocean liner *Queen Mary*, a local Long Beach Harbour landmark, is under threat as a floating hotel. Boasting an interesting past and several fine restaurants, hopefully the Queen will continue her faithful service. Adjacent to her on pier J is the Catalina Island ferry terminal, with fast boats to the island resort. For sportfishing, a whale-watching trip or a harbour cruise try Queen's Wharf, which also offers restaurants, a fish market and picnic area.

Popular waterfront shopping areas include Marina Pacifica Mall and Shoreline Village, the latter with a turn-of-the-century feel. Those in search of romance should make for **Naples Island**, a community planned around canals where gondoliers ply the waters of the Rivo Alto Canal.

Orange County

Named after the citrus groves which grew here, **Orange County** attracts millions annually to its resorts and theme parks. In Buena Park, Knott's Berry Farm has been an attraction since the 1920s while **Anaheim** boomed when Disneyland opened in 1955.

Anaheim Area Visitor & Convention Bureau offers information on Orange Country attractions while the 9,000-seat convention centre arena is used for concerts and sporting events. Near the Santa Ana River, **Anaheim Stadium** sports California Angels baseball (April-October) and Los Angeles Rams football (August-December) with guided tours daily except during events. **Los Alamitos Race Course** to the east offers year round thoroughbred, quarter horse and harness racing.

DISNEYLAND

Continuously being refurbished and improved, **Disneyland** remains as fresh and even more entertaining than when opened in 1955. Eight themed areas are packed with Disney characters, adventures, fun-packed rides and truckloads of Disney memorabilia.

First comes **Main Street USA**, turn-of-the-century small-town America through Disney-tinted glasses. Behind the façades are well stocked shops and Disney support services, such as First Aid and Lost Children. Out front, Main Street is plied by horse-drawn trams

Disneyland Tips

Arrive early as ticket sales commence *before* posted opening hours, and when parking note parking lot, row and position plus that hire car registration number to save a long search later. Disneyland eateries range from ice-cream parlours and snack bars to gourmet restaurants, but no food can be brought into the park. If using the picnic area west of the main entrance do get hands stamped for same day re-entry.

City Hall has the daily events schedule — check times first then plan your time accordingly, enjoying the popular rides early before queues build. Guests with limited time may opt for a 3.5 hour guided tour; book at City Hall. Shops, especially in Main Street, get crowded towards the end of the day so buy early and use storage lockers on Main Street. When planning the visit remember that crowds are smaller off season and midweek, but opening hours are extended in summer months and selected holidays when additional events such as Main Street Electrical Parade, Fantasmic! and Fantasy in the Sky fireworks are staged.

Physically disabled guests should write ahead or visit Main Street's Carefree Corner for the useful *Disabled Guest Guide*. Pushchair and wheelchair rental are also available here.

Parents should remember that all theme parks get very crowded, so make sure that you know where your child is at all times.

and double-decker buses while the Disneyland Railroad circumnavigates the entire park.

Main Street leads to Central Plaza, jumping off point for the 'themed lands'. In exotic **Adventureland** birds, flowers and tikis star in a tropical revue, whilst youngsters love exploring Swiss Family Treehouse and embarking on the Jungle Cruise. New Orleans Square hosts the spook-tacular Haunted Mansion and the ever popular Pirates of the Caribbean, an audio-animatronics adventure classic. A new Critter Country favourite is Splash Mountain, which combines a hi-tech thrill ride with Brer Rabbit and Song of the South. For footstompin' family fun, check out the Country Bear Playhouse. Performances vary seasonally, with a special show for Christmas.

Frontierland recalls the good old, bad old days of the American West. Parents — do encourage children to get involved in those gunfights. Attractions include Big Thunder Mountain, a rollercoaster of a railroad, and the Golden Horseshoe Jamboree (book early). The waters at Frontierland are plied by a riverboat and a sailing ship (high season and selected weekends), plus a selection of rafts and keelboats.

Sleeping Beauty Castle, a Disneyland landmark, is found in **Fantasyland**. A place where storybooks come to life, Fantasyland is geared for the younger set and hosts numerous attractions and rides. In peak season parents should either arrive early or perhaps leave this area until evening, as such classic rides as King Arthur Carrousel and Dumbo the Flying Elephant were not designed for the hordes that descend on Disneyland today.

Tomorrowland looks forward to the days of interplanetary travel with an inexperienced robot pilot in Star Tours and the wild warp-speed Space Mountain. Newly opened is **Mickey's Toontown**, where guests meet Mickey and cartoon friends in a three-dimensional cartoon environment. On weekends and holidays the high-tech Fantasmic! is presented thrice nightly. In this 22-minute extravaganza, Mickey Mouse battles an evil monster snake and fire-breathing dragon which sets even the Rivers of America alight.

For a more relaxed family holiday at Disneyland visit the park over several days and stay at the Disneyland Hotel, which is connected to the park by monorail. The reduced hassles offset the costs, and the Disneyland hotel offers additional entertainment and a choice of fine dining while the youngsters are enjoying Disney Character Meals in Goofy's Kitchen.

KNOTT'S BERRY FARM
Knott's Berry Farm in Buena Park is the 'other' theme park. Begun ✳ as a roadside fruit stand, Knott's became famous for home-made jams, preserves and chicken dinners when it opened in the depression years. As queues for the home-style cooking grew, Knott added an old Western ghost town as a diversion.

Still owned by the Knott family, this monster of a park has five themed areas and features over 165 rides including the wildest roller coasters, a twenty-storey Parachute Sky Jump and Bigfoot Rapids — plus live shows throughout the day. Native American heritage is explored at Indian Trails and visitors can try beading and sand painting. Prospectors can pan for gold at the ghost town and the younger set just adore Camp Snoopy. The park's innumerable shops supply everything from Snoopy memorabilia to those old-fashioned jams and preserves, while some two dozen restaurants and eateries serve up something for everyone, including those chicken dinners that save moms all that hard work.

*The Sleeping Beauty
Castle at Disneyland*
© The Walt Disney Company 1993

*Knott's Berry Farm
offers the wildest rides*

OTHER ORANGE COUNTY ATTRACTIONS

Near Knott's Berry Farm the **Movieland Wax Museum** features over
250 cinema and television stars in realistic sets including the original
costumes and props where possible. Then step back in time to
1093AD for Medieval Times, a four-course dinner extravaganza
where jousting by armoured knights is just part of the entertainment.
Others include Wild Bill's Western Dinner Extravaganza, an all-
American menu of food and Western fun, and King Henry's Feast,
with an evening of comedy, magic and juggling acts next door in
Anaheim.

Just east of Knott's Berry Farm the **Museum of World Wars &
Military History** houses the largest collection of military uniforms in
the USA, plus weapons, firearms and memorabilia from 1776 to 1945.
If toy soldiers, teddy bears and dolls from around the world are
preferable, visit **Hobby City Doll and Toy Museum**. This half-scale
replica of the White House also contains hobby, craft and specialist
collector shops.

Like some cross between an amphitheatre and an overgrown
greenhouse, the unique architecture of **Crystal Cathedral** in Garden
Grove hosts interdenominational church services which are tel-
evised around the world. Southeast and across the Santa Ana River
is **Bower's Museum**, which explores the culture and art of the
Americas and Pacific Rim. Nearby **Santa Ana Zoo** includes a children's zoo and playground while to the southwest South Coast Plaza
boasts an impressive line-up of international designer stores and
gourmet restaurants. Hourly shuttles run from many Anaheim
hotels to the South Coast Plaza and other major shopping malls.

Costa Mesa is queen of the Orange County performing arts,
boasting the South Coast Repertory Theatre and the 3,000-seat
Orange County Performing Arts Center, which hosts concerts, musicals, symphony, opera and dance.

For something different visit the **Richard Nixon Library and
Birthplace** in **Yorba Linda**. In the farmhouse built by his father are
shown films, interactive video displays, and exhibits concerning the
life and works of former President Nixon. Meanwhile Orange
County Fairgrounds hosts a huge open-air flea market on weekends
and speedway races summer Friday nights.

Santa Catalina Island

Usually shortened to **Catalina Island**, this lovely 21 mile (38km)
island became a popular resort when owned by chewing-gum
magnate William Wrigley. Today most of the island is owned by the
Santa Catalina Island Conservancy, who aim to preserve the natural

beauty of the area. Lying 22 miles offshore, the island offers a respite from city bustle and plenty of sea-clean air.

The only town, **Avalon**, has an attractive Mediterranean-style harbour and a palm-fringed sandy beach. The Visitor Information Center across from the pier offers full details on the island and activities. Charter boats provide deep-sea fishing and diving while tours include glass-bottomed boat trips and a 40-minute casino tour.

 Built by Wrigley, this large edifice now houses **Catalina Island Museum** which focuses on Indian and later island history. A pleas-

 ant 1.7-mile uphill walk (or bus ride in season) leads to **Wrigley Memorial and Botanical Garden**, which features cacti, succulents and native plants.

 Outside Avalon, much of the island is as discovered by the Spanish, and is popular for hiking, (free permit obtainable from the Conservancy office), riding and guided hunting in season. Camping is by permit only (advance reservations required). Transport around Avalon is limited to golf carts and bicycles, while the rest of the island is restricted to tour buses, bicycles (permit required), horses or foot.

A daily boat service operates year-round to Catalina from Long Beach and San Pedro, while a seasonal schedule is available from Redondo and Newport Beaches and San Diego. Year-round helicopter flights are offered from Long Beach Harbour and San Pedro, while seaplanes and airplanes operate from Long Beach Municipal Airport. Catalina Island can also be visited from Los Angeles cruise ships, many of which sail on to Mexico.

The Inland Empire

East of the Santa Ana Mountains is the Inland Empire, a diverse area comprising mountains, desert, fertile valleys and prosperous towns. Visitors may choose from outdoor activities such as hot air ballooning, hiking, camping, and skiing — in winter locals love to water ski then hit snowy mountain slopes on the same day. The Inland Empire Tourism Council provides information on the entire area.

 A major commercial hub and country seat, **Riverside** grew with the successful navel orange industry and still thrives today. Museums of note include the **California Museum of Photography** and an

 earth sciences museum specializing in fossilized flora and fauna at **Jurupa Cultural Center**. Housed in the 1912 post office, **Riverside**

 Municipal Museum examines local history including the founding of the citrus industry while **Riverside Art Museum** offers art exhibits and a restaurant. Youngsters enjoy **Castle Park**, a 27-acre amusement park featuring a huge video arcade, 4 miniature golf courses and a selection of rides.

The town's architecture evidences its early prosperity, a fine example being the beautifully restored 1891 Queen Anne **Heritage House**. The impact of the Chinese community on the citrus industry is recalled at **Chinese Memorial Pavilion** while to the west, high on Mount Rubidoux, are the Father Serra Cross and Tower of World Peace. **California Citrus State Historic Park** contains a producing citrus grove while the **University of California Riverside Botanic Gardens** has 39 acres of dry-climate plants, many blooming between January and May.

Lake Perris State Recreational Area to the southeast offers a variety of watersports, hike, bike and horse trails, plus a full service marina and snack bar. In **Perris** the Orange Empire Railway Museum displays railroad and trolley equipment and offers rides. Planes of Fame Museum at **Chino** airport exhibits military aircraft with a special selection of gliders dating back to 1896.

The college town of **Claremont** is home to the Kenneth G. Fiske Musical Instrument Museum and its collection of rare historical and ethnic musical instruments. Raymond M. Alf Museum specializes in paleontological remains including a diverse selection of fossil footprints, while native Californian plants are the focus for 85-acre Rancho Santa Ana Botanic Garden (most colourful February-June). Escape higher inland temperatures at **Raging Waters** in Frank G. Bonelli Regional County Park. Features include water slides, a large wave pool, river rapids ride and children's pool.

Redlands is home to **Asistencia Mission**, an outpost for Mission San Gabriel reconstructed between 1928 and 1937 and today housing a museum and small chapel. The adjacent Victorian three-storey **Edwards Mansion** offers a self-guided tours and also serves as a restaurant while nearby **San Bernardino County Museum** examines the region's history, geology and natural history with an outstanding mammal and bird collection. The 1932 Lincoln Memorial Shrine contains memorabilia on the life and times of Lincoln and serves as a memorial to the president and the Civil War.

North of bustling San Bernardino city, **San Bernardino National Forest** covers some 660,000 acres of blue lakes overlooked by mountains reaching over 11,000ft (3,350m). The resort centres of Lake Arrowhead and Big Bear Lake in this idyllic retreat may be reached from San Bernardino via the 40-mile scenic Rim of the World Drive (SR18). Affording some of Southern California's finest views the drive passes **Skyforest**, where Santa's Village entertains the youngsters with a fairytale village full of rides, a petting zoo and gift shops. SR38 is a scenic route back to Redlands while SR18 continues to **Victorville**, where the Roy Rogers and Dale Evans Museum houses guns, movie memorabilia and even Roy Rogers' horse and dog, Trigger and Bullet.

Adjoining San Bernardino National Forest, the **Silverwood Lake State Recreation Area** contains a reservoir popular with birdlife and outdoor enthusiasts alike. The nearby **Angeles National Forest** in the San Gabriel Mountains is like San Bernardino Forest with half the visitors. Hiking trails vary from easy nature trails to the strenuous Pacific Crest Trail (Mexico to Canada), and to really escape summer crowds head for San Gabriel Wilderness.

Winter brings snow, and ski areas in San Bernardino National Forest include **Bear Mountain** and **Snow Summit** (both downhill) and **Snow Valley** and **Snow Forest** (downhill and cross-country). Angeles National Forest offers **Ski Sunrise** and **Mountain High**, both catering for downhill skiing.

In western Angeles National Forest is the famous **Mount Wilson Observatory**, with a small astronomical museum and observation gallery for the 100in Hooker Telescope. The Angeles Crest Highway (SR2) leads down to La Canada Flintridge where **Descanso Gardens** sports 100,000 camellias from around the world and a Japanese tea garden. October to March is best for blooms, and call ahead for details of horticultural events.

Hills of Fire

In the spring a colourful carpet of orange, yellow and blue awaits visitors to **Antelope Valley California Poppy Reserve**. Head north of Los Angeles on SR14 to **Lancaster**, following I Avenue west into the blazing countryside. The visitor centre offers exhibits, a film and information on the trails and flowers here. Refrain from picking the poppies, which here grow wild in their native habitat. A southern California sunset upon rolling hills of fire can end the perfect stay.

Additional Information

Regional Visitor Information

Anaheim Area Visitor & Convention Bureau
800 W Katella Avenue
Anaheim, CA 92802
☎ 714-999-8999

Inland Empire Tourism Council
PO Box 838
Skyforest, CA 92385
☎ 714-941-7877

Long Beach Visitors Council
One World Trade Center, Suite 300
Long Beach, CA 90831-0300
☎ 213-436-3645 or 800-234-3545

Los Angeles Visitors Bureau
515 S Figueroa St, 11th Floor
Los Angeles, CA 90071
☎ 213-624-7300

Riverside Visitors Bureau
3443 Orange St
Riverside, CA 92501
☎ 714-787-7950

Santa Monica Visitors Bureau
2219 Main St
Santa Monica, CA 90405
☎ 213-392-9631

**Visitor Information Center,
  Hollywood**
The Janes House
6541 Hollywood Blvd
Hollywood, CA
☎ 213-461-4213

**Visitor Information Center,
  Los Angeles**
695 S Figueroa St
Los Angeles, CA
☎ 213-689-8822

The Missions

Asistencia Mission
16930 Burton Rd
Redlands, CA 92373
☎ 714-793-5402
Open: 10am-5pm Wed-Sat, 1-5pm
Tue & Sun
Restored chapel, museum

Mission San Fernando Rey de Espana
15151 San Fernando Mission Blvd
Mission Hills, CA 91345
☎ 818-361-0186
Open: 9am-5pm
Gifts, museum, garden setting,
carillon rings hourly

Mission San Gabriel
537 W Mission Dr
San Gabriel, CA 91776
☎ 818-282-5191
Open: 9.30am-4.30pm except Good Friday, Easter, Thanksgiving Day, Xmas.
Grounds open, mission may be closed

Places to Visit

Anaheim Stadium
2000 S State College Blvd
Anaheim, CA 92806
☎ 714-937-7333
Open: tours hourly 11am-2pm
CA Angels (baseball) & LA Rams
(football), special events

Angeles National Forest
701 N Santa Anita Ave
Arcadia, CA 91006
☎ 818-574-5200
Park HQ. Free

Angels Attic
516 Colorado Ave.
Santa Monica, CA 90401
☎ 213-394-8331
Open: 12.30pm-4.30pm Thu-Sun
Victorian house with doll's houses
& toys, gifts

**Antelope Valley California Poppy
  Reserve**
15 miles W of Lancaster, on Avenue I
Lancaster, CA
☎ 805-724-1180
Opening times vary seasonally.
Admission during spring blooming
season. Interpretive centre, walks

Bolsa Chica State Beach
Pacific Coast Highway
North of Huntington Beach, CA
☎ 714-536-1454
Open: 8am-10pm
Beach, surf, swim, camp, cycle,
picnic, ♿

Cabrillo Marine Museum
3720 Stephen White Dr
San Pedro, CA 90731
☎ 213-548-7562
Open: noon-5pm Tue-Fri, 10am-
5pm Sat & Sun
Free admission, parking charge
Aquariums of native sealife, gifts, ♿

California Museum of Photography
3824 Main St
Riverside, CA 92501
☎ 714-787-FOTO
Open: 10am-5pm Tue-Sat, noon-5
Sun except major holidays
Photography, create a movie

**California Museum of Science
  and Industry**
700 State Drive, Exposition Center
Los Angeles, CA
☎ 213-744-7440
Open: 10am-5pm
Free (except IMAX theatre)
Innumerable hands-on exhibits,
gifts, IMAX, &

Children's Museum (of Los Angeles)
310 N Main St
Los Angeles, CA 90012
☎ 213-687-8825
Open: 2pm-4pm Wed & Thu,
10am-5pm Sat & Sun
Hands-on museum

Craft and Folk Art Museum
5814 Wilshire Blvd.
Los Angeles, CA 90036
☎ 213-937-5544
Open: 11am-5pm Tue-Sun
Workshops, gifts, restaurant

Crystal Cathedral
12141 Lewis St
Garden Grove, CA 92640
☎ 714-971-4000 (-4013 for tours)
Open: 9am-3.30pm Mon-Sat, 1pm-
3.30 Sun except Thanksgiving Day
& Xmas. All donations welcome
Cable TV church services, tours, &

Descanso Gardens
1418 Descanso Dr
La Canada, CA 91011
☎ 818-790-5571
Open: 9am-4.30pm except Xmas
Free on third Tue monthly
Camellia gardens, Japanese
gardens, tea house, tram tours, &

Disneyland
1313 Harbor Blvd
Anaheim, CA 92803
☎ 714-999-4565
Open: 10am-6pm Mon-Fri, 9am-
midnight Sat & Sun, extended
summer & holidays
Theme park, restaurants, gifts, &

El Pueblo de Los Angeles
Olvera St
Los Angeles, CA 90012
☎ 213-628-1274
Open: 10am-8pm, museums close
early. Free. Historic area, Mexican
shops & restaurants

Farmers Market
6333 W Third St
Los Angeles, CA 90036
☎ 213-933-9211
Open: 10am-6.30pm winter (-5pm
Sun), extended in summer
Shops & restaurants

Fisherman's Village
13755 Fiji Way
Marina del Rey, CA 90292
☎ 213-822-1444
Open: 10am-9pm, -10pm summer
Shops, dining, cruises & charter

**Gene Autry Western Heritage
  Museum**
Griffith Park, 4700 Zoo Dr
Los Angeles, CA 90027
☎ 213-667-2000
Open: 10am-5pm Tue-Sun, except
major holidays
Gifts, restaurant, cinema, &

**George C. Page Museum of La
  Brea Discoveries**
5801 Wilshire Blvd
Los Angeles, CA 90036
☎ 213-936-2230
Open: 10am-5pm Tue-Sun except
major holidays
La Brea Pit exhibits, gifts, tar pits in
park setting, &

Griffith Observatory, Planetarium Theatre & Laserium
2800 E Observatory Rd
Los Angeles, CA 90027
☎ 213-664-1191, for astronomic phenomena call 213-663-8171
Open: 12.30am-10pm, facility times vary. Free
Observatory, planetarium, gifts

Heritage House
8193 Magnolia Ave
Riverside, CA 92501
☎ 714-689-1333
Open: noon-2.30 Tue & Thur, -3.30 Sun
Queen Anne house

Heritage Square Museum
3800 Homer St
Los Angeles, CA 90031
☎ 818-449-0193
Open: noon-4pm weekends & selected holidays
Victorian buildings

Hobby City Doll and Toy Museum
1238 S Beach Blvd
Anaheim CA, 92804
☎ 714-527-2323
Open: 10am-6pm except major holidays
Dolls & toys in model of White House, gifts

Hollywood Bowl
2301 N Highland Ave
Hollywood, CA 90078
☎ 213-850-2000 (info)
☎ 213-480-3232 (tickets)
Various concerts, including Philharmonic July-Sept.
17,680-seat outdoor amphitheatre, picnic facilities, museum

Hornblower Dining Yachts
Mariners Mile Marine Center
2431 W Coast Hwy
Newport Beach, CA 92663-1779
☎ 714-646-0155
Sailings vary. Lunch & dinner cruises

Huntington Library
1151 Oxford Rd
San Marino, CA 91108
☎ 818-405-2100
Open: 1pm-4.30pm Tue-Sun, reservations required
Art, rare books, & botanical garden

Huntington State Beach
Pacific Coast Hwy
Huntington Beach, CA
☎ 714-536-1454
Open: 9am-10pm
Beach, surf, picnic, cycle, store, ♿

J. Paul Getty Museum
17985 Pacific Coast Hwy (Route 1)
Malibu, CA 90265
☎ 213-458-2003
Open: 10am-5pm Tue-Sun except major holidays. Free
Book parking space ahead. Replica Roman villa, antiquities & art collection, book shop, restaurant, ♿

Knott's Berry Farm
8039 Beach Blvd
Buena Park, CA 90620
☎ 714-220-5200
Open: 10am-6pm Mon-Fri, -10pm Sat, -7pm Sun, extended summer & holidays. Free entrance to shops & Mrs Knott's restaurant
Ghost town, Camp Snoopy, rides, food, gifts, ♿

Lake Perris State Recreational Area
17801 Lake Perris Dr
Perris, CA 92370
☎ 714-657-0676
Open: 9am-sunset
Hike, picnic, camp, swim, boat, fish

Lincoln Memorial Shrine
125 W Vine St
Redlands, CA 92373
☎ 714-798-7536
Open: 1-5pm Tue-Sat. Free
Artifacts & relics of Lincoln & Civil War

Long Beach Children's Museum
Long Beach Plaza
445 Long Beach Blvd
Long Beach, CA 90802
☎ 213-495-1163
Open: 11am-4pm Thu-Sat, noon-4pm Sun
Interactive play

Long Beach Museum of Art
2300 E Ocean Blvd
Long Beach, CA 90803
☎ 213-439-2119
Open; noon-5pm Wed-Sun (-8pm Thu), except holidays
Contemporary art

Los Alamitos Race Course
4961 Katella Ave
Los Alamitos, CA 90720
☎ 213-431-1361
Open: Tue-Sat, 1st post 7.30pm

Los Angeles County Museum of Art
5905 Wilshire Blvd
Los Angeles, CA 90036
☎ 213-857-6000
Open: 10am-5pm Tue-Fri, -6pm weekends. Free on 2nd Tue of month
Gifts, restaurant, lectures & films, &

Los Angeles State & County Arboretum
301 N Baldwin Ave
Arcadia, CA 91006
☎ 818-446-8251
Open: 9am-5pm except Xmas
Greenhouses & arboretum, tram & guided tours, &

Los Angeles Zoo
5333 Zoo Dr
Los Angeles, CA 90027
☎ 213-666-4650
Open: 10am-5pm, -6pm summer
Zoo, bus tours, food, gifts, &

Los Encinos State Historic park
16756 Moorpark St
Encino, CA 91436

☎ 818-706-1310
Open: grounds 10am-5pm, house tours 1pm-4pm, closed Mon & Tue. Grounds free. Former cattle ranch, picnic, house tours

Malibu Creek State Park
County Route N1
North of Malibu, CA
☎ 818-706-8809
Open: 8am-10pm, interpretive centre hours vary
Hike, picnic, camp, interpretive centre, part &

Malibu Lagoon State Beach
Route 1
Malibu Creek, CA
☎ 213-456-8432
Open: 8am-sunset
Adamson House historic exhibits, picnic, pier, surf, part &

Mann's Chinese Theatre
6925 Hollywood Blvd
Hollywood, CA 90028
☎ 213-461-3331
Hand & footprints of stars, first run feature films

Medieval Times
7662 Beach Blvd
Buena Park, CA 90622
☎ 714-521-4740, 800-826-5358

Movieland Wax Museum
7711 Beach Blvd
Buena Park, CA 90620
☎ 714-522-1154
Open: 9am-8pm
Waxwork stars, gifts

Museum of Contemporary Art
250 S Grand Ave
Los Angeles, CA 90012
☎ 213-626-6222
Open: 11am-6pm Tue-Sun, -8pm Thu. Free on Thursday after 5pm. Gifts, &

Museum of Flying
Santa Monica Airport
2772 Donald Douglas Loop North
Santa Monica, CA 90405
☎ 213-392-8822
Open: 10am-6pm Thu-Sun
Historic aircraft

Music Center of Los Angeles County
135 N Grand Ave
Los Angeles, CA 90012
☎ 213-972-7211
Performance times vary
Chandler Pavilion, Ahmanson
Theatre & Taper Forum

Natural History Museum (of Los Angeles County)
900 Exposition Blvd
Los Angeles, CA 90007
☎ 213-744-3466
Open: 10am-5pm Tue-Sun
Natural & Californian history,
gifts, cafeteria, ♿

Norton Simon Museum of Art
411 W. Colorado Blvd
Pasadena, CA 91105
☎ 818-449-3730
Open: noon-6pm Thu-Sun except
major holidays
Early renaissance art to mid-20th
century

Orange County Performing Arts Center
600 Town Center Rd
Costa Mesa, CA 92626
☎ 724-556-2787
Performance times vary
Symphony, opera, ballet &
Broadway shows

Orange Empire Railway Museum
2201 South A St, PO Box 548
Perris, CA 92370
☎ 714-657-2605

Open: 9am-5pm except Thanksgiving Day & Xmas
Train rides weekends & holidays,
museum, gifts

Pacific Asia Museum
46 N Los Robles Ave.
Pasadena, CA 91101
☎ 818-449-2742
Open: noon-5pm Wed-Sun except
major holidays
Asian culture, Chinese courtyard,
gifts

Queen's Wharf
555 Pico Ave
Long Beach, CA 90802
☎ 213-432-8993
Food, gifts, boat tours

Rancho Los Alamitos
6400 Bixby Hill Rd
Long Beach, CA 90815
☎ 213-431-3541
Open: 1pm-5pm Wed-Sun except
holidays. Free
Ranch house & outbuildings

Rancho Los Cerritos Museum
4600 Virginia Rd
Long Beach, CA 90807
☎ 213-424-9423
Open: 1pm-5pm Wed-Sun. Free
Ranch house, exhibits, picnic

Rancho Santa Ana Botanic Garden
1500 N College Ave
Claremont, CA 91711
☎ 714-626-1917
Open: 8am-5pm except major holidays
Free. Native Californian plants

Redondo Beach Marina
181 N Harbor Dr
Redondo Beach, CA 90277
☎ 213-374-3481
Beach, pier, restaurants, boat cruises

Riverside Municipal Museum
3720 Orange St
Riverside, CA 92501
☎ 714-782-5273
Open: 9am-5pm Tue-Fri, 1pm-5pm
Sat & Sun except holidays. Free
Natural & human history, including Native Americans

Roy Rogers/Dale Evans Museum
15660 Seneca Rd
Victorville, CA 92392
☎ 619-243-4547
9am-5pm, except Thanksgiving
Day & Xmas
Personal & professional effects

San Bernardino County Museum
2024 Orange Tree Lane
Redlands, CA 92374
☎ 714-825-4825
Open: 9am-5pm Tue-Sat, 1pm-5pm
Sun
County historical exhibits

Santa Monica Heritage Museum
2612 Main St
Santa Monica, CA 90405
☎ 213-392-8537
Open: 11am-4pm Thu-Sat, noon-
4pm Sun. Free
Period furnished rooms, history
exhibits, &

**Santa Monica Mountains National
Recreation Area**
30401 Augoura Rd, Suite 100
Augoura Hills, CA 91301
☎ 818-597-9192
Opening hours vary
Hike, camp, cycle, horse trails,
Indian museums, &

Shoreline Village
Shoreline Dr & Pine Ave
Long Beach, CA 90802
☎ 213-590-8427
Open: 10am-9pm, -10pm summer
Harbourside shopping, dining &
entertainment

**Silverwood Lake State Recreation
Area**
Highway 138, off I-15
Hesperia, CA 92345
☎ 619-389-2281
Open: 9am-sunset
Camp, fish, boat rentals, hike,
picnic, &

Six Flags Magic Mountain
26101 Magic Mountain Pkwy
Valencia, CA 91355
☎ 805-255-4111
Open: from 10am daily summers,
weekends & holidays rest of year
except Xmas
Myriad rides, children's section,
gifts, food, &

South Coast Botanical Garden
26300 Crenshaw Blvd
Palos Verdes Peninsula, CA 90274
☎ 213-377-0468
Open: 9am-5pm except Xmas
2,000 plant species, including
native Californian

Southwest Museum
234 Museum Dr
Los Angeles, CA 90065
☎ 213-221-2163
Open: 11am-5pm Tue-Sun (library
closed Tues)
Gift & book shop, research library,
part &

Topanga State Park
Entrada Rd, off Hwy 27
West of Santa Monica, CA
☎ 213-455-2465
Open: 8am-10pm. Hike, cycle

**Tournament House and Wrigley
Gardens**
391 S Orange Grove Blvd
Pasadena, CA 91184
☎ 818-449-4100
Open: 2pm-4pm on Wed from Feb-
Aug. Free
Rose Bowl memorabilia, Wrigley house

Universal Studios Hollywood
3900 Lankershim Blvd
Universal City, CA 91608
☎ 818-508-9600
Open: 8am summer, 9am other
times, closing times vary
Tours, stunts, gifts, food, amusements, &

University of California, Los Angeles (UCLA)
405 Hilgard Ave
Los Angeles, CA
☎ 213-206-8147
Walking tours from Visitor Center,
1417 Ueberroth Blvd

University of Southern California (USC)
Exposition Blvd & S Figeroa St
Los Angeles, CA
☎ 213-743-2983
Walking tours 10am-2pm Mon-Fri
(by appointment). Parking fee

Wells Fargo History Museum
333 S Grand Ave
Los Angeles, CA
☎ 213-253-7166
Open: 9am-4pm Mon-Fri except
holidays. Free
Historical exhibits, gifts, &

Will Rogers State Historic Park
14253 Sunset Blvd
Pacific Palisades, CA 90272
☎ 213-454-8212
Open: 8am-6pm, -7pm summer
except Thanksgiving Day & Xmas
Will Roger's home, trails, polo
field, picnic, part &

Transportation

Los Angeles County Transportation Commision
818 West Seventh St, Suite 1100
Los Angeles, CA 90017
☎ 213-620-RAIL

Long Beach Transit
PO Box 731
Long Beach, CA 90801
☎ 310-591-2301

RTD (Rapid Transit) Centres
419 S Main St (Main)
ARCO Plaza Level B,
    515 S Flower St (LA)
California Mart,
    1016 S Main St (LA)
4015 'B' Wittier Blvd (East LA)
3501 N Santa Anita Ave
    (El Monte Station)
6249 Hollywood Blvd (Hollywood)
14435 Sherman Way,
    Suite 107 (San Fernando Valley)
☎ 213-626-4455

7

SAN DIEGO

A string of surfing beaches leads south from Los Angeles to San Diego, passing engaging coastal communities and a selection of Spanish Missions. The ardent historian could happily spend days enveloped in the past, while world-class art galleries and museums abound. For the children there are the delights of San Diego Zoo and Sea World, and holidaymakers enjoy reliving the past at Old Town San Diego. Excellent shopping facilities are available and, when finally exhausted, avail of the near-perfect sunny climate — relax on the beach or take in the sea air with a cruise to Mexico from the first-class cruise ship terminal.

Coastal Orange County

Rush hours excepted, I-5 is the express route south to San Diego from Greater Los Angeles and Anaheim, while SR1, the Coast Highway, leisurely passes the beachside communities.

Bird watchers will enjoy **Bolsa Chica Ecological Reserve**, 1,000 acres of undeveloped coastal wetland with a 1.5 mile (2.4 km) loop trail. Beachgoers enjoy the wide expanses of sandy shore via popular Bolsa Chica and Huntington State Beaches. These are connected by a 7-mile (11km) long cycle path while cars are catered for with 2,500 parking spaces at each site (leave valuables in the hotel safe, not in the car or on the beach). Stock up on swimwear, surfboards and suntan oil at nearby Huntington Beach.

The city of **Newport Beach** offers 6 miles of sand and upmarket shopping at Fashion Island on Newport Center Drive. Newport Harbour hosts the sleek yachts and speedboats of the affluent nautical set — try out the lifestyle on the elegant Hornblower Dining Yachts or visit the free **Newport Harbor Nautical Museum**.

Newport Harbor Art Museum displays modern and contempo-

Mission San Juan Capistrano's chapel is the oldest building in California

rary works, while beachside Balboa offers more down-to-earth amusements and entertainment. Balboa also hosts harbour cruises past the luxury homes and excursions to Santa Catalina Island (see Chapter 6). Sporting a selection of bars and fast food restaurants, Balboa's only lack is parking space.

Inland at **Irvine** is the 20-acre Wild Rivers Waterpark offering over forty rides, water attractions and picnic areas, while the outdoor Irvine Meadows Amphitheatre holds evening concerts.

On the coast near the small **Crystal Cove** community is Crystal Cove State Park comprising 2,791 acres of wooded canyon and over 3 miles (5km) of shoreline. The shore-bound can explore tide pools, sandy coves or hike the 23 miles (37km) of trails while scuba divers delve into the underwater park.

Picturesque artist colony **Laguna Beach** celebrates its lifestyle with its Festival of Arts and Pageant of the Masters, a mid-summer celebration by local artists (reservations are recommended). The **Laguna Art Museum** focuses on Californian artists, displaying both historical and contemporary works.

Dana Point was named after the celebrated author of *Two Years Before the Mast*, describing life along Alta California over two hundred years ago. A replica of his ship, the *Pilgrim*, can be seen alongside the **Orange County Marine Institute**. Sea-life exhibits are supplemented with a whale-watching cruise from December through March. The official *Californian Tallship*, the 145ft (44m) long replica of an 1849 Revenue Cutter, is berthed here and available for day and overnight cruises.

The entrance to **Doheny State Beach** is located on Del Obispo Street in Dana Point. This includes a campsite and the very popular day use area for swimming and surfing — arrive early on summer weekends.

Inland from Dana Point is one of the highlights of the drive south. **Mission San Juan Capistrano** was founded by Father Serra in 1776 and is famous for the legendary return of the swallows each year on 19 March, St Joseph's Day. Visitors will find a delightful combination of restored buildings, historic exhibits, and peaceful gardens surrounding the ruins of The Great Stone Church. The delightful adobe Serra Chapel is the oldest building in California.

San Juan Capistrano town sports quaint shops, good Mexican restaurants and old adobe buildings. Non-drivers will be delighted to know the town is a quick hop from Los Angeles or San Diego via Amtrak. Near the station, old Capistrano Depot has now been restored as a very popular restaurant located conveniently just two blocks from the mission.

Coastal San Diego County

At the Orange and San Diego County border the countryside becomes less developed, with I-5 the only route south. Here **San Clemente State Beach** offers clifftop picnicking and campsites with trails leading down to a mile of beach popular for swimming and surfing. I-5 passes through Camp Pendleton Marine Corps base — enter via the main gate for a self-guided tour of several adobe buildings. **San Onofre State Beach** on the coast offers another rugged clifftop area with 3.5 miles (5.5km) of sandy beach below, plus excellent views of the adjacent nuclear power plant.

Civilization returns south of Camp Pendleton with **Oceanside**, where watersports predominate. One world and several national surfing championships are held here annually on one of the coast's finest surfing beaches. Unfortunately, both inexperienced and seasoned surfers/bodysurfers have broken their necks here, so extreme caution is advised. Those preferring to stay dry can spend a day sportfishing or hire a boat from Oceanside Harbor. Nearby Oceanside Pier has been restored, offering a variety of dining along with bait and tackle shops.

Travel 4 miles (6.5km) east on SR76 for **Mission San Luis Rey de Francia**, founded in 1798. Called the 'King of the Missions', this was one of the largest and most impressive. The elaborate white-facaded Moorish style church was completed in 1815 and after restoration is still in use. In the Friary garden is the first pepper tree brought from Peru, while a tiled stairway leads to an elaborate sunken garden with spring-fed lavanderia (laundry area). Traditional Spanish vestments are worn during the mission's fiesta in July.

Several more state beaches are passed en route to **Encinitas**, where a turn east on Encinitas Boulevard leads to **Quail Botanical Gardens**. Self-guided trails pass rare plants and areas of chaparral serving as a natural refuge for birds and small animals.

South of **Del Mar** is **Torrey Pines State Beach and Reserve**, offering miles of wide, sandy beach good for swimming, surfing, sunbathing and fishing. A car park and picnic area are provided at the state beach, but at the reserve parking is limited and picnicking prohibited. The state reserve offers a peaceful and secluded area for hiking scenic trails in addition to preserving the Torrey Pines. The reserve also contains one of the region's few remaining saltwater lagoons, while the visitor centre displays interpretive exhibits. Arrive in early Spring for the blossoming wildflowers.

Just within San Diego City limits is the well-to-do resort community of **La Jolla** (pronounced La Hoy-ah). Shopping is heavily fea-

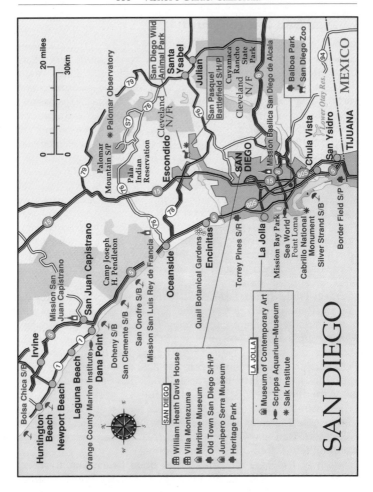

 tured here, the Coast Walk provides specialty boutiques, art galleries and some good seafood restaurants. Enjoy sun-drenched sandy beaches or explore sea-eroded caves along the rockier sections of coast. La Jolla is home to the respected **Museum of Contemporary Art** displaying works from 1955 to the present. Up the coast off La Jolla Shores Drive is the **Stephen Birch Aquarium-Museum**. The aquarium, featuring marine habitats from the Pacific Northwest, California and Mexico to the Indo-Pacific and exciting interactive exhibits, is administered by Scripps Institute of Oceanography, part

Into and Around San Diego

San Diego international Airport (Lindbergh Field) off Harbor Drive is served by major international and domestic airlines. Courtesy buses are operated by many hotels and motels — free telephones are located in the baggage areas of both terminals. Rental car booths are also here, though the free telephones may be used to contact shuttles for transport to pre-booked rental cars. Taxis are available from both terminals, as is the frequent and inexpensive public bus number 2 to downtown San Diego.

San Diego is connected via I-5 to Los Angeles and I-15 to Las Vegas, while the main route east is I-8. Most places of interest are spread out but easily accessed from the freeways, making the car a convenient form of transport around the city. Downtown metered parking is hard to find, but major attractions like Balboa Park, Sea World, and Old Town San Diego have separate parking.

The Amtrak depot is downtown at Broadway and Kettner Boulevard while Greyhound/Trailways operate from the main depot in San Diego on Broadway and 1st Avenue. Apart from connecting to other US cities, a daily service to downtown Tijuana (Mexico) is available.

The San Diego Metropolitan Transport System (MTS) serves the area from San Diego down to the Mexican border. The Transit Store on Broadway and 5th Avenue sells passes and multi-ride tickets as well as providing a comprehensive Regional Transit map of services, including the San Diego Trolley route — use it for your excursion south of the border.

Old Town Trolley offers a good introduction to the city, the full tour taking 1.5 hours and offering one-day unlimited on-off privileges. Gray Line Tours offer a selection of trips to city attractions and beyond.

Last but not least, with one of California's largest natural harbours and a first-class Cruise Ship Terminal, San Diego offers cruise opportunities along the coast and to sunny Mexico.

of nearby UCSD (University of California San Diego). Also here the scientifically-minded can tour the **Salk Institute**, one of the world's largest independent biological research centres.   ✳

Downtown San Diego

With so much to see and do in this sunny city it is best to plan a schedule. For information contact or visit the San Diego International Visitor Information Center or San Diego Visitors Information Center — addresses in the further information section.

Downtown's Convention and Performing Arts Center is on C Street, with Symphony Hall on B. Horton Plaza Center offers some of San Diego's finest department stores and restaurants in modern surrounds. The nearby sixteen-block **Gaslamp Quarter** was heart of downtown at the turn of the century and is bouncing back as a shopping and dining district with a Victorian touch. Saturday group tours leave from **William Heath Davis House** which is itself open for tours. **Villa Montezuma**, east of I-5 on K Street, was built in 1887 for musician, author and spiritualist Jesse Shepard. This elaborate Victorian Mansion with Queen Anne influence illustrates the luxury and sophistication of upper class boom-time San Diego. Visitors will enjoy the fabulous furnishings and stained-glass windows, and while there ask about the resident ghost.

Seaport Village along the Embarcadero (waterfront) offers a shopping, dining and entertainment experience. North along Harbor Drive are commercial fishing vessels, naval ships, and Broadway Pier followed by the Cruise Ship Terminal and the bayside **Maritime Museum**. This excellent museum has three fine ships: the square-rigged *Star of India*, reputedly the oldest merchant ship afloat; the *Medea*, a steam powered yacht; and the ferryboat *Berkeley*. The museum's exhibits and replica ships are displayed on the Berkeley, where volunteers can often be seen constructing additional models.

The Cruise Ship Terminal is the departure point for floating palaces which visit the other California — Baja, Mexico. One and two hour boat tours of San Diego Bay leave from Broadway Pier, passing ships of the Maritime Museum, San Diego skyline and Naval and merchant craft. Also accessible by ferry from Broadway Pier or by car on SR75 is the Old Ferry Terminal at Coronado, now a shopping and dining complex. Bicycle rentals and cycle path maps are available for those wishing to explore. One building worth a visit is the **Hotel del Coronado**, a huge wooden Spanish-Mexican style structure built in 1888 and used as a setting for numerous films. For swimming or sunbathing try **Silver Strand State Beach**, 4 miles (6.5km) south of Coronado on a sandspit which gives a choice of ocean surf or calm bayside beach.

Old Town San Diego

The city was founded in 1769, commencing with the Presidio. As numbers of settlers increased many moved down the hill to build houses and by 1821 the beginnings of Old Town, the first European settlement in California, were firmly established. Now preserved as

pedestrianized **Old Town San Diego State Historic Park**, the area is
part living history museum and part carnival, with tours starting
from the park visitor centre at Robinson-Rose House on Old Town
Plaza. The majority of adobe homes and historic structures in the
park and surrounding area are free, as are the 2pm guided tours.
Brochures are also available at the visitor centre for a self-guided tour
— if possible set aside a day to explore this area.

The history of the buildings is known in detail and many of those
destroyed in the great fire of 1872 have been reconstructed. Interesting buildings include adobe structures and some very early wood-
frame prefabricated houses. Wood not being a Southern Californian
commodity, even the San Diego Union Building was shipped
around the Horn from Maine.

Old Town San Diego preserves the appearance of the Mexican and
early American period from 1821 to 1872. The reconstructed Racine
and Laramie's store once again brims with cigars and tobacco, while
the small re-created Wells Fargo Office is complete with stagecoach
and Gold Rush era coins. One building which should not be missed
is the **Seeley Stable**. For a small admission charge there is an
informative slide show on early San Diego (thrice daily) and a
commendable collection of horse-drawn vehicles, Western memorabilia and Indian artifacts dating back 3,000 years. The nearby Black
Hawk Smithy and Stable demonstrates its time-honoured skills
midday on Wednesdays and Saturdays. Facing the Robinson-Rose
House across the plaza is **La Casa de Estudillo**, an extensive adobe
started in 1827 by the presidio commander. This interesting museum
is furnished in period and provides an insight into the lifestyle of a
successful family.

Within the park is Bazaar del Mundo, a colourful collection of
Mexican-style shops and restaurants surrounding an open-air courtyard. Here one may dine al fresco while sipping a *margarita* and
listening to a *mariachi* band.

Not all historic buildings lie within Old Town State Historic Park
and it is well worth taking a stroll along San Diego Avenue, past the
Catholic church, to the **Whaley House**. This 1856 two-storey mansion, said to be the oldest brick structure in southern California, was
used as the San Diego County Courthouse from 1869 to 1871. Now
restored to its original condition, the courtroom and living quarters
are furnished in period, as is the Derby-Pendleton house on Harney.
The old adobe chapel is on Conde Street while El Campo Santo, the
historic Catholic cemetery, is between Old Town and San Diego
Avenues. On Harney and Juan Streets is **Heritage Park**, a Victorian
area of houses containing San Diego's first synagogue.

Behind Old Town is Presidio Hill, site of the first mission and fort. **Junipero Serra Museum** constructed in 1929 commands an excellent view from its tower gallery, with photographs of old San Diego on display for reference. The museum traces the development of pre-American San Diego in exhibits and art and is sometimes mistakenly identified as **Mission San Diego de Alcala**. The first Alta California mission was sited where the large cross now stands, but was moved further inland by Father Serra. Although destroyed by an earthquake in 1803, the restored mission church on its site was completed 10 years later and today is easily accessed from I-8's Mission Gorge exit. Self-guided tape tours are available, and the mission museum contains artifacts uncovered in archaeological digs on the site.

Balboa Park

Site of several international expositions, **Balboa Park** is the undisputed gem of San Diego parks. A free tram services sections of the

Sample Mexican food at Bazaar del Mundo in Old Town San Diego

park but the 1,400 acres are best explored on foot. Parking is busy but plentiful, especially in the northeast corner near **San Diego Zoo**. Founded after the 1915-16 Panama-California International Exposition using animals imported for this event, the zoo is renowned for its hundreds of exotic species in natural settings. An optional 40-minute guided bus tour introduces visitors to the 100-acre zoo, with the deluxe ticket also including an educational children's zoo and rides on the Skyfari aerial tram. Plan to spend a full day and time visits around the informative animal shows. A restaurant and various eateries are available, and visitors may re-enter the zoo the same day after having their hands stamped. Next to the zoo is a carousel and miniature railroad, and adjacent to this is the colourful **Spanish Village** — replete with Hispanic and other artisans and their works.

An exceptional assemblage of museums and art galleries await visitors to Balboa Park — to do full justice allow at least two days as opening times are limited from 10am to 4 or 4.30 pm. A comprehensive map and guide is available for a small charge from Balboa Park Visitor Center in the House of Hospitality. A reduced price passport allows access to up to four museums, but check participating museums before purchase. Most museums give one free Tuesday per month on a staggered basis — check their schedules at the centre. Even those unwilling to spend sunny Southern California days indoors will enjoy the Spanish Colonial Architecture and pleasant gardens.

The **Ruben H. Fleet Space Theater and Science Center** is a world class complex containing an Omnimax theatre, where films are projected onto a huge dome. The educational hands-on Science Center is fun for all the family, while unusual scientific puzzles, games and books are sold in the large gift shop next to the Space Theater Cafe.

The **Natural History Museum** has an informative section on southern Californian desert, seashore and ocean ecology, including well produced dioramas. Nearby Casa de Balboa houses four small museums; the **Hall of Champions** full of sporting memorabilia, the **Museum of Photographic Arts** and its ever-changing exhibitions, the informative **Museum of San Diego History**, and fine working examples of a popular hobby at the **Model Railroad Museum**.

Next to Casa de Balboa is the House of Hospitality which contains the visitor centre and Cafe del Rey Moro offering full meals and cocktails in a delightful setting. Opposite, a large lily pond reflects the free **Botanical Building**, originally a Santa Fe railway station now displaying tropical and sub-tropical plants.

The adjacent elaborate Spanish Revival building houses the **San**

🏛 **Diego Museum of Art**, offering a rich selection of baroque and Italian Renaissance works as well as American art, nineteenth-century European paintings, and an extensive Asian collection which has been expanded to include Moghul works. For art in the sun try the Sculpture Court and Garden where refreshment is available in the café. Classic European Old Masters, American eighteenth- and nineteenth-century works of art and Russian icons are beautifully displayed at the free but excellent **Timken Art**
🏛 **Gallery**. Diagonally across Plaza de Panama is the free **San Diego Art Institute**, with changing exhibitions of contemporary works.

Nearby **California Tower** houses the 100-bell carillon — listen for the quarter-hourly chimes. The tower also houses the fascinating
🏛 world-class **Museum of Man**, where exhibits explore man's cultures. Emphasis is on artifacts tracing the history of Indians in the Americas, while the Wonder of Life Building examines the miracle of human development and birth.

❋ Behind the California Tower is the **Simon Edison Centre for the Performing Arts**, which comprises the Old Globe Theatre, Cassius Carter Centre Stage and Lowell Davies Festival Theatre. These three theatres stage a variety of productions throughout the year, each celebrating the Old Globe Theatre Festival in summer when Shakespeare's works are the prime focus.

❋ From Plaza de Panama the Mall leads to the tranquil **Japanese Friendship Garden**, while the adjacent **Spreckels Organ Pavilion** houses the world's largest outdoor musical instrument. Donated to the city at the opening of the Panama-Pacific Exposition, there is seating for 2,400 with free concerts at 2pm on Sundays.

❋ Taking Pan-American Road West, the **Houses of Pacific Relations** are cottages representing some thirty nations with ethnic music and dance on Sundays. Across is the UNICEF International Gift Shop, displaying an assortment of gift ideas from around the world. Further on the Palisades Building incorporates the Recital Hall, Puppet Theatre and Balboa Park Management Center, the latter having information on park activities and special events. Fronting
🏛 onto Pan-American Plaza is the **Automotive Museum**, where over sixty classic cars are on display.

🏛 The distinctive structure of the **Aerospace Historical Center** holds a vast array of early flying machines, including a replica of Charles Lindberg's *Spirit of St Louis* made by the San Diego company which constructed the original. Modern flight, including space travel, is also well covered, with inventors, pioneers and heroes remembered in the International Aerospace Hall of Fame.

Starlight Bowl hosts a variety of performances throughout the year, including the San Diego Civic Light Opera summer season. Found off the beaten track on Park Boulevard is the Centro Cultural de la Raza which promotes Native American, Mexican and Chicano cultures with visual arts, performances and exhibitions.

Mission Bay Area

Found north of San Diego Bay, activity oriented **Mission Bay Park** has a visitor centre on East Mission Bay Drive which highlights places of interest. Boat and bike rentals are offered in several locations, while accommodation is available in the area's resort hotels and campers get a waterfront setting at Campland on the Bay.

The main attraction is **Sea World**, where killer whales Shamu and family welcome guests to this, the original Sea World. Packed with educational exhibits and a variety of entertaining shows, the San Diego Sea World has been continuously improved, and each year offers a thrilling new act or three. Allow for a very full day and plan visits to the informative exhibits around the many shows. Arrive early at performances for the best seats, and remember that lower rows of seating can get drenched — sit higher to protect cameras but send children down to enjoy the splash-filled antics. By the nature of its shows, Sea World is unlike the other theme parks in requiring far less queueing and plenty of opportunity to sit down. Even so, wear comfortable shoes as considerable walking is required between performances, and don't forget that shows often change in the evening, offering additional value. To re-enter the same day get hands stamped at the exit.

South of San Diego

Cabrillo National Monument on Point Loma offers excellent views over San Diego city and harbour. This monument to the first European to discover California has a visitor centre with films and exhibits on Cabrillo's voyage and includes a refurbished 1885 lighthouse. There are interesting walks, an overlook good for observing California grey whales between December and February, plus tide pools to explore (check with rangers for times and precautions).

Found midway between San Diego and the Mexican border on the San Diego Trolley route, **Chula Vista** offers fine dining and shopping in its downtown area and at the Chula Vista Center. The interesting **Chula Vista Nature Interpretive Center** is accessed via a shuttle bus from the E Street car park, one block west of I-5. Marshland habitat is explored through trails, an observation tower and a visitor centre offering hands-on exhibits and nature films. East

The Spirit of St Louis was made in San Diego

Meet Shamu and family at Sea World, in Mission Bay Park

Getting to Tijuana and Mexico

Local tour operators offer trips from San Diego; alternatively take the San Diego Trolley from downtown right to the border. Those with their own vehicles may drive into Tijuana, but *Mexican* car insurance must first be purchased, and the fast-paced mêlée is a deterrent to all but the craziest drivers. Car rental companies generally do *not* allow their cars into Mexico — leave the car back in San Ysidro, the US border city.

A Mexican permit is only required if venturing beyond Tijuana, so once across the border either continue on foot (turn right and follow the crowd over the footbridge crossing the Tijuana river), take a taxi (agree the fare first), or catch one of the frequent if rather rickety buses for the short hop downtown. Converting currency is optional as dollars are universally accepted, but do check the exchange rate. US customs permit $400 worth of purchases, including one quart of liquor per adult.

Picture identification is required when returning, and visitors from abroad must ensure their visa allows multiple entries to the US, otherwise they are not permitted to return. Those who entered America under the Visa Waiver Program and any who did not obtain a multiple-entry visa should not visit Tijuana — if unsure check first on the *American* side.

of Chula Vista near Lower Otay Reservoir is the new year-round Olympic Training Center.

Border Field State Park adjoins the Mexican border, preserving sections of the Tijuana River Estuarine Reserve, a rare and pristine area currently under threat from pollution.

South of the Border

For an exciting side-trip join the 40 million people who anually cross the border into Baja, Mexico. **Tijuana**, one of Mexico's largest cities, offers colourful entertainment and fine restaurants, but its prime attraction to most is the shopping. Free port status keeps prices down, and bargaining is de rigueur in smaller shops. Although not mandatory, haggling can be good fun and the ideal situation is when both parties come away feeling satisfied.

Along Tijuana's Avenida Constitucion in the old downtown area are the twin towers of **Nuestra Senora de Guadalupe Cathedral**, which illustrate typical Mexican church architecture. This is a popular local shopping area while one block west Avenida Revolucion is the old tourist shopping street with its numerous arcades selling clothing, jewelry, handicrafts and curios. Here one is invited into restaurants and bars selling inexpensive cocktails, especially *margaritas*, and some offer a *mariachi* band for entertainment.

Waiters are happy to explain unfamiliar Mexican dishes, which in 'Tijuana border cuisine' can be hot but are not usually volcanic. Real Mexican food can be found and is invariably tasty, often involving a selection of condiments to spice up dishes to suite individual taste. The less adventurous will find many other cuisines are available, from American fast food to the occasional Italian or French restaurant. Whenever possible, choose a balcony table to dine or enjoy an ice-cold drink, then enjoy the spectacle below. The colourful locals go about their daily life, jostling on the sidewalks and hooting at other traffic, while the tourists don *sombreros* and have photographs taken astride zebra-striped *burros*. Before leaving downtown try the Mercado de Artesanias for its numerous craft and clothing booths.

Tijuana Cultural Center, a modern complex near the Rio Tijuana, displays interesting archaeological and historical artifacts, folk art and handicrafts in its museum. Also within the complex is a concert hall offering varied music and drama and the **Omnitheater**, housed in an 85ft dome presenting Mexican history and culture. Other facilities include a cafeteria, restaurant and handicraft shops.

For a south of the border shopping mall try the Plaza Rio Tijuana opposite Tijuana Culture Center. With three large department stores, plentiful speciality shops, several restaurants and a cinema it rivals those to the north. Across Paseo de los Heroes is Plaza Fiesta, with small shops and eateries, and Plaza del Zapato which specializes in shoes. Nearby is the colourful Mercado M. Hildago (public market) with fresh produce, arts, crafts and liquor stores.

Sports are varied and include both dog and horse racing at **Agua Caliente Racetrack**. Betting is also available for Jai Alai, a lightening-paced ball game played at **Fronton Palacio**, while golfers can try a round at the **Club Social Y Deportivo Campestre**. Spanish influence is manifested at the two bullrings, **El Toreo** and **Plaza Monumental (Bullring-by-the-Sea)** from May through September.

Escondido

Found 30 miles (48km) north of downtown San Diego, **Escondido** can be visited as a day trip or en route to the California desert, as highlighted in the next chapter. Their Heritage Walk offers a historical complex containing a diverse selection of old buildings, while 8 miles (13km) east on SR78 is **San Pasqual Battlefield State Historic Park**. The latter remembers one of the few bloody battles of the

Mexican-American War with a video and museum containing dioramas and maps. Next to this is **San Diego Wild Animal Park**, where African and Asian animals roam 2,150 acres of natural environment viewed from a monorail and at lookouts along a walking trail. Lawrence Welk Resort Theatre 7 miles (11km) north of Escondido offers a 330-seat dinner theatre and museum with exhibits on this inventor of 'Champagne Music'. Several Californian wineries offering tours and tastings can also be found around Escondido.

In the hills west of Escondido and northeast of San Diego is the white stuccoed church of **Santa Ysabel**. This outpost of San Diego Mission was founded in 1818 and rebuilt in 1924. North on SR79 leads towards the Pala Indian Reservation where the church of **Mission San Antonio de Pala**, an outpost of Mission San Luis Rey, has been restored and is still used by Native Americans.

SR 6 climbs 6,100ft (1,859m) **Mount Palomar** to the famed observatory, where images from the 200in Hale telescope are exhibited in the free Greenway Museum. The advantages for which this site was chosen — clear skies, elevation above coastal fog and remoteness from any city lights also benefit visitors to **Palomar Mountain State Park**. Found by taking SR7, this peaceful and remote area offers an interpretive walk, hiking trails through coniferous woodland and a small campsite. Mount Palomar lies within the 420,000-acre **Cleveland National Forest**, which encompasses four wilderness areas and several mountain recreation areas. Ranger stations offer information on naturalist programs, trails, camping and winter sports.

East from Santa Ysabel SR78 passes apple and pear orchards before reaching the small turn of the century mining town of **Julian**, centre of an 1870s gold rush. The **Julian Pioneer Museum** illustrates that era with photographs and artifacts, while the guided tour run by Eagle Mining Company explains methods of mining used here.

Cuyamaca Rancho State Park in the Peninsular Range is surrounded on three sides by Cleveland National Forest, and contains landscapes varying from pine and deciduous forests to chaparral and meadows. A good place to get away from it all, over half of the park is designated wilderness area with more than 110 miles (177km) of hiking trails. This former rancho was home to Native Americans for many centuries, a history outlined in the park headquarters museum on SR79. That period ended with the 1870-1891 gold rush, a chapter illustrated at the Stonewall Mine ruins near Cuyamaca Lake. The park's natural history is displayed in the visitor centre at Paso Pichaco campground.

If time permits, return to San Diego or Los Angeles via the Desert tour outlined in the next chapter.

Additional Information

Regional Visitor Information

Huntington Beach Conference & Visitors Bureau
2100 Main St, Suite 190
Huntington Beach, CA 92648
☎ 714-969-3492

Newport Beach Conference & Visitors Bureau
3700 Newport Boulevard, Suite 107
Newport Beach, CA 92663
☎ 714-675-7040

San Diego International Visitor Center
11 Horton Plaza
San Diego, CA 92101
☎ 619-232-1212

San Diego Visitor Center
2688 E Mission Bay Dr
San Diego, CA 92109
☎ 619-276-8200

San Juan Capistrano COC
31682 El Camino Real
San Juan Capistrano, CA 92675
☎ 714-493-4700

The Missions

Mission San Antonio de Pala
Route 76, PO Box 70
Pala, CA 92059
☎ 619-742-3317
Open: 10am-3pm Tue-Sun except Thanksgiving Day & Xmas
Restored chapel, museum

Mission San Diego de Alcala
10818 San Diego Mission Rd
San Diego, CA 92108
☎ 619-281-8449
Open: 9am-5pm except Thanksgiving Day & Xmas
Rebuilt 1st mission, museum, gifts

Mission San Juan Capistrano
Ortega Hwy & Camino Capistrano
San Juan Capistrano, CA 92675
☎ 714-493-1424
Open: 8.30am-7pm summer, else 7.30am-5pm
Swallows, chapel & church, gifts, museum, garden

Mission San Luis Rey
4050 Mission Ave
San Luis Rey, CA 92068
☎ 619-757-3651
Open: 10am-4pm Mon-Sat, noon-4pm Sun
Restored mission, museum

Mission Santa Ysabel
PO Box 129
Santa Ysabel, CA
☎ 619-765-0810
Open: 7am-dusk. Donation
Chapel, museum

Places to Visit

Aerospace Museum
2001 Pan American Plaza
San Diego, CA 92101
☎ 619-234-8291
Open: 10am-4.30pm except major holidays
Vintage planes to space capsules, gifts, &

Border Field State Park
Monument Rd
Imperial Beach, CA
☎ 619-237-6766
Open: 9am-5pm
Visitor centre, walks

Cabrillo National Monument
Cabrillo Memorial Dr
San Diego, CA 92106
☎ 619-557-5450

Open: 9am-5.15pm, extended in summer
Visitor centre, lighthouse, whale spotting, gifts, part &

California Tallship
c/o Nautical Heritage Society,
24532 Del Prado
Danta Point, CA 92629
☎ 714-661-1001
Tours, sailings

Chula Vista Nature Interpretive Center
1000 Gunpowder Point Dr
Chula Vista, CA 92010
☎ 619-422-2473
Open: 10am-5pm Tue-Sun except major holidays. Free
Films & exhibits, trails through marsh

Cleveland National Forest
c/o 880 Front St, Rm 5N14
San Diego, CA 92188
☎ 619-557-5050
Wilderness areas, hike, camp.

Cuyamaca Rancho State Park
SR 79, East of I-8
Descanso CA
☎ 619-765-0755
Open: 9am-dusk
Visitor centre, museum, camp, picnic, hike

Doheny State Beach
Off Pacific Coast Highway
Dana Point, CA
☎ 714-496-6171
Open: 9am-dusk
Beach, swim, camp, picnic, bike trail

Hornblower Dining Yachts
Mariners Mile Marine Center
2431 W Coast Hwy
Newport Beach, CA 92663-1779
☎ 714-646-0155
Sailings vary
Lunch & dinner cruises

Horton Plaza
324 Horton St
San Diego, CA 92101
☎ 619-239-8180
Shopping, restaurant & theatre complex

Huntington State Beach
Pacific Coast Hwy
Huntington Beach, CA
☎ 714-536-1454
Open: 9am-10pm
Beach, surf, picnic, cycle, store, &

Junipero Serra Museum
2727 Presidio Dr, Presidio Park
San Diego, CA 92138
☎ 619-297-3258
Open: 10am-4.30pm Tue-Sat, noon-4.30 Sun, except major holidays
Reconstructed mission, museum, gifts, views

Laguna Art Museum
307 Cliff Dr
Laguna Beach, CA 92651
☎ 714-494-6531
Open: 11am-5pm Tue-Sun
Works of Californian artists

Lawrence Welk Theatre & Museum
8860 Lawrence Welk Dr
Escondido, CA 92026
☎ 619-749-3448
Open: museum 10.30am-5pm
Museum free
Dinner theatre, Lawrence Welk Museum, accommodation & dining

Maritime Museum
1306 N Harbor Dr
San Diego, CA 92101
☎ 619-234-9153
Open: 9am-8pm
Tall ship, ferry, steam yacht, exhibits, gifts

Museum of Contemporary Art
700 Prospect St
La Jolla, CA 92037
☎ 619-454-3541
Open: 10am-5pm Tue-Sun except
major holidays & 2nd week August

Museum of San Diego History
Casa de Balboa, 1649 El Prado,
Balboa Park
San Diego, CA 92138
☎ 619-232-6203
Open: 10am-4.30pm Wed-Sun
San Diego history, gifts, &

Natural History Museum
El Prado, Balboa Park
San Diego, CA
☎ 619-232-3821
Open: 10am-4.30pm, -5pm
summer, except major holidays
Free 1st Tue in month
Native natural history, gifts, &

**Old Town San Diego State
    Historic Park**
4002 Wallace St
San Diego, CA 92110
☎ 619-237-6770 or 6766
Open: visitor centre 10am-5pm,
other times vary
Most buildings free
Historic buildings, plaza, gifts,
food, part &

Orange County Marine Institute
24200 Dana Point Harbor Dr
Dana Point, CA
☎ 714-496-2274
Open: 10am-3.30pm except
holidays, ship tours summer Sun.
Free except ship tours
Exhibits, replica ship *Pilgrim*

Palomar Observatory
Off County Rd S6
Palomar Mountain, CA 92060
☎ 619-742-2119

Open: 9am-4pm except Xmas. Free
Observatory visitor's gallery,
museum

Quail Botanical Gardens
230 Quail Gardens Dr
Encinitas, CA 92024
☎ 619-436-3036
Open: 8am-5pm (-6pm summer)
Free. Gardens, bird sanctuary

**Reuben H. Fleet Space Theater &
    Science Center**
1875 El Prado, Balbao Park
San Diego, CA 92103
☎ 619-238-1168 or 1233
Open: 9.30am-9.30pm
Omnimax theatre, hands-on
science, gifts, food, &

San Clemente State Beach
Avenida California
San Clemente, CA
☎ 714-492-3156
Open: 9am-sunset
Beach, surf, picnic, camp

San Diego Museum of Art
Balboa Park
San Diego, CA 92112
☎ 619-232-7931
Open: 10am-4.30pm Tue-Sun
except major holidays
Free 3rd Tue in month
Comprehensive collection, gifts, &

San Diego Museum of Man
1350 El Prado, Balboa Park
San Diego, CA 92101
☎ 619-239-2001
Open: 10am-4.30pm except major
holidays. Free 3rd Tue in month
Exhibits, gifts, part &

San Diego Wild Animal Park
15500 San Pasqual Valley Rd
Escondido, CA 92025
☎ 619-747-8702
Open: 9am-dusk
Monorail, food, gifts, shows, &

San Diego Zoo
Balboa Park
San Diego, CA 92112
☎ 619-557-3966
9am-4pm, -5pm summer
Zoo, children's area, tours, food,
gifts, part &

San Pasqual Battlefield State Historic Park
15808 San Pasqual Valley Rd
Escondido, CA 92025
☎ 619-238-3380
Open: 10am-5pm Thu-Mon
Visitor centre & museum, &

Scripps Aquarium/Museum
8602 La Jolla Shores Dr
La Jolla, CA 92093
☎ 619-534-6933
Open: 9am-5pm. Donations
Aquarium, exhibits, tidepool

Sea World
1720 S Shores Rd
(Exit I-5 west onto Sea World Drive)
San Diego, CA 92109
☎ 619-226-3901
Open: 9am-dusk, -11pm summer &
selected holidays
Exhibits, shows, petting pools,
gifts, food, &

Simon Edison Center for Performing Arts
Balboa Park
San Diego, CA 92112
☎ 619-239-2255
Numerous productions
Old Globe Theatre, Carter Centre
Stage & Davies Festival Theatre

Timken Art Gallery
Balboa Park
San Diego, CA
☎ 619-239-5548
Open: 10am-4.30pm Tue-Sat, 1.30-
4.40pm Sun. Free
American & European works, gifts,
&

Torrey Pines State Beach & Reserve
PO Box 38
San Diego, CA 92008
☎ 619-729-8947 or 755-2063
Open: 9am-sunset
Beach, visitor centre, walks, reserve

Villa Montezuma/Jesse Shepard House
1925 K St
San Diego, CA 92102
☎ 619-239-2211
Open: 1-4.30pm Wed-Sun except
major holidays
Victorian home, tours, gifts

Wild Rivers Waterpark
8800 Irvine Center Dr
Laguna Hills, CA 92653
☎ 714-768-9453
Open: daily mid-May to Sept
Water rides, food, gifts, amusements

8

THE DESERTS

Southeastern California is one of the state's most geographically diverse areas, with altitudes ranging from 282ft (86m) below sea level in Death Valley to snow-capped peaks over 11,000ft (3,350m). Although known for the desert, vegetation varies from coniferous forests in the western mountains to 'wet desert' plants like the Joshua tree down to the cacti and specialist plants that survive in the desiccated eastern desert. The three main Californian deserts —

Anza-Borrego is America's largest state park

Desert Precautions

Explore and enjoy desert areas (avoiding the extremely high summer temperatures if at all possible) but remember to carry *at least* a gallon of water per person per day and in hot weather take walks only in early morning or evening. To protect against extremely sharp spines and the sun, wear sturdy shoes (*not* sandals), long-sleeved cotton shirt, long trousers, a hat, sunglasses and sun screen. Do not put hands or feet into holes or burrows and avoid vegetation near water where rattlesnakes and scorpions shade themselves during the day. Be alert for flash floods if storm clouds gather and never venture into remote areas

alone. If leaving the main highways inform a ranger or friend and, if travelling by car, start with a full fuel tank and remain in the shade of the vehicle in case of breakdown — *do not* attempt to walk for help. On very hot days avoid using the air conditioning, particularly on the long climb out of Death Valley. Taking precautions beforehand enables visitors to more fully enjoy the fascinating life which abounds in the 'inhospitable' desert.

Imperial Dunes

Great Basin, Mojave (Mow-ha-vee) and Colorado (part of the Sonoran Desert) — each have their own character with unique plants and animals. Those visiting Anza Borrego Desert State Park will discover that not all the palm trees are situated in the sunny desert resorts like Palm Springs and Las Vegas. Then again these desert resorts have much more to offer than just palm trees...

Travellers following the itinerary inland from San Diego in the previous chapter can continue east on SR22 to Anza-Borrego, while those looking for places of interest en route from Los Angeles to Las Vegas can skip forward to the section on Palm Springs and take up the narrative from there.

♣ **Anza-Borrego Desert State Park**, east of Cleveland National Forest and largest state park in the contiguous United States, offers an excellent introduction to desert California. Situated on the edge of the Colorado Desert with elevations varying from sea-level to 6,000ft (1,829m), it boasts numerous hiking trails, over 500 miles (805km) of unsurfaced roads and no less than twelve wilderness areas. The landscape is varied with canyons, *arroyos* (dry gullies), colourful badlands and stark white salt deposits. Vegetation ranges from junipers and pinyon pines in the Peninsular Range to fan palms, cacti and succulents at lower levels.

Anza-Borrego is especially colourful in springtime, when cacti and wildflowers put on a brilliant display. Whilst many interesting birds and animals are to be found here, this is one of the last refuges of the desert bighorn sheep (*borrego* in Spanish).

Full details of the park's 600,000 acres and ranger-led activities are available at the semi-subterranean visitor centre just west of Borrego Springs. Exhibits and a 25-minute slide show introduce the region (beware the arctic air conditioning). This is a good place to get information on road conditions before venturing into the wilder areas, or better still experience the desert backroads by jeep tour from Borrego Springs. The largely undeveloped, varied terrain of nearby
❄ **Ocotillo Wells State Vehicle Recreation Area**, east of Anza-Borrego on SR78, is heaven-on-earth for off-road motorcycle, all-terrain-vehicle (ATV), four-wheel drive (4WD) and dune-buggy drivers.

If time is short, head north to Palm Springs. Those interested in rural California and its clash of cultures can try **Calexico** and **Mexicali**. Respectively found north and south of the Mexican border, these sprawling towns have a strong Spanish-Mexican influence. The surrounding area is heavily irrigated for agriculture, while to the east this gives way to real desert at **Imperial Sand Dunes**. Do not be surprised if these large, wind-sculpted dunes seem reminiscent of the Sahara — they have been used as movie settings from *Lawrence of Arabia* to *Mad Max*. Photographers should protect cameras from drifting sand and drivers should avoid the temptation to go off-road unless they can afford hefty towing charges.

The Salton Sea, actually 200ft (61m) below sea level, was accidentally created in 1905 when water being diverted from the Colorado

River to Imperial Valley went awry. The **Salton Sea National Wild-life Refuge** on the southern shore is the bird-watcher's habitat, with salt marshes, freshwater ponds and nesting grounds for over 200 bird species. On the northeast shore **Salton Sea State Recreation Area** provides a visitor centre showing a 15-minute video on the formation of one of the world's largest man-made inland seas — 35 miles (56km) long and 15 miles (244km) wide. Exhibits also cover the local Cahuilla Indians. Popular pastimes include swimming, boating, angling, bird-watching, hiking, and camping at primitive or semi-developed sites. North of the Salton Sea is the Coachella Valley, an area wrested from the Colorado Desert. Agriculture is important in the southern portion, with produce including dates, citrus fruit and feed crops. However most visitors head for the northern section, which contains the desert resorts.

Palm Springs

A favourite haunt of Hollywood stars since the 1930s, **Palm Springs** shows off its heritage via the Celebrity and Gray Line tours past movie stars' homes and elite country clubs. Found due west of Los Angeles on I-10, Palm Springs is a popular destination in its own right, and a useful stopover for those following the triangular desert tour through Lake Havasu and Las Vegas.

The intensely green lawns, tennis courts and golf courses of Palm Springs and the adjacent desert resort communities are watered from massive underground reservoirs. This conglomeration of resorts literally sprang up from the desert, and today offers everything to those in search of a little luxury in the sun. Resort and spa hotels abound, many with tennis and golf facilities and few without a swimming and therapeutic pool or two. Palm Springs shopping is world class — browse around Palm Springs Mall, The Courtyard or try the 'haute couture' of Desert Fashion Plaza.

Palm Springs offers the visitor more than high-class hotels, upper-crust country clubs and well watered lawns. The **Heritage Theatre** in the Desert Fashion Plaza presents the 38-minute film *Main Roads, Back Roads and Indian Trails — The Palm Springs Story* while the excellent **Palm Springs Desert Museum** features western American art, contemporary art, sculpture gardens, Indian artifacts and the natural history of the area. It also encompasses the Annenberg Theatre which caters for the performing arts.

The Village Heritage Center in the heart of Palm Springs contains three museums. **Ruddy's General Store Museum**, recreating the atmosphere of a 1930s general store, is open year round while the

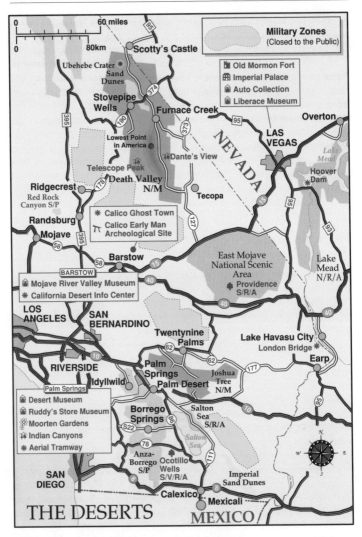

THE DESERTS

McCallum Adobe and Cornelia White's House are open mid-October until June.

* The **Oasis Water Resort** offers respite from the desert heat with its 21-acre waterpark, seven waterslides, the large wavepool for surfers and the Whitewater River inner tube ride for the more relaxed. Food, swimwear, gifts and board rentals are available and, for an extra fee,

get fit at the Oasis Health Club. The Swim Center on Sunrise Way and
Ramon Road offers more traditional swimming with its Olympic-sized pool and children's section, lawns and sun decks.

Those interested in the desert itself will enjoy **Moorten's Botanical**
Garden, which displays desert plants from around the world. Nature trails give information on these and Indian lore — keep an eye out for native desert birds and animals. Longer walks are available
through the scenic **Indian Canyons** to the south and west of Palm Springs. Settled centuries ago by the Agua Caliente Cahuilla (Kah-wee-ah) Indians, they benefited from the hot and cold running springs which supported considerable plant and animal life. Still owned today by their descendants, the toll road leads from the end of South Palm Canyon Drive to the canyons — a peaceful respite from resort living. **Palm Canyon**, 15 miles long, is lined with Washington palms some 2,000 years old. **Andreas Canyon** offers unusual

Escape to the cool of the mountains on the Palm Springs Aerial Tramway

rock formations and evidence of Indian occupation while the less visited **Murray Canyon** is quieter, offering better chances to spot wildlife. Tours of the canyons, some emphasizing Native American lifestyle, are available through Desert Adventures. Alternatives include horse rental from Smoke Tree Stables and Ranch of the 7th Range, or cycle hire from Burnett's Bicycle Barn and Canyon Bicycle Rentals and Tours. Get a bicycle trail map from the Palm Springs Recreation Department.

For a different perspective on the desert, Palm Springs Aerial Tramway in the north of Palm Springs lifts visitors up the 8,516ft (2,596m) San Jacinto Mountain for magnificent views, 54 miles of trails and a winter ski centre. Food, cocktails and gifts are available, and many take the tram or drive up into the mountains to experience the change from desert to snow (dress warmly). Other popular activities include balloon rides and helicopter tours; the Palm Springs Desert Resorts Visitor Bureau keeps a list of reputable operators.

Nearby **Palm Desert** was established as a hot-springs resort and sports numerous attractions. Start with the excellent 1,200-acre **Living Desert**, which includes Eagle Canyon wildlife exhibit and endangered species breeding centre, botanical gardens, exhibits on Native American culture, hiking trails and picnic areas. For Indian artifacts visit **Cabot's Old Indian Pueblo Museum**, a four-storey Hopi Indian-style building constructed over a 20-year period by Cabot Yerxa. The museum incorporates a trading post, rock shop and art gallery.

Palm Desert's largest shopping mall, Palm Desert Town Center escapes the desert heat with Ice Capades Chalet, its Olympic-sized skating arena. Another shopping area of note is the 2-mile stretch of El Paseo between SR74 and Portola Avenue. Billed as a world-class shopping street, it presents an eclectic selection of clothes shops, art galleries, jewelry stores, beauty salons and restaurants. While in Palm Desert check current productions at the **Bob Hope Cultural Center**. This incorporates McCallum Theatre for the Performing Arts, known for its variety of musical entertainment.

The Palms-to-Pines Highway (SR74) offers a scenic drive up through San Bernardino National Forest, with temperatures much lower than the desert below. The SR243 turnoff leads to Idyllwild, a small mountain village and year-round outdoor recreation centre. To complete the circle, follow SR243 down to I-10, passing the forest of wind-driven turbines which power the desert communities.

The Desert Triangle

The quickest route to Las Vegas (preferable in the heat of mid-Summer) is to return west on I-10 then head north on I-15. But those with time to explore hidden desert nuances must experience **Joshua Tree National Monument**. Arrange accommodation in the desert resorts or at Twentynine Palms before setting out, unless camping, in which case bring plenty of water.

If staying in Palm Springs leave early with a full fuel tank, heading east on I-10 and starting at the Cottonwood Springs entrance to Joshua Tree National Monument. The visitor centre offers maps and information on the 870 square mile national monument. The park protects an important buffer zone between the dryer Chihuahuan Desert and the higher and thus marginally more humid Mojave, where Joshua Trees grow (this large member of the yucca family was likened by Mormon pioneers to Joshua with his arms raised in supplication). Joshua Tree National Monument has plenty of these 'trees' and interesting panoramas with scenic overlooks, but also offers many activities for the adventurous. Hiking outside summer is excellent (carry plenty of water), while the jumbled masses of smooth granite boulders make for excellent rock climbing and the perfect backdrop for those primitive campgrounds.

Places of interest include Cholla (Choy-ya) Cactus Gardens, where one learns that these 'Teddy Bear' cacti are far from cuddly. Watch the flora closely here through the transition from Chihuahuan to the 'wetter' Mojave desert. Take in the broad panorama of Keys View and a walk through a former cattle rustler's hideout in Hidden Valley. Check with rangers before attempting the geology tour or other dirt road treks, as rental cars offer less ground clearance than four-wheel-drive vehicles. The Oasis Visitor Center near Twentynine Palms has interesting exhibits and helpful rangers for those planning to venture into the wilderness areas.

From Twentynine Palms SR62 leads east across the Mojave Desert, where the lifeblood of Southern California, the Colorado River Aqueduct, can be seen. In Earp take Parker Dam road north and cross the Colorado River Dam into Arizona, where watches should be advanced one hour. SR95 north leads to desert resort **Lake Havasu** and London Bridge, brought stone by stone from England. This planned resort has a 'Tudor English Village' next to the bridge, and many hotels have access to local golf courses. Head north on SR95, east on I-40 to Kingman, then north again on US93 for the massive **Hoover Dam** and the surrounding **Lake Mead Recreation Area**. Explore the lake's natural surroundings before returning west.

Joshua Tree National Park is a climber's paradise

Desert flora and fauna are well adapted

Las Vegas, Nevada

For a dramatic entrance, reach **Las Vegas** under cloak of night, when the glittering **Strip** sets the desert sky afire with colourful cascades of light and water and starbursts of neon as each casino tries to out-dazzle the competition.

Casual visitors believe that a good casino is determined by the quality of the food, the beauty of the cocktail waitresses, and the big name entertainment. But to the millions of gambling retirees who frequent the casinos, the number one priority is 'Super-Loose Slots'. Casinos have them, laundramats have them — even instant Wedding Chapels have them. Slot professionals wear gloves and carry *big* buckets, smartly pumping silver dollars into those machines in the hope for more. But casinos also have crap tables and roulette wheels, keno games and poker hands, with free sets of rules for the asking. Casino guests interested in learning a new game should watch a few players, find a quiet table, and talk to the croupier. In addition to advice newcomers occasionally receive 'practise chips'.

Las Vegas *is* famous for big name entertainment, and for the biggest shows it may be better to stay at that particular resort. Big casinos have free entertainment in their lounges, while people-

Colourful cacti bloom from February to April

watching or promenading along the Strip at night is excitement enough for many. Fine dining is available in large hotels, while firm favourites are the massive buffets offering hundreds of items for bargain-basement prices. The desert sun drowns the Strip's neon lights by day, but a wealth of recreation lurks around its borders.

Interesting rock formations and high desert animals are found along the drive and trails of **Red Rock Canyon**. Hire horses at **Bonnie Springs Ranch** in the canyon, which re-lives Nevada past with an Old West town and staged gunfights. **Overton**, founded by Mormon pioneers, is gateway to **Valley of Fire State Park**. Shifting rays of sunlight set rugged canyon walls alight, especially at sunrise and sunset. Various groups of Indians inhabited the area, and **Lost City Museum of Archeology** has restored sections of Pueblo Grande, remnants of an early civilization that vanished, possibly re-emerging as the Chaco Canyon and Mesa Verde cliff dwellers of the Four Corners area.

Returning to Las Vegas, the **Old Mormon Fort** has seen the transition from frontier outpost to railway town to gambling mecca. In sharp contrast are the **Imperial Palace Auto Collection** and **Liberace Museum**. Sightseeing flights from nearby McCarran International Airport offer a bird's-eye view of the **Grand Canyon**.

Death Valley

Death Valley Chamber of Commerce and a visitor centre are located to the west of Las Vegas in the quaint town of Tecopa. Death Valley was discovered in 1849 when a group of prospectors got lost whilst trying to find a short-cut to the Californian gold fields. After abandoning their wagons and eating the oxen they finally escaped on foot, giving the 120 mile (193km) long valley its present name. The best time to visit **Death Valley National Monument** is mid-October to mid-May — avoid summer as recorded temperatures in the valley have reached the desiccating high of 134°F (56.7°C) making it the hottest place in the USA. Restrictions may apply to hire vehicles, especially motorhomes which may not be insured for recovery in case of breakdown — so check before entering the valley.

The main sights may be seen in one long day, but if more time is available the full beauty of this varied and rugged terrain can be better appreciated.

In the centre of the valley Furnace Creek offers many facilities including a post office, fuel and campsites but remember these will be many degrees warmer than sites at higher altitude. **Furnace Creek Visitor Center** provides information on Death Valley's history, natural history, attractions and ranger-led activities through exhibits, audiovisual programs and leaflets. More than 900 plant species grow within the park, including twenty-one only found in this region. Spring is a popular time to visit, especially after a winter with higher than normal rainfall when plants burst into bloom. Best times are mid-Feb to mid-April for cacti, succulents and others on the valley floor, to early June for wildflowers at higher elevations. Regulations prohibit the picking of any flower or plant.

Desert animals are mostly nocturnal as the temperature falls rapidly at night, while larger beasts such as the desert bighorn occupy higher, and thus cooler, climes. Surprisingly five species of pupfish and eight of water snails inhabit the brackish spring-fed pools here.

The geology of the area is particularly interesting. Fault zones here have created one of the largest vertical rises in the USA between the valley near Badwater and Telescope Peak in the Panamint Range at 11,049ft (3,368m). Sudden flash floods in canyons cause erosion and form large alluvial fans, the drying of ancient lakes left huge salt deposits and volcanic activity has coloured the land whilst sand dunes evoke feelings of 'real' desert. As this is a protected area no rock or mineral samples may be collected.

The **Borax Museum** covers the important mining operations in Death Valley. This 'white gold' is an important chemical in many industries and can still be mined in Death Valley.

Nearby **Furnace Creek Inn** and **Furnace Creek Ranch Resort** form two oases in the desert. Green lawns, palm trees, an 18-hole golf course, tennis courts and sumptuous warm spring-fed pools all add to the luxury once enjoyed by 1930s stars such as Clark Gable. Those flying in by private or chartered aircraft from Las Vegas have no problem getting around as a variety of bus and carriage tours are offered. The more energetic may walk or hire a horse or bicycle. Cycles are not allowed on hiking trails but must use roads. Pick up a list of suggested routes from the visitor centre. Four-wheel-drive jeep rentals are available from the Furnace Creek service station to explore a number of popular dirt roads. Get a map and check conditions at the visitor centre or ranger station before venturing out — remember to carry plenty of water. Backcountry camping is subject to certain restrictions. Again check with rangers before embarking on an overnight trip.

There are very few maintained hiking trails in Death Valley. Two of these, Telescope and Wildrose Peaks are the only ones not discour- aged in summer while ice-axes and crampons may be required in winter. Most other hiking routes are cross-country — check condi-

Salt deposits form Death Valley's 'Devil's Golfcourse'

tions and obtain topographical maps from the visitor centre before setting out.

A popular attraction in Death Valley is **Scotty's Castle** which appears as a mirage out of the desert. This large, rambling Spanish-Moorish style building was erected by Chicago businessman Albert Johnson as a retreat from city life. His friend, Death Valley Scotty spread the rumour that he owned the mansion and in fact lived on there after Johnson's death. Thus it became known as Scotty's Castle. Arrive early on holiday weekends as the regular hour-long ranger-led tours may be filled before noon. The grounds and picnic area are free and facilities here include a snack bar, gift shop and fuel.

After visiting Scotty's Castle detour the 8 miles (13km) to **Ubehebe Crater** (Yoo-ba-hee-bee) which was formed by a violent volcanic eruption which left a pit nearly half a mile wide and 500ft (152m) deep. Those with jeeps may drive for a further hour and a half down the rough road to the dry lake bed where a hike leads to wind-blown moving rocks which leave tracks across the mud flat.

The village of **Stovepipe Wells** offers a store, lodging, campsite, restaurant and petrol station. Named after a freshwater spring marked by a stovepipe, the area has some picturesque rippled sand dunes. **Harmony Borax Works**, constructed in 1882, has been restored and is open to visitors. Borax loads weighing as much as 40 tons were hauled out by the famous twenty-mule-team wagons, one of which is displayed here.

Dante's View at 5,478ft (1,669m) offers a fantastic view of Death Valley from Badwater across to Telescope Peak which is often snow-capped and on a clear winter's day beyond to 14,375ft (4,381m) Mount Williamson in the Sierra Nevada. Remember the temperature will be appreciably (15-25°F) cooler up here.

In the valley a gravel road leads to the **Devil's Golfcourse**, a large area of salt pinnacles from 3 to 5ft thick. Nearby **Badwater Basin**, named for the brackish water, is 282ft (86m) below sea level, the lowest point in the USA. A notice high on the valley wall marks sea level. The one-way loop of Artists Drive is a must for the geology enthusiast while the colourful Artists Palette which is passed on the way can be enjoyed by anyone.

From Death Valley SR190 climbs steeply through the Panamint Mountains, affording panoramic views back into the valley and leading to SR178. From SR178 a dirt road leads to **Trona Pinnacles**, one of the best examples of tufa in the USA with some reaching as high as 140ft (43m). There are over 500 of these oddly shaped calcium carbonate structures originally deposited in Searles Lake, which has since dried up.

Maturango Museum in the centre of Ridgecrest has displays on the cultural and natural history of the area, a gallery featuring changing art exhibits and a hands-on discovery section. The gift shop carries a selection of books on the region and local crafts. Activities organized by the museum include lectures, Saturday adventures and local field trips (enquire in advance).

South of Ridgecrest is the Rand Mining District which has produced gold, silver and tungsten. Empty stores and buildings evidence the former prosperity of **Randsburg**, and the General Store has an antique soda fountain which still produces the taste of yesteryear.

West on SR14 is the colourful **Red Rock Canyon State Park**, setting for many Western movies. For best effect visit early morning or evening to explore fossil-rich canyons, vivid badlands and Indian petroglyphs in this 4,000-acre park with a primitive campground.

18 miles southwest of Randsburg on the California City road is the 40 square mile **Desert Tortoise Natural Area**. This contains a large population of the desert tortoise, the official Californian state reptile, with best viewing late March to early May when they feast upon wildflowers. A kiosk provides information while a self-guided trail leads through the area. Do not approach too close or otherwise disturb these endangered tortoises.

Southwest, at the intersection of I-15, I-40 and SR58 is **Barstow**, a late nineteenth-century mining town. Once a Santa Fe railroad depot, Barstow Station today forms an interesting period setting for shops and restaurants. The **Mojave River Valley Museum** preserves and interprets the heritage of the valley through photographs, archaeological finds, Indian artifacts and local field trips. The California Desert Information Center, managed by the Bureau of Land Management and Barstow Area Chamber of Commerce, has informative exhibits on the flora and fauna of the high desert. Drop in for information on weather, road conditions and recreational opportunities. Also available here are off-road maps and local area information on events, including those at **Calico Ghost Town**. Found ten miles northeast of Barstow, a rich silver strike in 1881 led to the founding of Calico. Despite the removal of over $13 million dollars worth of ore, when the price of silver fell in 1896 the town was abandoned until 1950, when it was purchased and restored as a tourist attraction. Several original buildings remain amongst those reconstructed along the single street and part of the Maggie Mine has been renovated for tours. Features include a museum, playhouse theatre, tram ride, railroad and shooting gallery. Period stores sell gifts, food and drink and there is an adjacent campground.

5 miles (8km) away is **Calico Early Man Archaeological Site**, an 卬
excavation begun by Dr Louis Leakey in 1964 which has revealed
more than 12,000 stone tools claimed (controversially) to date back
over 200,000 years. If proven, this is the oldest prehistoric tool site in
the Western Hemisphere. There is a visitor centre and site tours are
offered.

From Barstow I-15 and I-40 pass respectively to the north and
south of the **East Mojave National Scenic Area**. This scenic area
encompasses the Providence Mountains State Recreation Area
which contains the **Mitchell Caverns Natural Preserve**. Daily tours ✳
through these limestone caves pass stalactites, stalagmites,
flowstone and other interesting formations. Return to Western California via I-15.

Additional Information

Regional Visitor Information

**Barstow Area Chamber of
    Commerce**
831 Barstow Rd, PO Box 698
Barstow, CA 92311
☎ 619-256-8617

**California Desert Information
    Center**
831 Barstow Rd
Barstow, CA 92311
☎ 619-256-8617

**California Deserts Tourism
    Association**
37-115 Palm View Rd, PO Box 364
Rancho Mirage, CA 92270
☎ 619-328-9256

Palm Springs Desert Resorts CVB
Atrium Design Center, 69-930
Highway 111, Suite 201
Rancho Mirage, CA 92270
☎ 619-770-9000 or 1992

**Twentynine Palms Chamber of
    Commerce**
6136 Adobe Rd
Twentynine Palms, CA 92277
☎ 619-367-3445

Places to Visit

Anza-Borrego Desert State Park
PO Box 299
Borrego Springs, CA 92004
☎ 619-767-4684
Visitor centre, guided walks, books
Reduced facilities in summer

**Bob Hope Cultural Center/
    McCullum Theatre for the
    Performing Arts**
73-000 Fred Waring Dr
Palm Desert, CA 92260
☎ 619-340-2787
Call for production times

Cabot's Old Indian Pueblo Museum
67-616 E Desert View
Desert Hot Springs, CA 92240
☎ 619-329-7610
Open: 9.30am-4.30pm Wed-Mon
Hopi-style building, Pueblo art. Free

Calico Ghost Town
PO Box 638
(10 miles north of Barstow)
Yermo, CA 92398
☎ 619-254-2122
Mine tour, tram, gifts, food,
amusements

Death Valley National Monument
National Park Service
Death Valley, CA 92328
☎ 619-786-2331
Visitor centre, camping, hike, borax
mine. **Hot** in summer

Indian Canyons
S Palm Canyon Dr
Palm Springs, CA 92262
☎ 619-325-5673
Open: 8.30am-5pm, closed Jul & Aug
Hike or hire horse on Indian land

Joshua Tree National Monument
74485 National Monument Dr
Twenty-nine Palms, CA 92277
☎ 619-367-7511
Visitor centres, camp, picnic, hike

Living Desert
47-900 Portola Ave
Palm Desert, CA 92260
☎ 619-346-5694
Open: 9am-5pm, closed summer
Desert plants & animals, gifts, ♿

Maturango Museum
PO Box 1776
Ridgecrest, CA 93555
☎ 619-375-6900
Open: 10am-5pm Tue-Sun
Exhibits, art gallery, gifts

Mitchell Caverns Natural Preserve
PO Box 1
Essex, CA 92332
☎ 619-389-2281
Tours 1.30pm, also 10am & 3pm
weekends, closed summer

Moorten's Botanical Garden
1701 S Palm Canyon Dr
Palm Springs, CA 92262
☎ 619-327-6555
Open: 9am-5pm
Desert plants, palm oasis

Oasis Water Resort
1500 Gene Autry Trail
Palm Springs, CA 92264
☎ 619-325-SURF
Daily in summer, weekends to Oct

Palm Springs Aerial Tramway
1 Tramway Rd
Palm Springs, CA 92262
☎ 619-325-1391
Open: 10am weekdays, 8am
weekends, closed early August
Aerial tram, gifts, food, picnic,
mule rides

Palm Springs Desert Museum
101 Museum Dr
Palm Springs, CA 92262
☎ 619-325-7186
Open: 10am-4pm Tue-Fri, -5pm Sat
& Sun. Free 1st Tue of month
Art, gifts, theatre, ♿

Red Rock Canyon State Park
4555 W Ave G (Main Office)
Lancaster, CA 93536
☎ 805-942-0662
Camp, hike, picnic, ranger
programs in spring & fall

Ruddy's General Store
221 S Palm Canyon Dr
Palm Springs, CA 92262
☎ 619-327-2156
Open: 10am-4pm Thu-Sun, noon-
6pm weekends only in summer

California Fact File

Accommodation

Hotels and Motels

Californian hotels and motels typically charge by the room, with a small surcharge for additional occupants. Older hotels usually offer only single, twin, or double beds; while more modern hotels and motels typically have rooms with two double beds — great value for families or couples travelling together. The management can often supply an additional single bed or crib, but this should be verified while booking. Most rooms have private bathrooms, telephones, television, and air-conditioning.

Prices and services vary according to hotel/motel chain, location, the season, and whether AAA (American Automobile Association) or Senior Citizen discounts are available. Visitors from abroad will find that many chains have pre-paid voucher schemes. These offer excellent value, but ensure that the hotel coverage is suitable. Surcharges may apply to guests in up-market hotels or major cities. Most pre-paid schemes must be booked before departure, but fly-drive brochures often list one or two participating chains.

Hotels and motels with a restaurant may offer American Plan (full board) or Modified American Plan (half board). Those without often give the American continental breakfast — donuts and coffee — free in the lobby. Efficiencies are a special type of hotel/motel room where cooking facilities are available, varying from a hot plate and sink to full kitchens complete with garbage disposals and ice makers.

Toll-free telephone numbers for major hotel/motel chains who can supply details of their hotels are listed below, but before booking check available discounts, and also restrictions if travelling with children or pets.

Best Western International	800-528-1234
Budgetel Inns	800-428-3438
Clarion & Comfort Inns	800-228-5150
Days Inn	800-325-2525
Econo Lodges of America	800-446-6900
Embassy Suites	800-362-2779

Hilton Hotels	800-445-8667
Holiday Inns	800-465-4329
Howard Johnson's Motor Lodges	800-654-2000
Hyatt Hotels	800-233-1234
La Quinta Motor Inns	800-531-5900
Marriott Hotels & Resorts	800-228-9290
Omni Hotels	800-843-6664
Quality Inns	800-228-5151
Ramada Inns	800-228-2828
Scottish Inns	800-251-1962
Sheraton Hotels & Motor Inns	800-325-3535
Susse Chalet Motor Lodges & Inns	800-258-1980
Super 8 Motels	800-843-1991
Travelodge Hotels	800-255-3050
Westin Hotels & Resorts	800-228-3000

Condominiums

These are apartments, often high-rise, with one or more separate bedrooms, giving greater privacy than one room *efficiencies*. They typically have one or more bathrooms and a kitchen/lounge/dining room area with a fold-out double bed or two. Agencies in popular resort areas specialize in renting condominiums, usually requiring visitors to stay by the week or month. They can be found via local newspapers or 'Condo for Rent' signs.

Resorts

Top class cuisine, entertainment, and accommodation are offered by most resorts, with enough extracurricular activities to satisfy the most ardent sporting enthusiasts, health fanatics, and people people. Some of California's best resorts are exclusive hotels nestled in a pro-designed golf course.

Bed & Breakfast and Guest houses

Brought back by American visitors to Britain, the B&B has become popular in many areas, although bargain motels often offer the same facilities for less. Bed and Breakfast organizations have sprung up to ensure standards are maintained and to promote the concept, and their addresses may be obtained from the nearest California tourism office or the local tourist authorities listed at the end of each chapter.

Guest Houses are sometimes known as boarding houses, and

a large network exists throughout the USA. For details contact:

The Director
Tourist House Association of America
PO Box 355-AA
Greentown
Pennsylvania 18426

Youth Hostels and the YMCA
These provide inexpensive accommodation for all ages, although foreign visitors should become members of their own country's Youth Hostel organization before travelling. The YMCA is busy, especially during peak seasons, and should be booked well ahead to avoid disappointment and additional expense. Contact:

American Youth Hostels Inc.   or the YMCA via
1332 Eye Street NW   The Y's Way
Washington   356 West 34th Street
DC 20013-7613   New York, NY 10001
☎ 202-783-6161   ☎ 212-769-5856.

Camping
This is another popular way to see California. For those hiring a motorhome, many private campsites have full hookups, which include water, sewage, electricity, and a television cable. National and state parks and forests provide campsites in natural settings, with facilities ranging from full hookups to primitive sites, sometimes free in remote areas. The Woodall's or Rand McNally campsite guides, usually included with the hire, offer comprehensive lists of sites. Camping or tenting alongside the road may require special permission and is potentially dangerous. Campsites near major National Parks and cities may become fully booked in summer, while the southernmost areas of California and Nevada tend to fill in winter. Not all sites allow tents, but Woodall's produce a special guide for tenters.

Climate

California has not one, but many climates. Northern California has sunny summer days interspersed with occasional showers or fog. Snow-free coastlines and fast freeways to the major ski

Maximum and minimum temperatures

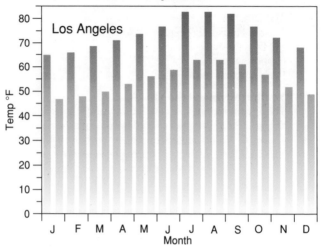

Average monthly rainfall

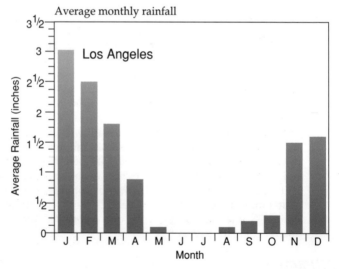

resORTS make for ideal winter recreation. Southern California varies from dry to desert, with winter and early spring being the best seasons to explore the desiccated interior. Average winter daytime temperatures are pleasantly warm along the

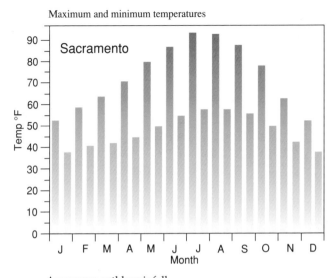

Maximum and minimum temperatures

Sacramento

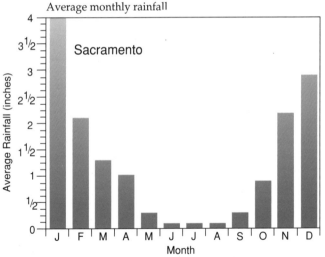

Average monthly rainfall

Sacramento

southern coast, with occasional cold snaps or rain showers. Spring and autumn are excellent times to tour the southwest, while summers are hot and dry.

Clothes

Dress is casual; only top restaurants insist upon a jacket and/or tie for men. One or two warm layers are essential, regardless of location or season — the hottest destinations have arctic air-conditioned restaurants, hotels, and shopping centres. Winter visitors in the north should bring or buy overcoats, boots or rubber overshoes with non-skid soles, gloves, and earmuffs or a hat. Winter sports participants should be prepared for cold weather, but business travellers and those visiting relatives are sometimes taken unawares.

Driving Styles and Tips

For pre-trip planning, the *Rand McNally Road Atlas (United States, Canada, and Mexico)* has state and city maps, distances between major cities, scenic routes and major sites of interest. The AAA (American Automobile Association) provides free maps and accommodation guides to its members and affiliated foreign club members.

Driving over California's excellent road network is enjoyable so long as the visitor has patience, as even the twelve-lane freeways get congested. Visitors may find distances deceptive but apart from major cities the roads are uncrowded, allowing drivers to travel further without undue fatigue.

Interstates in California are restricted access, multilane arteries between major cities; typically coloured blue or red on road maps. Green-coloured lines are turnpikes, which charge a toll but are otherwise similar to Interstates. Freeways are restricted access arteries into and through dense urban areas. Speed limits for limited access highways are normally 55mph, rising to 65mph in specified rural areas.

Californian highways are not necessarily multi-lane, and often cross towns rather than bypassing them. Traffic lights and strip development along urban highways slow traffic considerably. Speed limits are typically 45-55mph in the countryside, 15-35mph in urban areas.

Road numbering and signs can confuse the unwary. Signs for US Highways, Interstates, and Turnpikes have a numbered shield with three points at the top, and are respectively white, blue, and green. Even numbered highways go east-west, while odd numbered highways run north-south. To reduce confusion, road numbers within this guide are preceded by 'US' to designate a US Highway, 'SR' for a state or county road, and 'I-' for Interstates.

Emergencies

Breakdowns
In the event of a malfunction, coast onto the hard shoulder (breakdown lane), lift the car's hood (bonnet), at night use emergency flashers, and await assistance in a locked car. As soon as possible, notify the hire company and ask for a replacement. Personal protection insurance (PPI), if taken out, may cover hotel and incidental expenses while waiting. Members of an overseas automobile association can contact the AAA through the yellow pages or, for breakdown assistance, on 1-800-AAA-HELP.

Accidents
If involved in an accident, get the particulars of other drivers and any witnesses. State law requires the police to be notified if damage exceeds a nominal amount or in event of personal injury, and the hire company must always be informed. Some insurance policies become void if the driver admits liability, and saying, 'I'm sorry,' could be considered an admission of guilt. Always leave medical help to those who are trained and insured.

Illness and Injury
Medical insurance documents should be kept safe and preferably with the traveller. Call 911 (or 0 for operator) in emergency. Remain calm.

For non-emergencies the operator or medical referral agencies in the Yellow Pages can help the independent traveller, as can an overseas visitor's consulate. Advance payment may be required for those without medical insurance.

While hiking in remote areas, the group should have a minimum of three people so that one person can remain with injured while another goes for help. In the highly unlikely event of a bite from a poisonous snake or spider, always: remain calm, treat victim only for shock, and seek immediate medical attention. Permanent injury from a poisonous bite is highly unlikely, especially if proper medical attention has been sought without attempting a tourniquet or other treatment without professional advise. A course of rabies injections may be the outcome of feeding, petting, or molesting domesticated or wild fur-bearing animals. If bitten, seek a doctor immediately.

Theft and Lost Property
Common-sense rules on avoiding theft include using the hotel safe for valuables, reserves of cash or traveller's cheques, travel vouchers, and airline tickets. Dress casually, wearing the minimum of jewellery. Keep passports and reclaim forms separate from credit cards and traveller's cheques. Lock car doors and keep windows shut while travelling to prevent car theft and hand bag snatchers. Travel in groups, and check with hotel staff for areas of potential trouble (and local places of interest).

In case of theft, report details to police. Use travel or credit card insurance to replace lost or stolen articles. Contact the relevant embassy immediately if a passport is lost or stolen, and also for financial help in an emergency. Traveller's cheque replacement will be far easier if the company is represented in the United States. When notifying credit card companies of a loss, most companies have toll free numbers, while those abroad will accept a collect call. Several companies offer credit card protection schemes, where one call notifies relevant credit card companies.

California airports, hotels, and restaurants are very good with lost property, but also leave details with the police lost-and-found department.

Handicapped Facilities

Public buildings, national, and state parks must, by law, provide access facilities to the handicapped. In addition the major hotels and many private attractions, such as Disneyland, provide facilities and access for the disabled which are unsurpassed. However, planning is poor in some Californian towns and cities: sidewalks are nonexistent and pedestrians must cross at odds with turning traffic. Vehicular mobility is a must for the independent traveller, whether physically challenged or not, but there are alternatives: join a tour group, cruise on a ship, or stay in one of the many resorts. When requested, Walt Disney Company provides handbooks identifying special facilities within their theme park.

Major rental car companies such as Hertz and Avis can provide automobiles with special controls if contacted in advance. An increasing number of states include information regarding handicapped access to points of interest in their vacation planning guides.

For information on access to the great outdoors purchase a copy of the excellent *California Parks Access* from Cougar Publishing (☎ 800-735-3805, fax 619-738-0282, or write to Cougar Pass Publishing, PO Box 463060A, Escondido, CA 92046-3060). Note that this guide is also invaluable for those with young children.

National and State Parks and Forests

California's 'crown jewels' are on permanent public display. Her state and national parks, monuments and historic sites are open to all. Summers are usually the busiest periods in the north, spring and autumn bring cooler temperatures and fewer people while snowy weather in the mountains attracts winter sports enthusiasts. The deserts are best visited in cooler months with spring cactus and wildflower shows very popular. Avoid the summer heat if possible. National forests in mountainous areas boast some of America's finest ski resorts, often open for year-round recreation. Those who must visit a popular park at peak time should book accommodation or campsites months ahead.

Admission to most national parks is $5 per carload, valid for seven days. The Golden Age and Golden Access passes are free respectively to those over 62 years old and handicapped individuals, excluding foreign nationals, with discounts for campsites and certain tours. The $25 *Golden Eagle Pass* allows unlimited access — including foreign nationals — for one calendar year but gives no camping or tour discounts.

National Park Service information is available from the American tourist offices abroad, or from:

The National Park Service
PO Box 37127
Washington DC 20013-7127

California operates some of America's finest state parks including the high desert of Anza-Borrego State Park, the country's largest. Preserving important historic sites and native California habitat, the state park service offers everything from jogging/bike paths along golden beaches to the mining ghost town of Bodie, permanently in a state of 'arrested decay'. Information is available from:

California Department of Parks and Recreation
PO Box 2390
Sacramento, CA 95811
☎ 916-445-6477 (events)
    619-452-1950 (camp reservations)
    800-444-PARK (camp reservations)

Renting a Car

Renting a car is easy and inexpensive. Pre-booking an automobile via a fly-drive package or through a major rental company is safest, especially during peak season. Rent-a-Wreck style companies offer lower prices, but may sting unwary drivers with high mileage charges and/or inadequate insurance.

Third-party insurance is normally included in the price but CDW (collision damage waver) may not be. CDW pushes rental prices up $9 to $16 per day, but does insure against damage to the vehicle and loss of use charges. Travellers who utilize their own insurance policies may find themselves paying hire charges for damaged cars being repaired. PPI (personal protection insurance) provides additional liability coverage and may pay accommodation costs in the event of a breakdown or accident. Restrictions may apply to drivers under 25 years old, travellers without a major credit card, and anyone whose driving privileges have been revoked — they should inform the rental company or tour operator while booking.

Special insurance arrangements and permission will be required if crossing into Mexico — most hire companies forbid it — and private vehicles may go only if covered by Mexican insurance.

Renting a Motorhome

Seeing the United States by RV (recreational vehicle or motorhome) has become so popular that many Americans live permanently in these mansions on wheels. Hiring an RV is simple, with similar restrictions to car hire although additional limitations on access to such places as Death Valley may apply (check when booking). Both Cruise America and Go Vacations offer motorhomes which may be booked directly or through various travel agencies abroad.

The RV is ideal for groups and families who enjoy travelling together, whether or not they enjoy the 'great outdoors'. Far from spartan, these vehicles offer full kitchens, bathrooms, ample cupboard space, comfortable beds, and air-conditioning. Most come with a microwave and television, which can be linked to cable or satellite at many commercial campgrounds.

The temptation to hire the largest vehicle possible should be resisted. Wise 'RVers' chose a vehicle just large enough to meet their needs — a 35ft-motorhome is difficult to manoeuvre in tight spaces. Power steering and automatic transmissions help enormously, but drivers should practice in quieter locations before attempting a major city.

FOR OVERSEAS VISITORS

Currency and Credit Cards

The American unit of currency is the dollar, divided into 100 cents (¢), with coins in the value of: 1¢ (penny), 5¢ (nickel), 10¢ (dime), 25¢ (quarter), 50¢ (half dollar) and $1 (dollar). Bank notes are available in denominations of $1, $2 (rare), $5, $10, $20, $50, and $100. Larger notes exist in limited quantities, but many establishments will not accept notes larger than $20. Each bank note is the same size and colour, regardless of value, so take care to give the correct note and always check the change.

Bank hours are 9am to 3pm, Monday through Friday, except national holidays. Buy American dollars as cash or traveller's cheques before leaving home. American Express, Thomas Cook, and certain banks provide currency exchange, but in generally only in major cities, and tracking them down can waste valuable holiday time. Dollar traveller's cheques are treated as cash, and offer protection against loss. American Express are popular and widely accepted, while traveller's cheques from 'obscure' foreign banks may be more difficult to cash.

Major credit cards reduce the problems of currency exchange and dangers of carrying large quantities of cash. American Express, Diners Club, Visa, and Mastercard are the most popular, although a few establishments which accept Mastercard have refused to honour foreign Access Cards. Nonresident American Express card holders may cash foreign cheques (amount varies by card and country) once every three weeks. Dollar cash advances on a credit card may be obtained from participating banks and affiliated cash dispenser networks, although interest or transaction charges are levied. Certain ATM networks, such as the PLUS system, withdraw funds directly from home accounts without an interest penalty.

Customs

California is very strict on controlled substances (non-prescription drugs), meat, dairy products, fruit and vegetables. Check with the consulate or embassy before bringing firearms, ammunition or animals. British visitors should note that America does have rabies, and returning pets will be subject to extended quarantine.

There are no restrictions on the amount of currency brought into or taken from the United States, but a declaration form must be filled in when the value exceeds $10,000.

The following goods may be imported duty free into the USA:

Either 200 cigarettes, 50 cigars, 2kg of tobacco, or proportionate amounts of each; 1 litre of alcoholic beverage for those 21 years old or over; gifts up to a value of $100, which may include 100 cigars in addition to the tobacco allowance. Gifts must be available for inspection, and thus should not be wrapped. American Customs Officers are not chosen for their sense of humour — adopt a business-like attitude and save jokes for an appreciative audience.

Documents

Passports and Visas

All travellers visiting America from abroad, whether on business or holiday, must have a full passport valid for six months beyond the scheduled to return date. Canadian citizens and British subjects resident in Canada or Bermuda do not require an American visa if arriving from most Western Hemisphere countries. Mexicans arriving from Canada or Mexico do not require a visa if they are in possession of a form I-136.

A visa may not be necessary for nationals of the United Kingdom, certain EEC countries, and Japan when arriving by air or sea via a carrier participating in the United States Visa Waiver Program. Travellers intending to re-visit America are advised to apply for a visa and is necessary for those wanting to go 'south of the border' on a day trip. Those staying beyond 3 months must have a visa, as must students on exchange programs and citizens of countries not participating in the Visa Waiver Program.

Postal applications for visas are typically processed within 10 days, but for safety allow 4 weeks. Travel agencies can often obtain American visas within 48 hours, but acquiring an 'instant' visa by personally visiting the United States Consulate General may no longer be possible — check first. The standard multiple-entry visas are valid indefinitely, and will be transferred from an expired passport to a new one by presenting both passports when entering the United States. Visas may be obtained by writing to an American Consulate:

United States Consulate
  General, Visa Branch
5 Upper Grosvenor Street
London W1A 2JB
United Kingdom
☎ 071-499-7010

United States Consulate
  General, Visa Branch
1155 Saint Alexandra
Montreal, Quebec H22 I22
Canada
☎ 514-398-9695

United States Consulate
  General, Visa Branch
36th Floor
Electricity House
Park & Elizabeth Streets
Sydney, NSW 2000
Australia
☎ 02-261-9200

United States Consulate
  General, Visa Branch
4th Floor
Yorkshire General Building
Cnr Shortland & O'Connell
Auckland
New Zealand
☎ 09-303-2724

Upon admission to the United States, visitors have a departure form stapled to their passport. When leaving, especially if departing overland into Mexico, ensure the emigration official retrieves the form. The alternative is to be branded an illegal alien, making re-entry to America most difficult.

Driving Documents

For foreign visitors and Americans alike, the most popular way to see the United States is from behind a steering wheel. A valid driving license should always be carried with the driver. An International Driver's Permit is not necessary for those coming from an English-speaking country, and is invalid unless accompanied by a driving licence.

The AAA (American Automobile Association) has reciprocal arrangements with many non-American automobile associations and clubs. Visitors bringing proof of membership enjoy AAA services, such as free maps, trip-tiks (a series of detailed strip maps following the driver's intended route), area guidebooks, and breakdown help. AAA affiliated members may receive discounts from car hire companies, tourist attractions, and hotels. (Other discounts are often available to senior citizens, students, the military, and members of various travel clubs).

Essentials

Travellers taking medication should bring their prescription, which can be used for an emergency top up and also to prove the medication is prescribed. Replacement glasses or contact lenses and their prescription are also recommended. Electrical appliances must work at 110 volts and fit the US two/three pronged plug. European or British plugs, including 'Universal' electric shavers, will require an electrical socket adapter.

Drinking the water is not a problem, and water fountains are standard in most shopping centres and parks.

For travel security, one should make a list of telephone numbers, issuer's addresses, and identification numbers for passports, airline tickets, insurance policies, credit cards, travellers cheques, AAA or equivalent membership, and travel vouchers. Keeping the list secure and separate from the above items will greatly simplify replacing lost or stolen items.

Insurance

Good personal health and accident insurance is essential for medical coverage and general peace of mind. American hospital treatment is excellent, but it may be unobtainable unless proof of insurance is demonstrated or costs are pre-paid. Those with existing health problems should consult both their doctor and the travel insurance company to ensure they are adequately protected. Check that personal accident insurance indemnifies travellers against third party law suits.

Injections are not required to visit America, nor are vaccination certificates except where travellers have recently visited a country where yellow fever or similar is endemic. Bring or buy a small first aid kit, protection from the sun, and mosquito repellant.

For UK citizens a 24-hour emergency service is available via: British Consul General,
Suite 2700, 245 Peachtree Center Ave,
Atlanta, GE 30302
☎ 404-524-5856

Legal Advice
This is very expensive in California, and best avoided where possible. Purchased travel insurance should indemnify against personal law suites. If legal advice is necessary, check the yellow pages for legal referral specialists. Visitors from abroad should consult their embassy or consular offices.

Language

American accents vary, as does word usage compared to 'English'. Here are selected British words and their American equivalents:

British	American
biscuit	cookie
car boot	trunk
car bonnet	hood
car wing	fender
chips	french fries
cot (see single bed)	crib
crisps (potato)	chips
egg fried one side	sunny side up
egg fried both sides, yolk soft	over easy
egg fried both sides, yolk hard	over hard
grilled	broiled
ground floor	first floor
lift	elevator
motorhome	RV
pavement	sidewalk
post	mail
petrol	gasoline (or gas)
public school	private school
public toilet/convenience	rest room, bathroom
reverse-charge call	collect call
road	pavement
scone	biscuit
single bed	cot
sweet	candy
tap	faucet
tights	panty hose

Mail

Post Offices will hold mail sent to travellers for 30 days, so long as it is addressed with the recipients name and includes 'c/o General Delivery'. Most large cities have several post offices, with only one handling general delivery mail.

Holders of American Express Cards or Traveller's Cheques may have mail delivered to themselves care of *participating* AMEX offices, again held for 30 days. Mail should be addressed to the recipient and marked 'Client Mail'.

Note that some US addresses now use the new nine-digit zip code, which should not be confused with the telephone number.

Photography

Film is often less expensive in America than abroad, and most types are readily available. In major cities bargain if purchasing large quantities or buy from discount stores. Film prices increase significantly near major tourist attractions. Many theme parks offer free or rental cameras, usually courtesy of Kodak. Foreign visitors should check that process-paid film may be developed at home.

Hot sunny days turn cars into ovens, and can ruin film whether inside the camera or out.

Public Holidays

The following are public holidays:

New Year's Day	1 Jan
Martin Luther King Day	16 Jan
President's Day	Third Monday in February
Memorial Day	Last Monday in May
Independence Day	4 July
Labor Day	First Monday in September
Columbus Day	Second Monday in October
Veteran's Day	11 November
Thanksgiving	Last Thursday in November
Christmas	25 December

Sales Tax

Foreign visitors are often surprised to find their purchases cost more than the price tag indicates — State Sales Tax is automatically added at the till.

Telephones

The emergency code is 911, and if that fails, dial 0 for Operator. All American (and Canadian) telephones have a three-digit area code, and a seven digit phones number. Area codes are only used when calling between areas. The area code 800 is reserved for toll free calls, usually valid only from America or Canada. Major airlines, hotels and car rental companies have toll free numbers listed in the Yellow Pages. Long distance and toll free calls are normally preceded with 1.

Direct dialling of calls, even international ones, are possible from most hotels and public pay-phones. The international code 011 and the country code is followed by the phone number, minus the leading zero. To telephone 071-495-4466, the US Tourist Office in London, dial 011 (International Direct Dialling Access), 44 (the United Kingdom Country Code), 71-495-4466 (the London Number, less the leading zero).

Not all pay-phones are operated by AT&T, and rules for long distance dialling vary, but most phones provide instructions. International direct dialling from a public phone box requires a fistful of quarters, up to $10 worth for a short call. AT&T make calling home easier with their Direct Service. Collect or telephone credit card calls may be made to the United Kingdom by dialling 1-800-445-5667.

For directory enquires, dial 411 for local numbers, or the area code and 555-1212 for long distance numbers. To find the toll free number of an airline, hotel, or car rental firm, dial 1–800-555-1212 and ask for their number.

Time and Dates

California is in the Pacific Time Zone — 8 hours respectively behind (less than) Greenwich Mean Time. Daylight Savings Time comes into effect on the first Sunday in April, with the clocks moving ahead one hour, and reverts back to standard time on the last Sunday in October. Americans write their dates in the format month day, year. Christmas Day in 1999 is thus December 25, 1999, or in shorthand 12/25/99.

Tipping

15 percent is the standard tip for taxis, restaurants, and bar staff, while exceptional service or luxurious surroundings now command 20 percent. Restaurant service charges are not normal except for large groups, which then take the place of tipping. Cover charges are not service charges, and tips are still expected.

Toilets

Usually referred to in a hushed voice as the rest room, bathroom, or often the ladies' and men's room. Public toilets are found in shopping malls, large department stores, recreational parks, and at rest areas on major highways (often indicated on state maps). Fast food emporiums are useful in emergencies, although some now charge non-customers.

Tourist Offices

Main California tourist offices are at the following addresses. For those countries not listed, contact the American Embassy.

USA
California Office of Tourism
PO Box 9278, Dept A1003
Van Nuys, CA 91409
☎ 702-885-4384
or 800-237-0774

United Kingdom
United States Travel &
    Tourism Administration
PO Box 1EN
London W1A 1EN
☎ 071-495-4466

Australia
United States Travel &
    Tourism Administration
Suite 6106, MLC Centre
King & Castlereagh Streets
Sydney, NSW 2000
☎ 02-233-4055

Canada
United States Travel &
    Tourism Administration
Suite 602
480 University Avenue
Toronto, Ontario M5G 1V2
☎ 416-595-5082

Travel — Getting to California

Air

Many travellers reach California by air. The diversity of carriers, rates, and routes is bewildering, with many routes and packages. A travel agent can help decipher the offerings, but some general guidelines may help. Packaged tours generally offer the best value, without necessarily sacrificing the flexibility the independent traveller demands. A basic fly-drive package will leave the visitor in a rental car, this guide book propped open, with the whole of California ahead. Check before departing for hotel voucher bargains, which usually include a number of nights in a particular chain of motels at a special price. Those preferring a more fixed arrangement can still see more with a fly-drive or bus tour itinerary with places of interest, hotels, flights and transfers included.

Land

Travellers arriving in California overland via Mexico must have visas, unless they are Canadian Citizens, British Canadian Residents, Mexicans with form I-136, or naturalized Americans. The Visa Waiver Program does not apply to overland arrivals. Borders are friendly crossings and visitors occasionally have to prompt officials, especially about collecting the departure forms when leaving America.

Travel — Getting around California

Long Haul Public Transport

Air

America's air network has innumerable routes and carriers. Deregulation has increased competition between airlines, and the traveller often benefits with reduced rates. Numerous airlines give reductions for senior citizens, to whom they offer blocks of tickets for the cost of a few flights. Rates are significantly reduced when booking a week or more in advance if the return flight involves a weekend stopover — shop around. Non-residents should check for special deals available from local travel agencies, whether for a package holiday which visits several cities or a United States airline which offers reduced price air passes.

Rail (Amtrak)

Travellers booking from abroad may take advantage of Amtrak's USA Rail Pass. Each pass is valid for 45 days, allows unlimited stopovers, and takes in America's largest passenger rail network. The ticket may be valid for just one region or for continental USA, and the price varies accordingly. With the potential for unlimited travel comes restrictions, additional charges apply for luxuries such as sleeping car accommodation, and the large network can be difficult to negotiate.

Amtrak also offers packaged trips which include sightseeing tours of the major cities and national parks. Visitors from Australia and New Zealand should contact Thomas Cook, while Amtrak may be reached in the UK on (071) 978-5222. In America write to:

Amtrak
60 Massachusetts Ave NE
Washington,
DC 20002
☎ 202-383-3000 or 1-800-USA-RAIL

Greyhound Buses
Armed with a Greyhound Ameripass (purchased before leaving home) and a sense of determination, much of California can be seen by bus. The Greyhound (and participating carriers) network is extensive, but travellers may face poor public transport at final destinations, as the Greyhound network is city to city, not accommodation to attraction.

Short Haul Public Transport
San Francisco has the most options regarding public transport, with the world famous cable cars supplemented by the underground BART (Bay Area Rapid Transit) and an excellent bus system. Even Los Angeles has a belated but growing commuter rail network.

Motoring Laws and Tips
The essential law for foreign visitors is to drive on the right-hand side of the road. On multilane highways cars pass on either side — watch for speeding 'undertakers'. Unless otherwise posted, drivers at a red traffic light may turn right after stopping, but do not turn if interfering with other traffic or pedestrians.

One crucially important law relates to school buses. Whenever a school bus flashes red warning lights drivers going in *either direction* must stop! Children expect all traffic to come to a standstill, and often race across the road without looking.

Radar, airplanes and other methods of speed control are extensively used by the police forces. Intoxicated drivers and lead-footed speedsters will find that on-the-spot fines may be supplemented with prison and/or confiscation of the offending vehicle. Especially avoid speeding on turnpikes as the time-stamped tickets are checked when paying tolls at the other end, and fines are charged if the driver arrives too quickly. Tough policies on drunk driving means that drivers below the legal drinking age of 21 years old will lose their licence if any alcohol is detected.

Law breakers apart, driving is actually a very pleasant way to see California — the only way to see some parts. The most likely problem drivers confront is fatigue, caused by the temptation to go 'just a little further'. Rest stops (with toilet facilities) and pullovers (without) are plentiful along the interstates and scenic highways, and regular stops will refresh tired drivers.

Most California gas stations insist upon paying before pumping and the lower priced stations, often combined with convenience stores, will only accept cash and travellers cheques. Since the station attendant (and customers) would be at risk during a hold-up, chances are minimized by mechanically whisking paper money into a safe. The attendant thus cannot change large dollar bills or travellers cheques — bring small denominations.

A surcharge may apply for using credit cards, and at full service pumps a per gallon premium is charged in exchange for a windscreen wash, checking engine fluid levels and possibly the tyres, and a smile. Hire cars use readily available unleaded fuel, but older vehicles use difficult to find leaded fuel.

Weights and Measures

The American system of weights and measures was derived from the British Imperial system, thus they are similar if not identical. The metric system is making gradual inroads, but road distances are in miles, not kilometres. Produce, whether dry or liquid, usually has both metric and American weights or volumes indicated.

Liquid measure differs between America and Britain. 1 US Gallon=.833 Imperial Gallons=3.8 litres. Women's clothing sizes vary, with American sizes two less than the British. Thus a size 12 dress in Britain is only 10 in America, and a size 36 sweater is 34. Women's shoes are the opposite, so a dainty British size 4 becomes an American 6. Ounces and pounds are the same in the UK as the United States, but Americans do not use the stone.

INDEX